The Violences of Men

Some other books by Jeff Hearn

The Sexuality of Organization, co-editor with G. Burrell, D. Sheppard and P. Tancred-Sherriff, Sage Publications, 1989

Violence and Gender Relations: Theories and Interventions, co-editor with B. Fawcett, B. Featherstone and C. Toft, Sage Publications, 1996

Men as Managers, Managers as Men: Critical Perspectives on Men, Masculinities and Managements, co-editor with D.L. Collinson, Sage Publications, 1996

Unspoken Forces: Sexuality, Violence and ORganizational Worlds, with W. Parkin, Sage Publications, forthcoming

The Violences of Men

How Men Talk About
and How Agencies Respond to
Men's Violence to Women

JEFF HEARN

SAGE Publications
London • Thousand Oaks • New Delhi

SAGE Publications Ltd
6 Bonhill Street
London EC2A 4PU

SAGE Publications Inc.
2455 Teller Road
Thousand Oaks, California 91320

SAGE Publications India Pvt Ltd
32, M-Block Market
Greater Kailash – I
New Delhi 110 048

British Library Cataloguing in Publication data

A catalogue record for this book is available
from the British Library

ISBN 0 8039 7939 8
ISBN 0 8039 7940 1 (pbk)

Library of Congress catalog card number 98–060906

Typeset by Mayhew Typesetting, Rhayader, Powys
Printed in Great Britain by The Cromwell Press Ltd,
Trowbridge, Wiltshire

HQ1090
, H4
1998x

Contents

Tables and Figures

Tables

Figures

Preface

This is a book about men and men's violence to known women, about how men talk about such violence and how agencies respond to it.

As such, it is set within the context of social constitutions of men, violence and the relationship between men and violences. Importantly, in the UK and many other societies, there are massive ambivalences that remain around violence and its use. Violence is understood as a major, perhaps even the prime, form of power, and at the same time, violence is considered unfair, inappropriate, wrong-headed, as well as painful, damaging and sometimes illegal. The same people may think or say these two different things at different times, or even at the same time.

This kind of ambivalence persists in relation to the problem of men's violence to known women. Such violence may be ignored, accepted, condoned, whilst at the same time it may be seen as unfair, inappropriate, wrong-headed, as well as painful, damaging and sometimes illegal. It is a kind of legitimated taboo. It is also sometimes considered shameful, a sign of men's inadequacy, either of losing control of oneself or of not controlling women without the use of violence. In recent years there has been somewhat greater recognition of the inappropriateness of such violence by men – and in that sense the ambivalence has been lessened to some extent.

Ambivalence is important in other ways. For example, for men to talk about violence may be becoming both easier and more difficult for individual men, and the motivation for men to work against their own violence may also be a source of ambivalence.

Rather similarly I have experienced grave ambivalence in writing this book – between, on the one hand, a belief that it addresses urgent questions, is worth writing and needs to be finished, and, on the other, the unpleasantness of the task, the topic and the material. I have often been uncertain how to proceed and it has taken me longer than originally planned. Ambivalence, violence and writing are interconnected in complex ways.

Throughout this book, there are a number of themes that recur – debates on what is meant by violence in the first place; the importance of identifying and naming men's responsibility for violence; the persistent and close connection of violence with power, control and dominance; and, perhaps more surprisingly, real doubts about the notion of cause, at least in any simple terms, in explaining away men's violence to known women. Thus, for example, when I was coming towards the end of the study that is the basis of this book, an ex-student asked, 'So why are men violent to women?' As it was their graduation day, I didn't feel inclined to enter into a long analysis of the whys and wherefores, so I simply answered, 'Because they're men.' This was short and to the point. Men remain violent to women through social power and control, which, in some cases, is combined with physical size and strength, reinforced by social power and control that reduces intervention against them and that violence.

This book is a contribution to diminishing that power and control, and that violence of men to women and children.

Acknowledgements

This book has grown from research on men who have been violent to known women. The initial research was carried out between 1991 and 1995 with the funding of the Economic and Social Research Council. I am grateful to the Council and its officers for their support. The initial research was based at the Research Unit on Violence, Abuse and Gender Relations, Department of Applied Social Studies, University of Bradford. I am indebted to Jalna Hanmer, then Co-Convenor of the Research Unit, who directed the linked, but separate, project on women who have experienced violence from known men and who has provided invaluable discussions, personal concern and professional guidance; to Linda Arbuckle, the Unit Administrator, who provided indispensable, efficient and effective administrative back-up; to Roger Barford, John Davis, Mike Huett, Phil Raws and David Riley, for conducting interviews and talking through all the various issues that have arisen; to Lynda Gillah for transcription of tapes; and to John Lawler for statistical analysis. I also thank Linda Arbuckle, Valerie Bentley, Lynne Gerrard, Clair Ridley, Marina Sarjeant and Julie Trickey for typing parts of the text.

I would also like to thank Ann Oakley and Jennie Popay as Co-ordinators of the ESRC Initiative on the Management of Personal Welfare; the other researchers in the Initiative at London, Salford, Sheffield Hallam and York Universities; Detective Superintendent Gary Haigh, Julie Bedford and officers of the West Yorkshire Police; the West Yorkshire and other Probation Services; HM Prison Service; Leeds and Bradford Metropolitan Councils; Leeds MOVE/Men's Action Network; Leeds Domestic Violence Project; the Worth Project; Leeds Addiction Unit; the Crown Prosecution Service; Manchester, Lancashire, Durham and Cleveland Police Authorities; as well as members of voluntary agencies, doctors, psychiatrists, solicitors and other workers. I would also want to thank the men who agreed to be interviewed as part of this project – that act of thanks itself symbolizes the ambiguities and ambivalences of research into the violences of men.

The ideas and thinking developed in this book have been previously presented at several British Sociological Association Annual Conferences; the Political Studies Association Annual Conference; UMIST Gender Research Seminar, Manchester; the Universities of Bradford, Manchester,

Staffordshire, Leeds, London, Brunel, Cambridge, Helsinki and Tampere; the Institute of Public Policy Research; the ESRC International Conference 'Welfare: Whose Responsibility?'; ESRC Policy and Implementation Seminars; as well as a number of other policy and academic gatherings and conferences. I am grateful to all those who were present and who commented on those presentations.

I also wish to thank the other members of the ESRC Research Strategy Seminars on Violence, Abuse and Gender Relations, who provided major support and intellectual stimulation during the period 1991–4: Sylvia Bailey, Jackie Barron, Rebecca Dobash, Russell Dobash, Jalna Hanmer, Owen Heathcote, Marianne Hester, Wendy Hollway, Catherine Itzin, Tony Jefferson, Liz Kelly, Monica McWilliams, Mary Maynard, David Morgan, Russell Murray, Sheila Saunders, Betsy Stanko, Nicole Ward Jouve and Shantu Watt.

I would also like to thank all the other people who have given me support and assistance over the last few years in the development of this work. They include Thmes Ashraf, Trevor Butt, David Collinson, Margaret Collinson, Celia Davies, John Davis, Gareth Dawkins, Cath Dillon, Barbara Fawcett, Brid Featherstone, Elizabeth Harlow, Amy Hearn, Jay Jacobs, Molly Hearn, Tom Hearn, John Holt, Sajid Hussain, Liisa Husu, David Jackson, Taira Kayani, Ruth Lister, Mary Locking, John MacDonald, Paul McHugh, Bob Matthews, Antonio Melechi, Wendy Parkin, Deidre Quill, Pam Todd, Christine Toft, Hugh Valentine, Sophie Watson and Paula Wilcox.

The writing of this book took place initially at the University of Bradford and since 1995 in the School of Social Policy, Faculty of Economic and Social Studies, University of Manchester. I am grateful to all my colleagues and students at these two universities for discussions on the issues raised in this book and for their support more generally. Thanks are also essential to the librarians of the Universities of Bradford and Manchester, and of Bradford City Council. I also wish to thank Elina Haavio-Mannila and colleagues at the University of Helsinki, and Elianne Riska and colleagues at Åbo Akademi University for providing convivial working environments for the final completion of the book. I am especially grateful to Karen Phillips of Sage who has given patient support, helpful advice and consistent encouragement throughout the writing. I also thank Justin Dyer for his careful and creative copy-editing, and Jane Evans of Sage for managing the production process.

There remain the voices of the women who have experienced violence from men, voices that have been silenced and are now, in some cases, less so. Paradoxically, I hope that this research and writing will increase the voices of those and other women, and will contribute to freeing women from men's violences and their threat.

Part I

SETTING THE SCENE

1

Introduction

The Problem of 'Men'

Men, or 'men', are now on the political agenda – and about time too! In one sense men have, of course, always been there. Many, most, public political agendas have been men's, just as many, most, organizations have been full of men's groups for centuries. On the other hand, the way men are has been questioned before.[1] What is relatively new, however, is the extent to which 'men' have become problematic, contested, up for discussion, debate and dispute. In fact it is only with 'men' becoming problematic that 'men' are explicitly placed on agendas at all.

Thus, what we have here is the common paradox that something becomes a topic for study and critique when that topic is no longer coherent, certain, known, in fact is no longer a topic in itself. And that something in this case is 'men'. The placing of the topic 'men' on political agendas simultaneously solidifies it and contributes to its withering, its falling away. These agendas are not only political but also personal, popular, theoretical and professional.

This focus on 'men', this solidifying and falling away of 'men', is necessarily different for those who are or who are not part of the topic 'men'. Thus, for men to focus on 'men' is different for women or others to focus on 'men'. The solidifying and falling away of 'men' may be, for women, a useful naming of those in power and a useful contribution to the destruction of their power. For men, the solidifying may be all too appealing as a means to further power. This is illustrated profusely in the theories and practices of male liberationists, members of the male backlash against feminism, as well as those who naively repudiate or reinforce men's power. The falling away is for men more difficult.

Undermining what men are may be personally disconcerting, confusing, even frightening. It may also be unclear what political implications follow from this: in this scheme there are few certainties on what is the appropriate thing for men to do. It is also likely that the subversion of men may show up further and further cracks in the power of men, may contribute to the destabilizing of men's structural power. Similarly, this book is uncertain, theoretically. It questions the very ideas of 'knowledge' and 'theory'; in particular, it undermines the dominant connection between men's knowledge and men's theory, on the one hand, and 'knowledge' and 'theory', on the other.

Pro-Feminism

My own perspective on these questions is unreservedly, unapologetically, pro-feminist. This may be an obvious and very familiar position, or it may be new and strange to you. Pro-feminism has developed as an explicit perspective over many years, even many centuries, on the basis that men cannot be feminist(s), if feminism is understood as theory and practice by women for women. On the other hand, it is quite possible for men to relate positively to, to welcome, to learn from, to support and be supportive of feminism. This does *not* mean that men can just sit back and depend on feminists, nor does it mean that men can become quasi-feminists. It does, however, strongly suggest that if men are to take feminism seriously, as within a pro-feminist perspective, then one of the most urgent tasks, perhaps the most urgent one, is for men to change men, ourselves and other men. It is not our (men's) task to try to change women; they can do that themselves if they wish.

While pro-feminist work necessarily develops in close association with feminist work, the focus on men and changing men is a task that clearly is, and has to be, open to both women and men. This applies in personal, professional, political and academic forums. Thus, what has come to be called Critical Studies on Men, while informed by pro-feminism, is necessarily open to both women and men.

Critical Studies on Men

The idea of Critical Studies on Men has developed as a more appropriate framework for the recent growth of studies on men than what has been labelled 'men's studies'. Men's studies is a confusing and potentially dangerous way of conceptualizing studies on men. Not only are 'men's studies' ambiguous (studies *on* men or studies *by* men?), they are also far from new. Libraries are stacked full of men's studies – the academic disciplines *themselves*. Moreover, men's studies can be a way of excluding women, of creating (more) spaces for men (without women). Men's studies also carry no clear political perspective; they may be well intentioned, even pro-feminist, but they then can become places for the development of institutionalized relations to feminism or may even be anti-feminist, in design or outcome (see Hearn, 1989).

Within Critical Studies on Men (see Hearn and Morgan, 1990), the emphasis is on the critique of men and men's power and domination, not just the study of men. Accordingly, issues of sexuality, sexual violence and violence are central within this framework, not just another 'topic' within studies of men (see Hanmer, 1990). There are diverse strands within these developments. They include feminist studies that are looking in some detail at particular men, or men in particular situations (for example, Friedman and Sarah, 1982; Cockburn, 1983); gay studies, most obviously, though not exclusively, on gay men (for example, Weeks, 1977; Plummer, 1992); and pro-feminist responses by men to feminism.

Explanations of 'Men'

One aspect of theorizing on men, whether by women or by men, that is particularly important is the production of *explanations* of men. Men are an object to be explained, just like any other social phenomenon. There are a number of ways of approaching the task of explanation. First, all the various methodological and theoretical approaches in social science can be applied to the explanation of men, for example, symbolic interactionism, conflict theory. Second, and similarly, all the different approaches and perspectives in feminism(s) implicitly or explicitly suggest different accounts of men. Third, some broad distinctions can be made between psychological and psychoanalytic accounts that focus on the individual man; social psychological accounts which focus on interpersonal relations; cultural, sub-cultural and other socially specific accounts which draw on the specificities of particular kinds of men; structural accounts of the general social category of men; and accounts that are structurally defined in some other way, for example, in structured discourses. Although I realize that discourses about men, as about anything else, can be, indeed perhaps by their very nature are, *specific*, they are also structured in ways that transcend interpersonal, group or even cultural processes and dynamics.

For much too long men have been considered the taken-for-granted norm against which women have been judged to be different. Yet despite, indeed because of, this dominance, the social construction of men has often not been addressed. Men have been all too visible yet invisible to critical analysis and change. Like other superordinate categories and groups (the rich, white people, physically able, and so on), men have been strangely absent from explicit inquiry – and deconstruction. To put this bluntly, men need to be named as men (Hanmer, 1990; Collinson and Hearn, 1994).

Making sense of men necessitates placing men in a social context. This entails considering men's power relations to women in that general context.

Men's identity usually includes an acceptance of that basic power relation. To do so is a relatively simple way of affirming a sense of, first, being a boy and then being a man. Thus a common aspect of men's identity is a taken-for-granted acceptance of that power, just as it is also likely to involve an acceptance of being a boy, then a man. The psychological and social identity called 'man' says and shows power relations. It is *identical*. An important aspect of men's power and sense of power is the use, potential use or threat of violence. And men's violence remains a major and pressing problem.

Furthermore, men have *unities* with each other and *differences* between each other (Hearn and Collinson, 1993). Unities and diffferences exist both collectively, for groups of men, and individually, for individual men. It is very important to acknowledge the interplay of these unities and differences between men; the paradox of the recognition of men as a gender class and the deconstruction of the monolith of men; and, more generally, the usefulness of developing explanatory accounts that are simultaneously psychological and social, agentic and structural, material and discursive.

The Focus on Men's Violences

Men's violences may be to women, girls, boys, children, young people, each other, animals, life, ourselves. The term 'men's violences' is preferred to 'male violence' for several reasons. First, it is more precise: it attributes the violence to men. Second, it makes it clear that there is not any assumption of biological inevitability to the violence or a biological cause of the violence. Third, it removes the ambiguity that there might be a special form of violence that is 'male' that is only one part of the totality of violence of men. Fourth, it acknowledges the plurality of men's violences.

In this book, my primary focus is on men's violence to women, in particular, men's violence to known women, as wives, girlfriends, partners, ex-partners, mothers, other relatives, friends and neighbours. The extent of men's violence to women and known women is immense. This is not to say that all men are violent towards women all the time, in all societies, in all contexts or cases. It is, however, to recognize the pervasive presence of those violences by men to women. Indeed it is apparent that: 'The safest place for men is the home, the home is, by contrast, the least safe place for women' (Edwards, 1989: 214). Similarly, Dobash and Dobash (1992: 2) comment:

> It is now well known that violence in the home is commonplace, that women are its usual victims and men its usual perpetrators. It is also known that the family is filled with many different forms of violence and aggression, including physical, sexual and emotional, and that violence is perpetrated by young and old alike.

In considering men's violence to known women, I am particularly concerned with violence in 'intimate', usually sexual, that is, heterosexual relationships. A recent review suggested that: 'Estimates based on national and regional surveys . . . show that ten to twenty-five percent of British women have, at some time, during their life, been the victim of violence from a male partner' (Dobash et al., 1996a: 2).[2] However, even such figures needed to be treated with caution as they may under-report verbal, psychological and emotional violence and abuse, and rape, coercive sex and pressurized sex. When women point out that women are in most danger from the man they are in the closest relationship with, this means that we can see why it is that men are most dangerous to the women with whom they have the closest relationship. This effectively raises the question of the relationship of men's violence to women and men's heterosexuality and heterosexual relations.

Men's violences are being increasingly recognized for what they are – a severe social problem. Yet the recognition appears to do little to reduce men's violence to women, or, indeed, other kinds of men's violence. The problem of men's violence to known women has now been named, and men have been named as the problem. Men's violence to known women and the pain, both physical and emotional, of that violence have been made public. The focus upon men's violence to known women has become more conscious – in personal and political responses, in clarification of the law, in particular the making of such violence illegal, and in the changing of criminal justice and other policies.

Similarly, there is increasing concern with the way in which different forms of men's violence may be interconnected with each other, yet it is still far from clear to what extent it is analytically and politically useful to consider men's violences as a unified set of activities, as against a series of relatively discrete activities, with different characteristics, and thus demanding different intervention, policies and actions.

Kaufman (1987) has written of the triad of men's violence, between men's violence to women, to each other and to ourselves. This provides a simple but effective framework of thinking about the connections between these forms of violence. This can be done theoretically, politically and, indeed, personally. I have previously attempted to extend this relationship to include a fourth form of violence – men's violence to young people, including child abuse (Hearn, 1990). This clearly increases the combination and permutation of connections, and thus is difficult to conceptualize. However, it does have the advantage of including the specific dimension of men's violence and power in relation to age. The connections between men's violence to women and men's violence to young people are many, not least because the latter is always also the former, and the former is often the latter. This is especially so in the case of men's violence to mothers, whether or not in the presence of young people. An important task in studying, changing and abolishing men's violence is to make connections between different kinds of men's violences, whilst simultaneously recognizing their specific and special form in different situations.

To adopt this focus is not to play down women's experience but rather it is to *name* and *focus on* the problem – the problem of men as the major *doers* of violence to women, children, each other, and indeed to ourselves, whether in specific self-destruction and suicide or more generally men's self-reduction to 'not fully human', indeed to violence itself.

This necessitates for men a critical *relation to men*. For men to do this involves a challenge to the way we are; it involves a critique of ourselves, that is, first, personally; second, in terms of other men we are in contact with in our personal or public lives; and *also*, third, more generally and socially, towards men as a powerful social category, a powerful social grouping. So to focus on men, the problem of men, in doing this kind of work, whether it is research work or otherwise, is likely to have different implications for women and for men. It raises a variety of problems of how men are, how men behave, how men should behave, why men have power in society, whether that power is structured, personal or both, what different kinds of men are there, and how these current arrangements can be changed.

To put this rather bluntly, to focus on men and men's violence to women unsettles, makes problematic, the way men are, not just in the doing of particular actions of violence but also more generally. It raises question marks against men's behaviour in general. For example, how is it possible that men can be violent to women, perhaps over many years, and this can be part of a socially accepted way of being a man? How does violence relate to the social construction of different forms of masculinity in school, in sport, in work, in the media? What is the link between violence and dominant forms of masculinities? What is the connection between men and violence? What has violence got to do with men? How do we understand men and violence, men's violence? In raising these kinds of questions, two major themes need to be stressed: power and control; and the taking apart of what is usually taken-for-granted.

My Relation to Men's Violence

Like most issues in sexual politics and gender politics, 'the personal is political'. What I mean by this is several things: men's violence to women is certainly both a personal and a political problem; doing work on this problem may raise personal issues about one's own behaviour as a man both in private and in public; and in changing the situation, it is not just enough to rely on 'governed' policies. The actual occurrence of violence occurs personally and interpersonally. To stop violence necessitates both general policy change and changing individual men.

Violence is for me, thus, necessarily a personal and political issue. This is also so for most men, even when it is not recognized as such. My personal relation to violence is not a matter of direct physical violence, for that is not how I live. It is because of the physical intimidation of my presence as a man, my ability to be emotionally and verbally violent, as well as my potential physical violence. Furthermore, I, like other men, am defined at least partly in relation to violence. In other words, violence is a reference point for the production of boys and men. For these reasons, opposing violence is a key political priority for men.

While I have been researching and writing on men for many years, it is relatively recently that I have explicitly researched on men's violence. In retrospect, I think I avoided that explicit focus for several years. Thus, the neglect of the study of men's violence has been one of the shortcomings of much of men's studies on men. My own current interest in researching men's violences comes from a number of sources:

- the recognition of the centrality of (men's) violence within, for example, theoretical and historical work on patriarchy/patriarchies (Hearn, 1987, 1992b);
- the relationship of sexuality and violence within research on sexuality and organizations, including sexual harassment and thus violence (Hearn and Parkin, 1987, 1995; Hearn et al., 1989; Hearn, 1994c);
- the concern with child abuse arising from interest in childcare, teaching social work students and collective work with the Violence Against Children Study Group (Hearn, 1990; also see Hearn, 1988; Hearn and Parkin, 1989);
- the increasing prominence of public responses to violence by men, including practical and political organizing on this issue, partly as a response to feminism.

Within sociology and the social sciences more generally, the issue of violence, and particularly men's violence, is problematic, in the sense that a social science of violence is strangely unformed and unrecognized. Instead, the study of violence tends to be scattered between a variety of disciplines (sociology, criminology, jurisprudence, social policy, and so on) and a variety of sub-topics (crime, deviance, child abuse, sexual harassment, and so on). The topic of violence has been avoided, both in sociology in general, and in studies on men in particular.

My relation to men's violence is thus set within a wide web of personal, practical, working and biographical features. I bring these to doing research and writing on violence. They include my own relationship to violence, enacted, experienced and witnessed; the different meanings to me of different kinds of violence; the association of sexuality and violence (partly summed up in MacKinnon's [1983] phrase 'the eroticization of dominance'); my opposition to violence; the facts of where I have worked, whom I know, and so on. Working on violence is always for me a personal and political issue, even though it clearly has more general significance in relation to the power of men and the construction of masculinities. It is also a difficult area to work on, and an area of study and action that is demanded by a pro-feminist standpoint. This raises the question of the importance of political commitment against violence when working on and researching violence. Other areas of study on men that also demand attention, and are probably even more difficult, include state, corporate, institutional violences; militarism; corruption and organized crime.

One of the particularly difficult things I have had to struggle with in writing this book, and doing the research that led to it, is how to locate myself. My relationship with men's violence to known women and indeed with the men in this study is ambiguous. On the one hand, I can see myself at one end of a continuum of violence. On the other hand, my experience has been different to that of the men studied and I am not like them in terms of their own violence. For one thing, I have given a lot of time and attention to the topic; also I do not intend to use violence; and, third, I am politically opposed to violence, and especially men's violence to known women.

The Historical Construction of Men's Violence[3]

In attempting to 'make sense' of men's violence to women, it is necessary to consider the problem in a clear historical context. While my focus here and throughout is on the UK, the question of the historical construction of men's violence is of course relevant much more broadly. This is especially important in understanding how such violence has been accepted, condoned, normalized and ignored by both individuals and institutions. It has been seen as a 'private matter'. Individual men's perceptions of violence to women are themselves affected by the definitions and constructions produced and reproduced in agencies. The recent increase in recognition of the problem by state agencies has arisen from the actions of the Women's Movement, and in the UK case particularly Women's Aid.

Men's violence to women was an important focus of attention in both First Wave feminism (see, for example, Cobbe, 1878, 1894; Pankhurst, 1913) and Second Wave feminism (see, for example, Bristol Women's Studies Group, 1979; Coote and Campbell, 1982). In 1853 the British Parliament passed the Act for the Better Prevention and Punishment of Aggravated Assaults upon Women and Children, but this was not extended to Scotland or Ireland, and '. . . did very little to deter husbands from abusing their wives and children' (Steiner-Scott, 1997: 127). The basic Act of Parliament that defines violence to the person is the Offences Against the Person Act 1861. The relevant sections are 42 (common assault), 47 (assault occasioning actual bodily harm), 20 (unlawful wounding) and 18 (grievous bodily harm). However, this Act could not be said to operate in relation to men's violence to known women until subsequent reforms in the nineteenth and twentieth centuries.

Significantly, the reform of the legal treatment of men's violence to women within marriage that was made in 1878 followed shortly after the Cruelty to Animals Act of 1876. The latter Act extended to all animals the provision of the Cruelty to Animals Act of 1849 which had made it illegal to 'cruelly beat, ill-treat, over-drive, abuse or torture' any *domestic* animal

(c. 92, s. 2) (James, 1986: 601). Prior to 1878, the 'rule of thumb' had operated in the courts, whereby husbands were not permitted to use a stick broader than a thumb. The 1878 Matrimonial Causes Act allowed women to use cruelty as grounds for divorce. Magistrates were given powers to grant swift and cheap separation orders to women who could prove a *specific* incident of physical assault. In this way, state law had begun to claim, if only in word, some jurisdiction over men's violence in marriage, and so to recognize, if only implicitly, a distinction between violence and sexuality in marriage.

A number of other legal reforms were introduced towards the end of the nineteenth century. These included the Married Women's Property Act 1870, which gave wives the right to keep their own earnings; the Married Women's Property Act 1882, which introduced women's rights to keep property they owned in marriage or acquired later, even though no criminal proceedings could be taken against a husband whilst the 'partners' were cohabiting; the Maintenance of Wives Act 1886, which empowered magistrates in local courts to grant and enforce maintenance orders of no more than two pounds per week; and the Summary Jurisdiction (Married Women) Act 1895, which made it easier for women to gain protection of the court following persistent physical cruelty rather than a specific physical assault. In 1891, husbands lost their 'rights' to forcibly imprison their wives in the matrimonial home to obtain their 'conjugal rights' (*R* v. *Jackson*, Court of Appeal, 1891).

Despite these reforms and the formal equalization of women's and men's property rights in marriage, by the end of the nineteenth century in practice little had shifted the nature of men's authority relations over women in marriage. Men's day-to-day domination and authority was routinely reinforced by the state, for example, in the avoidance of intervention in 'marital disputes' by the police. Women's position was also generally weak in terms of divorce proceedings and the award and receipt of maintenance. Brophy and Smart (1982: 210) have summarized this situation as follows:

> She had no right to leave her husband without his permission and if she did he could physically restrain her. She had no right to maintenance if she could not prove her husband had committed a matrimonial offence . . . he could divorce her on a single act of adultery whilst she had to establish adultery combined with another matrimonial offence. . . . Any challenge by a wife to this authority, or to the principle of sexual monogamy resulted in the courts refusing to grant her maintenance. The magistrates courts . . . treated adultery as an absolute bar to maintenance for wives.

Thus while the picture was, to put it politely, mixed, the late nineteenth-century reforms did at least clarify the situation in terms of criminal law.

Second Wave feminism has led to the reappraisal of legal responses to violence. However, even in 1967 when the first Matrimonial Homes Act was passed, 'matrimonial violence was a non-subject' (Freeman, 1987: 38). The

Act was designed to preserve the rights of occupation of the non-owning and non-tenant spouse rather than to respond to violence. Following the establishment of the Women's Aid Federation in 1974 and the Parliamentary Select Committee on *Violence in Marriage* (Select Committee on Violence in Marriage, 1975), the Domestic Violence and Matrimonial Proceedings Act was passed in 1976, giving additional powers of injunction, including for the unmarried, and of arrest. Subsequent reforms, such as the Matrimonial Homes Act 1983, which strengthened the power of the ouster order, still, however, failed to produce a fundamental reform of state intervention in favour of women's freedom from violence (see Binney et al., 1981; Atkins and Hoggett, 1984).

In recent years, there have been uneven attempts to reform state policy and its implementation. Reform has occurred most obviously in police forces with the enactment of 'domestic violence' pro-arrest policies; the treatment of violence equally seriously regardless of its location or the relationship of the parties; and the creation of Special Units. In 1988 the Chief Constable of West Yorkshire issued a Policy Statement on Domestic Violence to all members of the Force, pledging a commitment to treat violence in the home as seriously as violence elsewhere. Other state agencies, notably the Probation Service and the Crown Prosecution Service, have also more recently given more attention to this problem.

The state, and particularly state agencies controlled by men, has made a series of concessions in response to men's violence to women. The state has thus sponsored particular social forms within the private domains. Increasingly but rather gradually the private powers of men – individual husbands and fathers – have been brought into the purview, and sometimes the control, of the state. Most importantly, legal and other state constructions of violence have generally served to play down its significance and to limit its definition, whilst at the same time there has been a gradually increased awareness and recognition of the problem in law, policy statements and, to an extent, in policy implementation.

The Growth of Research

This book follows the development of theoretical and practical research on men's violence to known women and indeed children. While the history of such violence is long, it was research in the post-war period that recognized the 'battered wife syndrome' (Walker, 1979), the cycle of abuse, and the field of 'domestic violence'. Feminist work has both built on these analyses and provided a critique of them, particularly those that attributed the cause of men's violence to women through 'learned helplessness' and other victim-blaming approaches (for example, Pagelow, 1981). Thus the field of study of men's violence to known women has been established. The frequency of such violence and the difficulty that many women face in gaining services and other material assistance from state and other agencies, in the effort to stop or move from such violence, have been explored (Dobash and Dobash, 1979; Binney et al., 1981). In this process, it has often been voluntary, community and women's organizations that have been at the forefront of organizing the provision of assistance to women who have experienced violence from known men. These practical and policy issues have then involved the interplay of individuals, families, voluntary sector agencies and the state (Dobash and Dobash, 1992). The way in which these interrelations have worked has been different for different women in different social situations – national, regional, urban, rural (McWilliams and McKiernan, 1993). For example, black women have experienced particular difficulties in gaining an appropriate response to men's violence from state agencies (Mama, 1989).

These practical, policy and research agendas have been strongly intertwined within feminist research. They have also closely interrelated with debates around the explanation of men's violence to known women. In general terms, there has been an historical movement from more individualistic explanation to explanation based on learning theory and the operation of family systems to explanations that locate men's violence as part of men's structural power within patriarchy.

While the problem of men who have been violent has clearly been very significant within much feminist work, it has been relatively unusual for this to be the main focus. This is of course not surprising as the priority has been to give support to women and assist in the improvement of their lives. There is, however, a much smaller literature which has discussed men's experiences of men's violence in specific locations, such as prisons (for example, Wooden and Parker, 1982), or of particular types of violence, such as rape (for example, Groth, 1979; Beneke, 1982; Scully, 1990) or pornography (for example, Kimmel, 1990; Stoltenberg, 1990). There is an additional literature that is directed towards practical and professional initiatives for working with men who have been violent towards women with a view to stopping that violence, and especially men's programmes (for example, Gondolf, 1985). Other more general texts on men and men's power have included chapters on men's violence and men's violence to women (for example, Segal, 1990). Less usual have been studies on men who have been violent to known women and have remained living in the community.

The Research Study[4]

This book arises from a three-year research project on men who have been violent to known women. This has usually meant wives, partners, co-habitees, girlfriends, lovers, but also included mothers, neighbours, and other friends and acquaintances. The study was based in West Yorkshire and involved interviewing 75 men, in some cases twice or more; of these, 60 men were included in the main study[5] (see Appendix). These interviews included detailed accounts from the men of what they had done; their understanding of why they had done this; the responses of family, friends and state and other agencies; their attitude to and relationships with women; what, if anything, they had done about their violence; and their hopes and plans, if any, for the future. The violences reported included rape fantasies; sexual wrestling; long-term verbal abuse; restraining, holding, blocking; throwing against the wall; slapping, hitting, striking, punching, beating up, attempted murder; murder; the use of sticks, knives and other objects and weapons; rape; abduction; torture; throwing and smashing things, for example, bottles, damaging property, houses, furniture, cars. In addition, about 130 follow-up interviews, questionnaires and examinations of case records were completed with agency staff who had dealt with their case, where the men gave permission. A linked, but separate, study of women's experiences of violence from known men, as well as follow-up interviews with agency staff, was conducted by my colleague Jalna Hanmer, using the same methodology and methods.

This Book

This book is an exploration of men's violence to known women. It has arisen from extensive research on the topic and draws on the research study just described and the issues that this study has raised. It considers what can be learned and what cannot be learned about men's violence to known women from what men say about their violence. The book also addresses what agency staff who deal with this have to say about it. It contains detailed interview material, research results, general surveys of the current issues in this field, as well as theorizing on the area. The research and the interview material is often complex, explicit, vivid, tragic, and sometimes shows alarming inconsistencies or 'logics' within the same interview. For example, one man explained that he was violent to the woman because he loved her so much; another because he was trying to stop her drinking; a third explained that if his ex-partner's current male partner hurt her he would attack him, and yet if he saw her he 'would kill her', and so on.

While this book derives from the research study, it is not just a direct account of it. Clearly this book is not an account of women's experiences of men's violence; that has been or can be produced by feminist research on women's experiences. Neither is it a comprehensive review of all men's violence, whether to women or to others. It is also not intended as a practical handbook against men's violences, even though it contains information and discussion which may be of interest to those working against such violence, whether personally and/or professionally. Rather it is intended as a contribution to a complex field and to opposition to an urgent problem.

The next two chapters set the scene by, first, reviewing approaches to the definition and explanation of men's violence to women and, then, outlining some of the major issues in studying and researching men's violences. Chapter 4 examines an important academic and political question, namely, the problematic connections between violence and talking about violence. The following four chapters show the various ways in which men talk about their violence to known women – in terms of the contexts of their violence; descriptions of their violence; forms of accounting for their violence; and the sexual and other subtexts of their talk. Chapters 9 and 10 concern what happens after the violence through the responses of agencies and the possible attempts by men to move away from violence. The final chapter reviews key issues for theory, policy, politics and practice that have been raised throughout the book.

2

Definitions and Explanations of Men's Violence

To analyse and to oppose men's violence means considering possible definitions and possible explanations of violence. This may seem obvious
enough. Debates, policies, politics and interventions against men's violence
are very much about *contesting* and *contested* definitions and explanations
of violence. However, there are dangers in reifying a particular definition of
violence as absolutely the most appropriate, and in explaining away
violence through particular explanations and causes. It is more important to
appreciate the changing definitions of violence through time and place – to
evaluate and contribute to the historical and cultural process of naming,
whereby different actions and structures have been *named* as violence.
Likewise, the aesthetic appeal of causes can be misleading as a way to
stopping violence. It is necessary to both interrogate explanations and
causes, and be wary of them and the ways they can be used and abused.
Furthermore, explanations of men's violence can be constructed for many
different reasons and in many different contexts. They can be produced by,
amongst others, social scientists, judges, lawyers, social workers and of
course individual men who have been violent, and individual women who
have experienced violence.

Theories and the contestations between them are vital, as they inform
practical agency interventions, the development of policy, the work of
professionals, and, significantly, the views of those involved, as both
violators and violated. Theories, causes and explanations of violence can be
re-used by men to explain away, excuse, justify or perpetuate men's
violences. There are numerous possible interplays between social scientific,
agency, professionals' and individual actors' theories and explanations of
men's violence. Men in contact with agencies may take on agency and
professional explanations, and especially so if those theories provide
individualistic explanations. More structural explanations are more difficult
to respond to and have further reaching implications for both agencies and
agency staff.

In this chapter I outline alternative approaches to men's violence to
women and possible explanations for these violences.

What is Violence? What are Men's Violences?

The definition of violence is contested. This contestation is itself part of the process of the reproduction of and indeed opposition to violence. This process occurs differentially and unevenly in different cultural and historical contexts. It has both short-term and local dimensions and long-term historical and global dimensions. Accordingly, in addressing the definition of violence, a broad view is necessary. Violence can mean many different things to different people; it can refer to or involve many different kinds of social actions and social relations. 'Violence' is sometimes used to include or exclude 'abuse', or to mean 'physical violence' or only certain forms of physical violence. The term 'violence' can be used precisely or vaguely.

Most importantly, violence is not *one thing*; it is not a thing at all. Violence is simply a word, a shorthand, that refers to a mass of different experiences in people's lives. And as a word, 'violence', like other words, can be used and abused – it can be reduced through nominalization (Kress and Hodge, 1979; Trew, 1979) and reification (Lukács, 1971). In the first case, 'violence' as a word can obscure power relations within the practical use of the word; in the second case, social relations in the case of violence are reduced to things without human agency, or even social structure.

Violence is not separated off from the rest of life; violence can be mixed up with all sorts of everyday experiences – work and housework, sex and sexuality, marriage, leisure, relaxing and watching television. Some men specifically separate violence off from other parts of life and their life, and treat it as some kind of separate activity. This in turn becomes part of the problem of the continuation of the violence.

What 'violence' is and means is both material and discursive: both a matter of the experience of change in bodily matter, and a matter of change in discursive constructions. It is simultaneously material and discursive, simultaneously painful, full of pain, and textual, full of text. Finding a definition of violence that works for all situations and all times is difficult. Violence, what is meant by violence, and whether there is a notion of violence at all, are historically, socially and culturally constructed. Historical and cultural constructions of violence are not just matters of local, relative variations; they specifically shape the personal circumstances and future courses of action available to women and men in relation to violence. More concretely, historical constructions of violence affect the way in which state organizations, the law and other institutions define violence. These in turn influence actual and potential policies on men's violence to women, thus structuring the lives of women and men. State and other organizations structure the meaning of violence through both inclusion and exclusion of actual or possible actions.

Definition can be approached from many different perspectives and interests. A necessary part of the definition of violence is the *recognition* of violence or the threat, potentiality or possibility of violence. *Recognition* may often, though not always, move from the individual to the group or collectivity, especially when individuals begin to share their experiences of violence and the possibility of violence.

While I do not think there is any one simple definition of violence, it is useful to consider the following elements in definitions of it:

- that which is or involves the use of force, physical or otherwise, by a violator or violators;
- that which is intended to cause harm;
- that which is experienced, by the violated, as damaging and/or violation;
- the recognition of certain acts, activities or events as 'violent' by a third party, for example, a legal authority.

All these elements are themselves historically and culturally specific. What is not named as violence in one situation or time may become named as violent elsewhere or subsequently. This, for example, is clear when what are at one time named as 'consensual' sexual-social relations are renamed as power relations, exploitation, abuse or harassment. Seen in this way, violence is an open-ended category, and especially so if the experience of violation is emphasized as part of definition.

Furthermore, violence is both interpersonal and structural. While the concept of interpersonal violence refers to *direct* violence from one person to another in an identifiable situation, what is meant by structural violence needs some attention. There are several different, though related, meanings of the term 'structural violence'. These are as follows:

- the structural pattern of individual and interpersonal violence, such as the societal patterns of men's violence to women in the home;
- the violent acts and effects of social institutions such as the state – more accurately referred to as institutional violence;
- the violent effects of inequalities, including those on a world scale, such as the distribution of famine;
- the violent effects of warfare and inter-nation and inter-community violence;
- the social structural relations of institutions when and where those social relations have historically been violent or have underwritten violence, for example, the social relations of fatherhood or capitalism.

All of these possible distinctions and definitions are relevant to men's violence to known women. Men's violences are those violences that are done by men or are attributed to men. The range of men's violences is immense. It spans the very particular and the global; the interpersonal and the institutional; the agentic and the structural. It includes violence to strangers and to known others. It includes violence to women, children, each other, animals, and men's own selves. It varies in form and in process. It includes physical, sexual, verbal, psychological, emotional, linguistic, cognitive, social, spatial, financial, representational and visual violences. It includes violence done, threatened violence and potential violence. It includes enacted violence in the present and accumulated or consolidated violence in the past and present. It also includes the interrelation and overlap between all these kinds of violences.

These various violences connect with the general question of the health and welfare of those involved – both the women violated and the construction of bodies of themselves and others. Violence involves the use of the body and the affecting of the bodies of others. These bodily violences provide the material grounds for further violences.

Explanations of Men's Violence to Known Women

The debate on why men do violence to known women has been long and varied. It has moved through shifts in discursive constructions, and the placing of men's violence in relation to both 'men' and 'violence'. Explanations of men's violence may be developed from a wide range of academic and disciplinary traditions, each with its own different traditions, conceptual, analytical and empirical building blocks.

There are very many different explanations of men's violence to known women. Biological explanations may emphasize 'hormonal patterns' and 'aggression'; sociobiology may conceptualize violence in relation to 'territory' and its 'defence'; psychology may introduce 'personality types' or 'disorders' and 'personal constructs'; psychoanalysis may hypothesize 'projection' and 'displacement'. Sociology, anthropology, political science and economics all tend to use concepts that are grounded in interpersonal, collective, institutional, structural or societal processes. These may include 'poverty', 'stress', 'alienation', 'sub-culture', and so on. With all of these explanations, there are problems. Moreover, while it is quite possible to identify individual, family, cultural, economic, structural and other causes or explanations of violence, the search for a final or original cause may be futile.

Nature and Biology

Constructions of violence have often been made with reference to 'Nature', 'nature' or 'the natural'. Men may be seen as, for example, naturally aggressive, and violence may be considered as naturally associated with men. Nature may also be invoked in terms of the justifications for such violence. Ideas of 'Nature' and 'the natural', whether as natural rights to do violence or natural explanations of violence, are very persistent in both everyday and professional discourses of violence, frequently underpinned by ideologies of biology.

Biological approaches have usually been founded on one or more of the following: instinct; territoriality and physical size; chromosomal difference; hormonal difference; human interventions on the biochemistry of the body. The emphasis upon instinct and territoriality, and indeed competition for food and sexual partners, has a long history in attempting to explain violence. In the 1960s this focus became particularly popular, largely through the work of Lorenz (1966) and Ardrey (1961, 1966). Importantly, these proponents of the links between explanations of animal behaviour and human behaviour, in this case violence, were immediately countered by a series of critiques from liberal, human, anthropological and other perspectives (see, for example, Montagu, 1968), as well as those more centrally located within sociobiology itself which point to the presence of the *independent* evolution of agonistic behaviour (social fighting) in each animal species (Vessey and Jackson, 1976).

The chromosomal explanation of violence, and particularly the violence of particular types of 'males', has followed research and intervention on intersexuality, of which there are 15 main variants (Annett, 1976). Particular interest followed research of chromosomal patterns amongst men in a 'maximum security hospital for mentally disturbed or subnormal men with criminal propensities', and the possibility that XYY men (that is, males with an XYY chromosomal structure) were strongly over-represented amongst such populations (Jacobs et al., 1965). While such men do on average appear to be larger in physique, to be more prone to severe temper tantrums when children, and to score lower on IQ tests, it would be simplistic to identify the root cause as hyperaggressivity resulting from their chromosomal pattern (Manning, 1989: 54). In a short and careful review, Manning (1989: 55) concludes:

> XYY men do have a number of handicaps to overcome; not all succeed and because the result is sometimes antisocial they, more often than their peers, end up in prisons. In Britain, there may be some 130 . . . in maximum security prisons but note there must be some 24,870 who are not. The huge majority of XYY males lead ordinary lives and the childhood problems which they have are not particularly intractable.

Another major line of biological research has been on variations in levels of testosterone, both between and amongst males and females. Testosterone is often represented as the *male* (androgen) hormone. However, while testosterone is produced mainly in the testes in males, it is also produced in the adrenal cortex and ovaries in females. It is responsible for the differentiation of male and female primary sex characteristics, with males having higher levels than females.[1] Furthermore, stature and musculature are both related to testosterone (Strand, 1983), which may also tend to increase the level for males. While some animal studies show a link between testosterone and aggression, this connection is complicated in many ways, for example, the aggression may be predominantly by males in the presence of females

(Keverne, 1979). In some animal studies, surges in testosterone appear to be followed by increased access to sexual partners and to food, and greater security from territorial infringement.

Furthermore, animal studies indicate that victory in struggles for dominance tends to increase testosterone, while defeat tends to decrease it. For humans, surges in testosterone occur at puberty, and also in sexual arousal. But testosterone also increases in a variety of other social situations, such as winning in sports, following successful athletic or fearful accomplishments, and even with social achievements or celebrations. However, this relationship between testosterone and dominance is not simple. Increases in testosterone have been found following *decisive* victories, such as winning tennis matches *decisively* (Mazur and Lamb, 1980) rather than just winning in itself. Similar conclusions have been found in wrestling matches (Elias, 1981). Outcome studies have also been completed amongst men, such as the following:

1   Men who had committed violent crimes at a younger age were found to have higher testosterone levels (Kreuz and Rose, 1972).
2   Men who committed violent crimes were found to have higher levels than other convicts (Dabbs et al., 1987).
3   Prisoners who were rated 'tougher' by other inmates were found to have higher levels (Dabbs et al., 1987).
4   Men who committed violent crimes and prisoners with higher status both had higher levels than other prisoners (Ehrenkranz et al., 1974).

In order to make sense of such variations in humans, Kemper (1990) has argued that there is a need to develop socio-psychoendocrinology, in which reciprocal links are recognized between testosterone, aggression, dominance/ eminence, social structure, and indeed sexual behaviour.[2]

Finally, in this section, we need to note those biologically based explanations of aggression and violence that are couched in terms of human intervention in the biochemical. This is most obviously the case with debates about the effects of steroids (Haupt and Rovere, 1984). Such interventions clearly at the very least suggest the need for social *and* biological explanation.

Towards the Social

Biological approaches to men's violence have tended to locate explanation in the biological body, human biological processes that transcend sex/ gender, or the nature of the biological male. Such explanations are usually open to criticism for neglecting questions of power, cultural and historical relativity, and morality. Similar criticisms can be directed at many psychological explanations of violence. Psychological approaches to men's violence have tended to locate explanation in the mind, mental processes that transcend sex/gender, or the nature of the male or masculine psyche. Either way, biological and psychological explanations generally do not address the interrelations of body and society, and of mind, body and society.

While 'nature' discourses remain popular in the media and in everyday conversation, in social science and many professional discourses violence is frequently located elsewhere. These discourses include those of social work, law and civil rights. In each of these, violence, and in this context, men's violence to known women, is in some sense 'social' rather than 'natural'. These arguments even apply to those versions of medical, psychiatric, psychoanalytic discourses that at the least recognize the social construction of the biological or physiological. More usually, violence is constructed as derived from social causes or liable to response from social intervention or in terms of its longer term effects. In other words, violence is usually constructed in terms of its antecedents or its postcedents, and much less often in terms of the immediate actions, behaviours, impacts and effects. There is a significant avoidance of constructing violence as itself, as something to be constructed as the prime focus, rather than the result of antecedents or the preliminary to postcedents.

Within the social discourses, men's violence to women is constructed as partly, largely or totally social in its origin, form, content and impacts, effects and traces. There are a number of different dimensions that might be used to categorize these 'social' accounts of men's violence to known women. These include variations between the individual, the group/family/network, the society; anti-feminism and pro-feminism; and disciplinary and professional 'traditions'.

Many theories and analyses of violence have at their centre debates about the very nature of *the social* – the relationship of individual and society; of social order and social conflict; of mind and body; of the internal and the external; and above all the place of violence in the social. There are thus a number of difficult, and implicitly gendered, dilemmas to be engaged with:

1 Violence can be understood as a biological or a social fact.
2 Violence can be constructed as part of the inherent 'badness' of people or an exception to the inherent 'goodness' of people.
3 Violence can be something taken on by individuals from the social or something placed upon individuals by the social.
4 Violence can be expressive of internal needs or instrumental to achieve external ends.
5 Violence of one party, in this context particular men, can be considered as separate from or in relation to the violence or potential violence of others.
6 Violence can be a means of maintaining social structures or of disrupting social structures.

A simple but useful framework for the analysis of explanations of men's violence to known women is that outlined by Gondolf (1985), drawing on the work of Bagarozzi and Giddings (1983) and Gelles (1983). Gondolf's framework presents three major theoretical explanations as follows:

> Psychoanalytic themes [that] focus on stress, anxiety instilled during child rearing . . .; social learning theories [that] consider the abuse to an outgrowth of learned patterns of aggressive communication to which both husband and wife contribute . . .; socio-political theories [that] hold the patriarchal power plays of men oppressing women to be at the heart of wife abuse. (Gondolf, 1985: 27)

These and other social approaches are now examined in more detail.

Psychoanalysis and Psychoanalytic Explanations

Psychoanalytic explanations of men's violence to known women have often relied on notions of 'intrapsychic conflict, personality disorders, denial mechanisms, developmental deficiencies/impaired ego, narcissism, traumatic childhood, masochism' (Dankwort, 1992–3: 35). The violence itself is often *not* the focus of attention; rather 'the dynamics' are. Violent behaviour may be constructed as psychologically expressive rather than instrumental in the maintenance of control. Freudian and neo-Freudian theories have analysed violence as located primarily *inside* the person, to the extent that observing the violence of other people, or even expressing one's own anger, or at least mild versions of anger, may tend to reduce violence.

Some psychoanalytic theories have been heavily criticized for reducing violence to the product of a determined individual personality outside of social relations or even for attributing violence to the personality of the victim. For example, abused women have sometimes been described as masochistic or of tolerating or even seeking out abuse, following their treatment as children. In such an argument, the undervaluing of girls as children might be seen as explaining women's tolerance of abuse and violence from men in their adult lives. In the worst case, the focus of attention shifts from the violating man to the violated woman. A well-quoted study of this type is that by Snell, Rosenwald and Robey (1964). In their research on 12 couples, they concentrated on the women, whom they described as:

> Domineering, masochistic, frigid, aggressive, indecisive, masculine, passive, over-protective of their sons, and emotionally deprived . . . [needing] . . . periodic punishment for their 'castrating activity'. (Pagelow, 1981: 115)

Whilst much psychoanalytic writing has been both Freudian in inspiration and anti-woman (or at the least not feminist/pro-feminist), there has been increasing concern with the interaction of feminism and psychoanalysis. This has provided a new genre of writing about men's violences, from what can be described as feminist psychoanalysis or psychoanalytic feminism, that uses psychoanalytic concepts and epistemologies without the anti-feminism of some earlier psychoanalyses.

Meanwhile, men's violence towards women may be explained through their own childhood experiences, and, in particular, their attempts to assert an 'exaggerated masculinity' as compensation for their fears of femininity. Craib (1987) has very helpfully considered the implications of feminist psychoanalytic work for the explanation of male dominance. He contrasts the account given by Chodorow (1978) in *The Reproduction of Mothering* with that of Eichenbaum and Orbach (1984) in *What Do Women Want?* In the former, men's dominance derives in part from the development of a rigid ego created in response to the demands of coping with separation from the mother and identifying with an 'absent' father. In the latter, men's dominance derives from men's dependency and its denial through dominance. These contrasts are found in earlier psychoanalytic work. For example, Suttie (1935), writing over fifty years earlier, argued in *The Origins of Love and Hate* that it was the 'taboo' on tenderness imposed on boys that led to their differentiation from females and forced their development to proceed by and towards violence. Their own violent change produces their change of others through violence. Echoes of this theme are found in Jukes's (1993) book *Why Men Hate Women*, in which the difficulty of boys' relations with their mothers is seen as remaining a persistent potential, and, for him, an almost inescapable source of hate and violence for men into adult life.

The dependency problematic has been taken up more fully by Benjamin (1988) in *The Bonds of Love*. For her '[d]omination begins with attempts to deny dependency' (1988: 52), and 'the root of domination lies in the breakdown of tension between self and other' (1988: 53). Thus, domination, including violence, is the result of complex dynamics, in particular, the exaggerated maintenance of difference with each saying or *overstating* 'I am not you' (1988: 57) – whereas in her analysis, 'I am you' at least to a larger extent than 'I' and perhaps 'you' realize. Domination and desire are not for her opposites: domination does not repress desire; rather domination and violence use and transform desire – the bonds of love. Her analyses are centrally about intersubjectivities between people, rather than splitting and other processes of intrasubjectivity in relative isolation. She thus provides a very interesting way of developing psychoanalytic theory in a social and political context.

These apparent contradictions between different elements of psychoanalytic theory are of course not necessarily insoluble. For example, an apparently over-rigid 'ego' could be a compensatory response to a fragile 'ego'; alternatively, an over-rigid ego may obscure or even bind together aspects of the personality that are apparently fragile. Much here depends on what *kind of reality* is assumed to be relevant in the investigation of the person. Is it the reality of deep structures, in that the apparent is always or nearly always assumed to be underlain by the less apparent, the immanent? Or is it the reality of the more explicit personality structure, so that what is revealed as dominant is indeed more real? These two interpretations of the personality illustrate some of the difficulties of interconnecting psychoanalysis and realism, both in general, and specifically, in relation to men's violence to women.

Psychoanalytic approaches remain very powerful and influential. They figure in both social science explanations of men's violence to known women and professional explanations in social work, health, therapeutic and related occupations. They are also sometimes taken up by individual men themselves following their interaction with such professionals.

The Social Individual, Social Roles and the Social Environment

While biological, psychological and psychoanalytic theories of violence and men's violence have been and continue to be important within the social sciences and many spheres of social intervention, more socially located theories have gradually become increasingly significant. These have often included accounts of the following features, explicitly or implicitly:

1 *The individual who can change to become both more and less violent over time, in relation to changes in social circumstances.* This might be summarized as a social constructivist social psychology of the violent and potentially violent individual.
2 *The relation of the individual to the social order through a concept of social role.* The notion of social role is distinct from people; it is a relatively stable, yet changeable, form of social expectations, including that violence has a meaning independent of individuals. The notion of social role derives from the analogy of social life as drama, with people playing roles in both.
3 *The immediate social environment through a concept of either culture or system operating at the level of the family or beyond.* Such a concept assumes it is useful to consider the relations between people as having such an importance that they produce the context, means and values for further violence or indeed its reduction.

Thus it might be argued that it is men with particular *social* dispositions, rather than particular psychological dispositions, who are prone to violence. An example of such a social disposition might be the propensity of some men to drink alcohol or drink alcohol excessively, which may then be assumed to 'explain' the violence. However, while some small-scale studies have noted the use of large amounts of alcohol by many men before physical violence to known women (for example, Bergman and Brismar, 1992), great caution needs to be exercised in seeing alcohol, or indeed drug use, as a direct and independent cause or explanation of men's violence to known women (see Kantor and Straus, 1987; McGregor and Hopkins, 1991; Dobash and Dobash, 1992).

More generally, Rosenbaum and Maiuro (1989: 168–172), in outlining what they call 'eclectic approaches with men who batter', put forward a number of 'guiding principles' for understanding and indeed changing men who use violence and abuse, including:

Abusers do not enjoy being abusive.

Batterers often have negative attitudes toward women, which contribute to the occurrence of aggression in marital relationships.

Abusers generally lack non-violent alternatives for expressing themselves or for achieving desired goals within their marital relationships.

Abusers are frequently saddled with [sic] traditional, patriarchal notions that men are expected to be dominant, omniscient, omnipotent, and infallible.

This is clearly an outline of a particular kind of *social individual*. It is also very close to the description of a stereotype of the typical batterer that is criticized by Gondolf (1985: 28). On the other hand, the focus on the individual is important politically and morally. Thus Rosenbaum and Maiuro (1989: 172) conclude that: 'Marital aggression is an individual's problem, most commonly the man's. Marital discord is a couple's problem.' This represents an interesting compromise between a moral political focus on the individual, and a relational, even systemic, view of 'the couple'.

Social Learning Theory, Socialization and Cognitive-Behavioural Analysis

Thus within the social sciences not all approaches that focus on the individual are narrowly psychological or psychodynamic in orientation. A well-developed framework is to explain men's violence as learned behaviour. This involves the focus on violence as external sense data that are observable and reproduced, replicated or imitated over time. Whereas in some psychoanalytic theories, observing others' violence and indeed expressing anger, at least mild forms of anger, is constructed as cathartic, thus reducing violence, according to social learning theories, observing violence and expressing anger is likely to lead to further violences. While Freudian and related theories construct violence as internally driven, social learning theories construct it as externally derived. On the other hand, both kinds of theory have one major feature in common, namely, their reference back to the importance of past experiences, and specifically childhood experiences. The assumption that it is early experiences that form the basic personality could be justified, in terms of either psychoanalytic or social learning theorizing.

Interestingly, the logic of learning theories can be developed to argue that violence by parents produces violence in children and then as adults, or that aggressive violence can be used by parents to punish and restrict the aggression and violence of the child, and thus the adult. In the latter argument, the continuation of violence into adulthood is an indication of a learning deficiency, rather than a learning proficiency (Mowrer and Lamoreaux, 1946; Eysenck, 1964). The paradox here is that if (some) adults do not learn to use aggression and violence for the purposes of punishment and reprimand, then children and thus future adults are likely to become more or really or inappropriately violent.

What we are centrally concerned with here is the attempt to understand violence by way of intergenerational relations, so that patterns 'learned' between a person and their parents are assumed to be repeated by that person with their children, and so on. The *exact* process by which this is assumed to take place is often less than clear: it might involve personality formation, cognitive structuring, behavioural reinforcement and modelling, or some permutation of these. In particular, the precise nature and relationship of psychological, cognitive, behavioural and social processes in socialization theories around violence is often left unstated.

The most important set of theories that attempt to address this question of the detailed social psychological processes by which learning and socialization are reproduced is cognitive-behavioural analysis. Cognitive-behavioural analysis focuses on the particular forms of learning that have taken place for particular individuals, which in turn it is assumed constitute the longer term processes of reproduction of violence through intergenerational learning and socialization. These particular forms of learning are 'behavioral in that they are structured and emphasize alteration of functional (intentional and consequential) aspects of behavior. They are also cognitive in that they focus on the verbal-symbolic mediators of the battering behavior' (Hamberger and Lohr, 1989: 58). They involve 'basic behavioral repertoires' (Staats, 1975), which include emotional-motivational, verbal-motor and language-cognitive repertoires, through which language controls behaviour, in this case, violence (Hamberger and Lohr, 1989: 58–67). Hamberger and Lohr (1989: 66) conclude that 'by using the concept of basic behavioral repertoires, battering behavior can be seen as purposeful, goal-directed, and self-produced patterns of behavior that are under the control of the batterer'. These social psychological processes derive from the more general principles of social learning theory.

Probably the most influential of the social learning theorists of violence is Bandura (1973, 1977). He has analysed the origins, instigators and maintaining conditions and regulators of aggression. Goldstein (1989: 124) follows this view in arguing there are three main arenas where aggression is to be learned: the home, the school and the mass media. Learning may be direct following the reinforced practice of aggression, or vicarious by the observation of others behaving aggressively and being rewarded for doing so.

There are a wide range of empirical studies which provide some support for social learning, socialization and cognitive-behavioural theories. Some of these have been usefully summarized by Campbell (1993) in her book *Out of Control*. She reports:

> Couples who argue the most are those who are the most likely to become violent.[3] Husbands who push their wives are those most likely to move on to slapping and punching. The best prediction of an individual's likelihood of criminal violence is his criminal violence last year.[4] Violence seems to beget violence, rather than decrease it. (Campbell, 1993: 8)

In discussing the specific problem of men's violence to known women, she continues:

> One of the strongest predictions of wife beating by men is whether they were exposed to violence in the house as children[5] . . . the boy who observes his father's violence is three times more likely to beat his own wife when he marries.[6] The boy learns that aggression pays. (Campbell, 1993: 105)

In contrast to the idea of direct or vicarious *learning* of violence, an alternative interpretation is presented by Hotaling and Sugarman (1986). They suggest that most of the men whom they studied who had been violent to wives had been *traumatized* as children either by being abused or by observing the abuse of their mother. The idea of trauma reproducing violence allows for an intrapsychic model of violence or a composite model containing social learning and psychodynamic insights. Whichever interpretation is preferred, attention is again directed to inter-generational processes in the reproduction of violence. This standpoint makes way for a wide range of subsidiary concepts, such as 'inter-generational transmission', 'the cycle of violence', and 'cultures of violence'.

Despite this kind of evidence, there are a number of difficulties with learning theories and socialization theories. I have already noted that the exact process by which this social learning or socialization takes place is often unclear. It is often as if the individual is an undifferentiated and unproblematic being who either learns changes in accordance with what is observed, or is changed through learning from that which is to be observed. The emphasis in social learning theory tends to be from the individual to the observable, and in socialization theory from the observable to the individual. Cognitive-behavioural analysis attempts to describe the detail of either social learning or socialization. Either way, these are relatively simple formulations of how violence works and is reproduced.

Learning/socialization models rest fundamentally upon the relative isolation of the individual from the processes of their differentiation in and by social structures. While it is difficult to refute the idea that people *learn* about violence from a variety of sources, claims for this being a general theory of violence tend to rely on correlational analyses of the experiences and actions of individuals out of the context of social structures.

However, the main problem with these kinds of theories is their under-theorization of gender. If boys who observe violence are more likely to be violent subsequently, why is this not also the case for girls? Or, to put this another way, is witnessing violence as a child relevant for understanding the violence of the violating man but not the violation of the violated woman (see Roy, 1982)? It is clear that the supposed individual is in fact a gendered individual; any learning (of violence or indeed anything else) is done in ways that are thoroughly gendered. Thus, not only may boys learn that violence is possible and is performed by older males, but that this is done in the context of male domination more generally. What is actually called 'social learning' or 'socialization' is itself imbued with gender and gendering, for example, in what is *valued* and what is *not valued* differentially by gender and for genders.

Reactive Theories: Frustration, Stress and the Blocking of Social Roles

While learning theory stresses the change in the individual following obser-vation of others' behaviour, and socialization theory stresses how the behaviour of some people provides the context and stimulus to adjustment and change in the socialized or socializable person, another set of theories focuses on violence as a *response* to external conditions. In this view, violence is reactive to threats to relatively given or relatively stable social roles and social goals. In this kind of account, the individual, his or her social goals and his or her social role are *privileged* as relatively given, in relation to which violence is formed, is performed and may indeed temporarily disappear. Violence is seen as not so much an aberration as a reaction, expressive and/or instrumental, to that which is given but changing. In the face of this, further change (that is, violence) is produced by and for the individual or social group.

Reactive theories of violence can be psychological or sociological in focus. Aggression and violence can be explained as a response to psycho-logical frustration, 'emotional illiteracy', individual stress, social stress, or economic and political deprivation. Despite such differences in emphasis, essentially the same argument can be used to 'explain' violence – that violence, men's violence, comes not because men learn to be violent, but because men use violence when their goals are blocked and other means of proceeding (such as non-violent alternatives) are unavailable or ineffective. This *resort* to violence can be further 'explained' in various ways – as a return to infancy, a movement to an innate or expressive violence, an instrumental means to successful achievement or as something that cannot be helped.

The main genre of reactive theory on men's violence to women is stress theory. This has been particularly influential in the American literature in relation to both child abuse and men's violence to women (Gelles, 1974;

Straus et al., 1980). In this approach, factors such as low income, unemployment, part-time employment and the greater number of children are related to violence towards children and 'between spouses'.

A rather similar interpretation is sometimes found in explanations of men's violence to women that see it as a reaction to men's alcohol use/abuse. Whilst acknowledging there is an association between the two, Horsfall (1991: 85–86) also notes some of the difficulties in seeing alcohol as a direct cause of violence. These include the possibility that both may have a similar aetiology through other personal, social or structural conditions. She concludes: 'If their [men's] gender identification is positional, their self-esteem shaky, work or sport are closed to them or work is a frustration in itself, then drinking with the "boys" may make them feel like "men". Behaving in an authoritarian way at home may also provide a similar opportunity' (Horsfall, 1991: 85)[7]. However, even this kind of interpretation leaves open why it is that men, or some men, might respond to these situations in these ways, and why the social structuring of 'boys' and 'men' takes these particular forms.

The Significance of Terminology

Significantly, reactive approaches often use degendered terminology, such as 'spouse', 'marital', 'parent', so leading to an *apparently* degendered analysis. What is of crucial importance in stress-based theory is the way in which stress is seen as a separate causal factor,[8] whereas in fact change is a constant feature of 'family life' and potentially stressful. Moreover, why is it that stress causes men to be violent and not women to the same extent?[9]

The terminology used in conceptualizing violence is very important – empirically, theoretically, politically. Indeed the terminology used often indicates the explanation of violence that is assumed to operate (see Poon, 1995; Pringle, 1995: 99–100). The term 'domestic violence' remains the most popular way of talking of men's violence to known women throughout much of the world. This is especially so in the UK, in journalistic discourses, and in policing. The terms 'conjugal violence', 'marital violence' and 'family violence', are also widely used, particularly in the United States, in therapeutic discourses and family therapy. They take the family or the conjugal or marital relationship as their empirical focus, conceptual assumption and theoretical framework. In doing so they make the political problem somewhere other than men or the man in question.

While some family-focused approaches draw attention to the relational context of violence, they can also divert attention from who does what to whom, and thus from the naming and recognition of *men's* violence. On the one hand, it is important to acknowledge the relational nature of gender and the relational context of violence, but it is equally important not to reduce violence to the product of 'the relationship'. Unfortunately this is not always the way in which relationships have been conceptualized in family violence or family therapy studies. More often there has been an attempt to locate the problem of violence in the family 'as a whole' as a system or a structure. The danger in conceptualizing the field as 'family violence' is that it implies that it is 'the family' that does the violence. 'The family' does not do violence: violence is done by people, usually men, albeit within violating relationships, including those of families.

Environment, Cultures and Systems: Family Culture, Subcultures and Cultural Theories

Social learning and socialization theories lead very easily, and reactive theories slightly less easily, onto theories of violence that prioritize a notion of 'culture' or 'system'. Violence may be understood as produced and reproduced through learning, socialization, modelling, imitation, and this in turn can be conceptualized as producing an environment of violence that operates over time, for example, across generations, and also above and beyond individuals through social relationships. These temporal and social continuities produce the environment of violence that transcends the individual and the particular violences of the individual. This 'environment' can be thought of as a 'culture' with its particular norms and values (as in the idea of sub-cultures) or 'system', with its particular systemic characteristics (as in the idea of family system).

The advantages of these kinds of shifts are that they provide a way of moving beyond a focus on the individual and towards the consideration of social relations. They also raise important questions of continuities across time and space, social or physical. This is clearly stated in the following:

> Family systems theory provides a framework for examining how both parties are caught in a negative cycle of violence. The wife is not blamed for being the 'victim' nor is the husband accused for being the 'victimizer', since neither partner may know alternative behaviors. Since the abusers often have been physically or sexually abused as children (Gelles and Cornell, 1985), they are also 'victims' of the intergenerational transmission of violence. Thus, in the recursive cycle of violence, victim becomes victimizer who is again victimized. (Geffner et al., 1989: 107)

On the other hand, systemic theory, especially in the form of marital and family systems therapy, focuses on the interactive dynamics *between* the violator and the violated. As such, there is a danger of reducing the people, the man and the woman, to parts of a degendered system.

Hybrid Theories: Stress, Inequality and Subculture

Interestingly, reactive theories of men's violence may sometimes be combined with proactive theories, like learning theories. Lees and Lloyd

(1994: 9) have summarized this combined approach of 'stress, inequality and subculture', as follows:

> Social structural stress is another theory, often used in collaboration with social learning theory, to explain the beating of women. Integrated into this approach is the notion that social stress is associated with unequal access to resources, especially for the poor. In this view, individuals who are under stress resort to violence as an outlet for frustrations, which may result from one incident or a slow build-up of incidents. In his article 'Social Class, Social Learning and Wife Abuse' Peterson (1980) suggested that his study of 602 married, or formerly married, women showed:
>
> 1 Conjugal violence is a response to either private or structural stresses. Private stresses are caused by conditions other than the individual's position in the social structure.
> 2 Conjugal violence is a learned behaviour. This behaviour is either learned in the family of origin or learned by contact with, and acceptance of, norms existing in certain lower-class groups that define violence as legitimate in certain situations.
>
> However, stress and poverty by themselves are not sufficient to explain the violence, as many poor families are not affected. Also, woman battering and stress occur right across the social spectrum, although it is thought that stress and violence is greatest amongst the lower classes.

This kind of theorizing thus brings together elements of learning, reactive stress and environmental cultural theories. It may even be argued that in introducing questions of economic class inequality such approaches are moving towards more structural analysis. This is, however, not necessarily extended to the structural analysis of relations between men and women, or indeed around (hetero)sexuality.

Multicausal Explanations

Following on from hybrid theories of men's violence, the next staging post of explanation is the multicausal. Again Lees and Lloyd (1994: 10–11) are helpful in summarizing this approach and some of its shortcomings:

> Some theorists have recently attempted to combine some or all of the theories so far discussed in order to achieve a more comprehensive understanding of woman beating. Edleson, Eisikovits and Guttmann (1985) argue that terror is the major feature of the battered woman's life, rather than beatings which might only occur spasmodically. They looked at the many empirical studies undertaken of woman battering and suggested they fell into five areas:
>
> 1 Violence in the man's family of origin
> 2 Chemical abuse and violence

3 Personal characteristics
4 Demographic and relationship variables
5 Information on specific violent events

In another multi-causal explanation, Straus (1977) identified seven inter-
acting factors:

1 High levels of conflict inherent in the family form
2 High levels of violence in society
3 Family socialization into violence
4 Cultural norms legitimating violence between family members
5 Violence integrated into the personality and behavioural script
6 Sexist organization of society and its family system
7 Woman puts up with beatings because of various structural and ideological
reasons

This list lacks any suggestion that patriarchy plays some part. Straus justifies this
because, as she [*sic*] puts it: 'even though men are dominant, their dominance does
not protect them from violence by other men'.

This is a rather strange argument when it is woman battering under discussion,
as there may be other reasons for male-to-male violence. If the concept of
patriarchy is used, rather than the term 'sexist society', male-to-male violence is
explained as having to do with the hierarchical structure of society. When one
examines the other six factors in detail, it is apparent that patriarchy is the back-
drop within which they too operate. The combination of factors that Straus
identifies seems to be a useful breakdown of the elements of patriarchy.

There are other problems with these hybrid and multicausal approaches.
They can be vague and imprecise, both analytically and in moving responsibility away from individual men. Both cultural and systemic approaches
can also be a means of avoiding gender and of avoiding naming men as
men. To put this rather differently, such theories do not usually deal adequately with questions of social structure, including gender relations but
also other social relations.

Violence as Structured Oppression: The Sociopolitical Critique
of Patriarchy

In most of these social and cultural perspectives on violence, women and
men remain conceptualized as relatively autonomous individuals within the
liberal society or as bearers of sex roles. This means that a relatively simple
understanding of gender is in use. However, feminist studies in particular
have emphasized how men's violence to known women can be understood
as part of the system of structured power and oppression that constitutes
patriarchy and patriarchal social relations (see, for example, Yllö and
Bograd, 1988). Similarly, structural analyses of gender power may be

interlinked with analyses of structured power relations around class, race and other social divisions and oppressions.

Just as writers such as Brownmiller (1975) and Dworkin (1982) have argued that men's violence, in the forms of rape and pornography respectively, are at the very heart of patriarchy, so too can men's violence to known women be understood in the same way. Individual violent acts of individual men, including assaults, rape, incest, murder, and so on, can thus be understood as gender class actions of men over women within the differential contexts of patriarchy. While such arguments, whether couched in sociological or political terms, are the subject of great debate, radical feminist ideas of this kind represent the most profound and solid challenge to men, men's power and men's violence.

Thus in this view a central notion for understanding men's violence to known women is that of patriarchy. The landmark statement of this approach is Dobash and Dobash's (1979) *Violence Against Wives: A Case Against the Patriarchy*. Here the structural and ideological character of patriarchy, as a hierarchical organization of social institutions and social relations, is analysed. It is this fundamental organization of society that locates people differentially, particularly by gender. Women are located in subordinated positions by both structural discrimination and ideologies that legitimate and rationalize that situation. This applies both in the family and in the public institutions of society. In this societal context, violence is a means of control for men over women and indeed children. Violence and its threat is understood as an attempt to diminish the power and resistance of women to men. This acceptance of men's control of and violence to women has often been sanctioned by law (see pp. 8–10). With the reduction of some of those 'legal specifications for the subjection of women . . ., men have resorted to force in order to maintain their position of privilege' (Gondolf, 1985: 33). Structural analyses may emphasize the place of patriarchal capitalism (Messerschmidt, 1986), sexual slavery (Barry, 1984), sexual terrorism (Sheffield, 1987), heterosexuality and violence in heteropatriarchy (Hanmer et al., 1989), and patriarchal social relations and male dominance in supporting violence (Hester et al., 1996).

Overly simple or one-dimensional models of the place of men's violence within patriarchy may themselves be criticized for neglecting historical change, cultural specificity, structural and sectoral differentiation and multiple oppressions. Instead more complex and differentiated models of patriarchy/patriarchies or public patriarchy/patriarchies have been developed. Men's violence within patriarchies, although persistent, is also variable and specific, rather than monolithic.[10]

These various kinds of structurally located approach are not necessarily distinct from the attempt to attend to the context-specific meanings of particular individual violent actions. Accordingly, Dobash and Dobash (1984) also argue for the need to analyse both the concrete nature of the event (including the source of conflict, resultant injuries, time, location and reaction of others) and the dynamic development of the event (including how it developed over time, the relevance of the relationship) in the wider social context of the individuals concerned.

This combination of structural and contextual approaches has been very influential in the development of women's organized responses to violence, policy debates and research, particularly in the UK around the operation of housing, legal, policing and welfare services. Women have organized various collective responses to the range of men's violences, including physical attacks, rape, sexual abuse of girls, and pornography. A very useful summary of women's initiatives has been provided by Hanmer (1996: 7–8). In discussing these, she concludes: 'In terms of personal experience, there is no necessary sealing off of one type of violence and abuse from another,[11] although the response of the state may involve attention to different aspects or the same aspects in different ways' (Hanmer, 1996: 8).

Importantly, these structural perspectives do not imply that women are passive recipients of men's violence. Rather it is the structural contexts that women and men occupy that are relatively historically determined. Within these contexts the response of state and related agencies to men's violence is crucial in constructing that violence over time. Women and men may make history but not in conditions of their own choosing. While women are confined by lack of alternatives (Schechter, 1982), they actively attempt to stop men's violence through various strategies until they find a combination of assistance that finally works (Bowker, 1983; Gondolf, 1985: 33). Women actively struggle to find ways to improve their situation: 'It can take women many years and agonizing emotional trauma to reach the point where they reformulate and resituate themselves in relation to cultural boundaries' (Hanmer, 1996: 15).

Difference and Diversity; Poststructuralism and Postmodernism

Reference has already been made to the importance of recognizing difference and diversity within structural analyses of patriarchy and patriarchal systems. The question of difference and diversity is particularly important in relation to men's violence to known women in terms of age, disability, economic class, gender, race and ethnicity, and sexuality (see, for example, Mama, 1989). Black feminists have highlighted the neglect of experiences of black women in much research on men's violence (Bhatti-Sinclair, 1994). Context-specific studies of men's violence also inevitably suggest differences among men and among women, albeit within definite structural relations. In a different way, structuration theory, in emphasizing the intersection of social structures and agency/action, also raises the theme of difference and diversity (Messerschmidt, 1993). These issues of difference and diversity between forms of violence, between kinds of men's violence, and between the experiences of different social groups defined by other social divisions and oppressions are a major theme of current research (see, for example, Rice, 1990; Kirkwood, 1993; Tifft, 1993; Pringle, 1995).

There is a limited development of feminist work on men's violence to known women that is inspired or influenced by poststructuralism, postmodernism, and feminist poststructuralisms and postmodernisms. The central themes here are the multiple interconnections, in no pre-determined or overly structural way, between power/resistance, agency/identity/the subject, and discourse/knowledge (Hollway, 1981; MacCannell and MacCannell, 1993; Bell, 1993, 1995; Fawcett, 1996). Accordingly, violence, including men's violence, is not a discrete area of study nor is it a separate object 'caused' or explained by some other subject or cause. Instead violence is multiple, diverse and context-specific; it is also formed in relation to and in association with other social forms, such as sexuality, family, marriage, authority. It is not a separate phenomenon, less still a separate thing; it is constructed in discourses.

While structuralist work on difference and diversity emphasizes the different structured contexts in which different social groups live, poststructuralist and postmodernist approaches tend to interrogate the very idea of difference. Accordingly, difference refers to a unity simultaneously divided from itself; differentiation between people, categories, divisions is also subject to de-differentiation. And interestingly, structuralist, poststructuralist and postmodernist approaches to violence are all in different ways becoming more concerned with international and global perspectives.

There is a gradual growth of interest in theoretical approaches that interrelate, and even transcend, divisions between individual, group, structuralist and poststructuralist perspectives. Increasingly, separate disciplinary and professional traditions are being superseded by interdisciplinary, multidisciplinary, inter-professional, inter-agency, inter-organizational and international approaches.

The Explicit Focus on Men

These various literatures on men's violence to known women have generally focused on violence as an *attribute of individuals*, on violence as a *process between individuals in a family relationship*, on violence as a *structural relation* or on *women's experiences of violence from men*. While they all to some extent attend to men's part in violence, this has often been indirect or at least not direct. Thus while these accounts can be *re-read* as about men and masculinities, an explicit focus on men as the doers of violence is more unusual.[12]

To conceptualize men's violence to known women as *the violences of men* may seem at first to be playing with words. However, seen in this way, men's violence becomes that which is done *by men*. This is an important emphasis, as a moral, political and theoretical construction that locates violence *in relation to* the social category 'men'. In recent, more critical approaches to men, men's power and domination are recognized as a central problem and violence is understood as one major element of that power and domination.

In placing the analysis of men's violence to known women within *the context of the analysis of men*, rather than within the context of violence or 'domestic violence', it is necessary to understand the social construction of men and masculinities, not only the nature of the violence itself (Newburn and Stanko, 1994; Collier, 1995). Each of the perspectives already outlined can be reinterpreted as possible explanations of both men and men's violences. Accordingly, different perspectives on violence – psychoanalytic, learning theory, sociopolitical critique of patriarchy, and so on – give different accounts of men and masculinities (Hearn, 1990). An explicit focus on men may therefore engage with the variety of ways in which men, masculinities and violences interrelate with each other – for men in general, for particular groups of men, and for individual men.

There is an increasing literature that addresses these questions. For example, Messerschmidt (1993) has argued that crime, including violence, is available as a resource for the making of masculinity, or at least specific forms of masculinity. The production and reproduction of masculinities is also detailed by Miedzian (1992) in her description of the significance of violence in the rearing of boys and sons (also see Jackson, 1990). Both Miedzian and Jackson do not simply chart the socialization of boys but also see the construction of masculinity of boys and young men within wider society as intimately interconnected with violence. Stanko (1994) has more recently spoken of the need to look simultaneously at masculinity/violence in analysing the power of violence in negotiating masculinities. While this may appear to be clearer in considering men's violence *to each other*, such a 'simultaneous yet negotiated' analysis needs to be extended to men's reproduction of violence/masculinity in relation to women.

The explicit focus on men is also emphasized by Pringle (1995) in his review of men's violence to women. He notes first that 'men tend to have a need to dominate and control', and, second, that 'structural factors play a part in the generation of men's physical and emotional violences' (Pringle, 1995: 100). Drawing particularly on the work of Tifft (1993) and Kirkwood (1993), he stresses that such violence is behaviour *chosen* by men, and is the product of choice within a *structural* context of hierarchical power arrangements.

Developing an Initial Framework

How do we develop a framework for thinking about, focusing on and naming the problem of men's violence to women?

The answer is both very simple and very complex. Men are members of a powerful social group and a social category that is invested with power. This has the consequence that membership of that group or category brings power, if only by association. As with other powerful groups, dominance is maintained and reproduced in a wide variety of ways, including persuasion, influence, force, violence, and so on. Men are the main *doers* of violence of all kinds – to women, children, each other, animals, ourselves. These kinds of violence used and done by men are organized and individualized, in public and in private, in deed and in text. All these forms of violence reinforce each other and form the contexts of each other. The doing of violence is dominance, is the result of dominance, and creates the conditions for the reproduction of dominance. Violence is a means of *enforcing* power and control, but it is also power and control in itself. Violence is often a means to an end – more obviously of men's control of women; and it is also *meaningful*, to some men at least, *as an end in itself.* In other words, some men simply enjoy violence, or at least say they do.

Men may use the range of forms of power and control available to those who are members of dominant categories. Sometimes this includes violence. Sometimes violence is not necessary to use as power and control are effective without that. Those men who are relatively more powerful may not need to use violence to keep control or they may use violence with less fear of retribution and response. Those men who are relatively powerful members of relatively less powerful groups of men may not need to use violence in their own cultural area (particularly if this is relatively immune to dominant forms of power) or they may use violence to assert their local power in that local situation. Less powerful men may use violence despite the likely response or may become subordinated and withdraw.

Men's violence to known women can be understood as standing at the centre of patriarchy or patriarchies, patriarchal relations and patriarchal institutions. It can be seen as in large part a development of dominant–submissive power relations that exist in 'normal' family life. Men may resort to violence when men's power and privilege are challenged or under threat (Dobash and Dobash, 1992), and other strategies have failed. Violent actions may be available as part of men's repertoire, but are most used at particular times, such as when women resist or when women do not do what men expect, in terms of childcare, housework, paid work, sexuality, and so on. Men's feelings of possible or potential loss of power in one sphere may also be acted upon in another sphere or relationship, where there may be less resistance.

To argue for such a perspective on violence is not to say that all men are violent all the time, or that it is only men who are violent. Rather it is men who dominate the business of violence, and who specialize in violence. And while women, as the receivers of violence, in some ways know more about the direct effects and experiences of violence than men, men remain the experts in how to do violence and in the doing of violence. Indeed the reproduction of dominance through violence does not necessarily refer to the reproduction of the dominance of the individual man concerned. It is quite possible that an individual man may cease violence to women through growing older, separation from the woman, imprisonment or killing himself.

Interestingly, a perspective on the 'normality' of men's violence within dominant masculinities and men's power within patriarchies is not necessarily at odds with psychological or social psychological accounts of men's violence. The fact that there are violent men is not the product of psychological traits – all men can be violent. However, violence, with its specific generic qualities of violence, is a powerful way of demonstrating that someone is a man. Just as Messerschmidt (1993) talks of crime as a resource for the making of masculinities, so the same can be said of violence. Being violent is an accepted, if not always an acceptable, way of being a man. Doing violence is, that is, is available as, a resource for demonstrating and showing a person is a man. These connections apply all the more so to men's violence to women, that is, violence by men to those who are different from men. Men's violence to women thus speaks and shows this difference. The difference is produced and reproduced in and through violence.

Seeing men's violence in this way means that violence can be considered in relation to the social category of men, men's structural location, and the tension between men as a gender class and differences among men. It also raises the question of how violence relates to different forms of masculinity. Different masculinities may, however, relate to violence, and particularly men's violence to known women, quite differently and distinctly. In some cases, men's violence to known women may be constitutive of masculinity: it may be a central and typifying, even symbolizing, feature; in other cases, men's violence to known women may be less obviously, more subtly, related. It may appear to contradict the dominant, overt form of masculinity yet may reinforce it through its presence, potential or threat. The interrelations of violences and masculinities can be simple or complex, unified or contradictory. The connections between violence and masculinity are everywhere – in the media, sport, film, representations of physical action, fantasy, and elsewhere.

Men's Violence to Known Women

So what is men's violence to known women? It shares some characteristics with other violence and other violence by men; it is also specific and with specific characteristics.

First, it is an inherently *gendered* way of men referring to themselves and to violence. Men's doing of violence to women simultaneously involves 'being a man' and symbolically showing 'being a man'.

Second, the violence is to *known* women as opposed to women who are strangers. This means that the women are known before the violence or that the violence is the first point of contact. The latter situation may at first sight appear to be less likely; however, on reflection, violence can be the beginning of a subsequent relationship, for example, in the use of verbal abuse to initiate social contact or the use of violence in a man's initial contact with a woman selling sex. This raises the more general question of to what extent heterosexual relations are necessarily harassing.

Known relations between men and women also involve other features. They will probably involve a history together; this may involve experiences about similar events, though experiences that cannot be said to be in common. Known relations also may well mean that there is likely to be contact of some kind in the future. There are many implications of this 'known-ness'. They include the fact that the violence occurs in association and sometimes in contradiction with other *knowledges* about the person, whether the man or the woman, the violator or the violated. For example, because of the existence of known relations, the man may *know* about the woman, the woman's past, perhaps her previous violation, the woman's strengths and weakness; similarly, the woman may know about the man, his past, his previous violence (and lack of violence), and so on. This inter-action of violence and 'other knowledge' is both a perceptual problem and a social relation that may create the possibility of further violation or indeed movement away from violence. Indeed it must be emphasized that violence is itself *a form of knowledge* – for both the violator and the violated. In doing violence, the man knows violence, has knowledge of and in violence; and similarly, in receiving violence, the woman knows violence, has knowledge of and in violence. To put this slightly differently, in such situations, the man knows the woman *through his violence*, and the woman knows the *man as violence*.

Third, and following the previous point, this kind of violence generally, though not always, occurs in the context of *intimate*, often marriage, relations (see Delphy and Leonard, 1992). Thus we are concerned here not only with the question of 'known-ness', but also with intimacy in all its various forms and expressions. Intimate relations involve confidences, trust, 'care', close personal and physical contact, conversation as well as sitting in silence. They may, though, clearly not necessarily involve sex, sexual activity, sexual potential and sexual meaning. In a general sense, for women, the closest relationship with a man is often the most dangerous and potentially dangerous. This close relation of danger and closeness is, of course, further complicated by the intimate association of 'pleasure and danger' for both men's and women's sexuality (see MacCannell and MacCannell, 1993). This kind of violence is indeed 'intimate' in many ways: it occurs in association with intimacy and the violence itself may be intimate, intricate, detailed, variegated, and based on intimate knowledge and knowledge of intimacy.

Fourth, this violence is predominantly violence in the context of *hetero-sexual* relations and relationships. Not only does this violence usually occur in association with past, present or future intimate relations, but these relations are themselves predominantly heterosexual. Just as this kind of violence is gendered, so too it is 'sexualed' (and often also sexualized). The hierarchy that is implicit and often explicit in heterosexuality and hetero-sexual relations (Zita, 1982) is shown and reproduced in men's violence to known women. The occurrence of violence in and around heterosexual relations contributes to the eroticization of dominance. Sexual and sexual-ized relations are continued, enforced and reproduced with and through violence, and the reproduction of violence and the violated is itself constructed as 'sexy' by the violator (Russell, 1993).

Fifth, this kind of violence often though not always occurs in relative 'private' isolation. It is enforced in specific locales, within the feudal mode of reproduction (Hearn, 1983, 1987). In this situation individual men can be both relatively separate from each other and part of a specific gender class or sub-class.

This combination of features makes men's violence to known women an especially complex social phenomenon to study and research, and it is to this particular set of challenges that I now turn.

3

Studying and Researching Men's Violence to Known Women

In thinking about, researching and working on and against men's violence to known women, issues of content and process are inextricably linked. Theories, explanations, forms of men's violence are not separated off from the *processes* of thinking about, acting against and researching violence. Throughout, questions of *how* to study and research, of methodologies and methods, are absolutely fundamental. It is not possible to take any single part of the research process for granted. For example, to make an arrangement by letter or by telephone or face to face with a man to talk with him about his violence can be problematic.

In some senses, this is just another piece of research; in others, it involves the questioning of research methods at every stage, and research methodology in every respect; it is swimming against the tide of the malestream. Standard textbooks and articles on research methods and methodology rarely address these practical issues of how to research men's violence to known women. At each stage of the research process, the appreciation and apprehension of the violence needs to be treated with caution and creativity. This includes the definition of the research problem, access to 'subjects', research methods, techniques of interviewing, the construction and delivery of questionnaires, the use of mixed methods, the analysis of data, the publication of results, and feedback to policy makers and others. Special attention has to be given to questions of safety and confidentiality, the gendering of the research process, the emotional effects of doing research, and other sensitive questions in doing research (Lee, 1993). Care has to be exercised in the assessment of empirical information, especially that from men talking about their own violence. Experience and interpretation, and their interrelation, have to be constantly understood and contextualized. Pure truth is not to be found here.

In this chapter I address some of these questions. First, I put these particular concerns within the broader picture of men critically studying men, multiple methodologies and the historical context of research. The next section summarizes the methods and methodology of this research. This is followed by attention to more detailed issues and difficulties, including the emotions of research. The final section addresses questions of knowledge and epistemology.

Men Critically Studying Men

For men conducting critical research on men, there are a number of specific issues and difficulties – personal, practical, political, methodological and theoretical.[1] First, there is the question of men's personal motivation to do the research in question, and the way in which the (gendered) researcher relates to the research process and the research problem. Of special import-ance for men working on men's violence are issues of commitment, energy, urgency. The issue of reflexivity in social science has a specific gendered significance in the gendered experience of the researcher.

Second, and closely linked, is the matter of men's political relationship to research. This includes the political relationship of men (researchers) to feminism (Hearn, 1992b), women's information, women's experience and women's research. This is both a question of broad principles/standpoints (as in pro-feminist stances by men) and practical decisions (as in decisions to apply or not to apply for certain research funds or for projects on certain research topics). It is also a matter of responding to research agendas set within feminisms (such as how to prevent men's violence) and contributing to politics and policies of assistance to women (such as policy change on men's violence to women). Such intentions do not resolve methodological and theoretical questions on the relationship of politics and knowledge, in this context of critical research by men on men.

Third, there are methodological and theoretical questions in men doing critical research on men. For example, what theories of epistemology and ontology are present or relevant in such research? What can be known by men? What cannot be known? And what is unlikely to be known? Just as with current debates around feminist epistemology and ontology, and par-ticularly the interrelation of feminism, modernism and postmodernism, it is no longer possible to just read off the truth value of particular statements; instead, experience, knowledge, politics and theorizing are in a continuing and changing relationship; both absolutism and relativism are flawed. Debates on feminist epistemology are often set in the tension between the material basis of experience and the fragmentation of knowledge. Such tensions may also apply to critical studies by men.

Partly in response to this *structuring of objectivity/subjectivity*, partly in the context *of self-validating* (rather than other-validating) *political practice*, and partly in terms *of an epistemology that creates knowledge from effects rather than essences*, there has been a strong attempt to assert the superior-ity of knowledge of the objectified, within feminism and elsewhere. Speci-fically, the route to knowledge and emancipation has often been constructed through subjectivity, rather than objectivity. So what does this mean for men, and for studies by and of men? If what is called objectivity is (perhaps in large part) a form of men's subjectivity, then a more direct, explicit and fuller resort to men's *subjectivity* may be a means to reconstituting objectivity in critical studies on men by men. There are, however, at least three problems with this explicitly subjectivist approach to men's knowledge of men. First, men's subjectivity is itself set within power: it may be, indeed, it is likely to be, self-reproducing of further dominance and rationalizations of dominance. Second, men and men's situations vary greatly. And third, such an understanding of men's subjectivity has to be placed alongside, and perhaps in contradiction with, understandings of women's subjectivity.[2]

Epistemological and ontological questions such as these can be considered both as immediate practical concerns and as more generalized analyses of power relations. Certain kinds of experiences may only be easily or directly known by men. This includes experiential knowledge of men-only situations and knowledge of men's *effects* on men. Certain kinds of activities, aspects, experiences of men, or even certain types of men, are not known about. There are definite gaps in knowledge. Some of these can be identified. These include those that are usually 'alone', 'secret' or 'private', for example, direct observation of men's violence to women in the home.

Other gaps are not necessarily known. By definition, some are difficult (perhaps impossible) to talk of; some are only apparent retrospectively. For example, what did we not talk about ten years ago that we do now? Such gaps in perception illustrate some of the problems of empiricism in researching men: How do we/I know there are gaps at all? Does this rely on 'intuition', limited/personal/shared information or shared knowledge? These difficulties illustrate the importance of linking together fragments of knowledge. In many respects, men's knowledge as researchers and/or researched remains *severely limited* by virtue of men's power locations as members of an oppressor class (or classes), relative to women's knowledge of the *effects* of men.

The need to problematize the association of knowledge and objectivity applies throughout critical studies on men by men. Men have dominated not only what has been studied, but also how that study is to be conducted, and what counts as knowledge. In particular, this has included the equation of knowledge and objectivity, and the downgrading of subjectivity as non-knowledge: processes that have been and are gendered. Much, most, of what has been and is considered objective knowledge has been and is pre-scientific; for example, in the neglect, the blatant ignoring, of issues of gender, sexuality and violence. What is called objectivity reaffirms and reproduces certain kinds of subjectivity, in terms of being subjects in discourse, feelings of objectification, and structuring of rules of knowledge.

These issues and difficulties cannot be 'overcome' just by getting the 'correct' methodology; less still by sheer determination and good intentions, important though they may be. Rather, they have to be lived with and recognized as continuing tensions and contradictions. In particular, it is always necessary to consider the *relationship* of critical studies by men on men to women's research, whether directly (for example, as collaborators and colleagues) or indirectly (for example, in previous or contemporary researches elsewhere). Men's research in isolation (from feminism) is likely to reproduce some of the 'knowledge' of anti-feminism.

Several methodological possibilities present themselves as ways forward in critical studies by men on men. First, there is the *macro approach* that locates men's knowledge in the context of world patriarchy. Second, there is the *micro approach* of in-depth investigations, as a means of increasing self-knowledge and knowledge of others. However, purely subjectivist approaches to men have to be treated with caution and understood socio-logically. Third, there are *more differentiated, contextualized approaches to men's subjectivities* that specify different rules for the understanding of men's subjectivities depending on the context of the experiences concerned. These offer the possibility for transcending subjectivity/objectivity in knowledge of men. Men's subjectivities may be understood as giving fuller information when they relate to men in *relatively* lesser power, especially when recounting the *effects* of other men upon men or boys; in contrast, men's subjectivities relating to men in relatively greater power need to be understood as giving less information, through rationalization, minimization, justifications and elaborations of power in accounts. Such differentiations become particularly important and complex when consider-ing multiple oppressions, for example, 'race' and gender, and reciprocal/ mutual oppression, for example, men's violence amongst peers. Fourth, there are *multiple methods*, as part of the broader concern with multiple perspectives (Grosz, 1987; Hearn, 1992b). It is unlikely that a single methodology will be able to encapsulate all that has to be said. Thus, this is more than just a bringing together of qualitative and quantitative methods. The movement to multiple perspectivism is a commentary on the nature of social reality, perception and politics: it is a call to undermine the grand narratives of the malestream.

The Historical Context of the Research

In trying to understand research on men's violence to known women, it may be useful to ask: Why is this kind of research being done now? What is the climate of sentiment, the structure of feeling about violence that makes it both easier and more shameful to talk about violence? In one sense this particular research is itself a response to feminist opposition to men's violence. It follows on from previous research conducted in West Yorkshire on women's experiences of violence from known men (Hanmer and Saunders, 1984, 1990, 1993). This not only has shown the scale of men's violence to women and children, but has also examined the policy impli-cations for more effective policing. Other innovations in West Yorkshire have included the establishment of Police Special Units for 'domestic violence and child abuse' (as well as for rape), the creation of Domestic Violence Forums in each urban area, bringing together representatives from

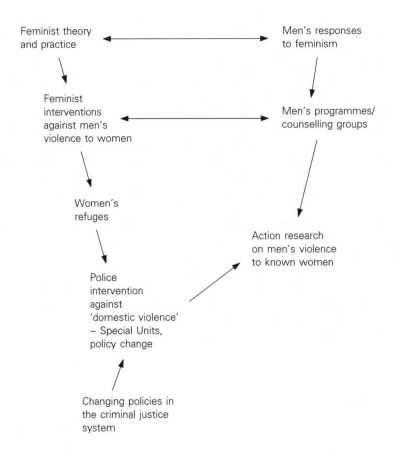

FIGURE 3.1   *The historical context of research*

statutory, voluntary and community organizations, and the development of inter-agency work around violence to women and children (see Figure 3.1).

My own concern with studying men's violence to women followed research on sexual harassment, child abuse and the changing historical form of patriarchies. This led to the decision, with Jalna Hanmer, to establish a Research Unit on Violence, Abuse and Gender Relations at the University of Bradford. We co-convened the Unit from 1990 until 1995. This provided an institutional framework for feminist and pro-feminist research on violence. In this context, research by women on women's experiences and research by men on men's experiences was conducted that was linked, but separate, and fully preserved confidentiality.

Research is historically specific. Certain kinds of research become more possible at certain historical, intensely political, moments. This research was facilitated by two kinds of agency initiatives: police policy recognizing the problem of men's violence to known women as being as serious as other violence; and the creation of a number of group-based men's programmes for men who have been violent to women. It was also facilitated by major support from women in setting up the research, and from a wide network of contacts in local agencies in West Yorkshire. Arguing that the historical time has come for particular kinds of action research to be done should not, however, obscure ongoing contradictions in that intervention. It may begin a process of not knowing, a process of which men do not fully have control.

Methods, Methodology and the Organization of the Research

The methodology and organization of this research have been based on various commonalities and differences between and within projects: one on women's experiences, one on men's experiences. There are specific issues for each project, independent of each other; there are also commonalities most obviously in terms of the overall methodology. The two projects have been jointly funded but separately organized in terms of access, interviewing, confidentiality. Both have used multiple methods: open-ended qualitative interviews; pre-coded structured interviews; qualitative analysis; quantitative analysis; as well as triangulation with agency accounts. The organization of the project on men is in the context of and in collaboration with feminist research.

The basic research design followed on from a US study of 60 women in a battered women's shelter, and their patterns of stress, coping and social support (Mitchell and Hodson, 1983). The whole study was in part (Project 1) a replication of the US study (Hanmer, 1993) in a British context; at the same time, these methods were applied, with minimum necessary adjustments, to men (Project 2). This book is concerned almost totally with the project on men's experiences. There were a number of differences between the Mitchell and Hodson study on women and this research on men:

- its application to men;
- unstructured interviews, as well as a pre-coded questionnaire;
- the study of agency policies and documentation;
- follow-up interviews with agencies with whom the men had had contact (where permission was given).

The research investigated how men talk about and understand or do not talk about and do not understand their own violence to women; the differences between women's and men's experiences in relation to men's violence; and the interrelation between individual accounts and accounts from agency personnel. The basic aim was to find out more about men's violence to women and contribute to the reduction and abolition of such violence.

Men were interviewed from a number of sources: following arrest by the police; from men's programmes; via probation officers; from prisons; from

TABLE 3.1 *Sources of interviewees*

Source	No. of interviews	No. in sample	No. giving permission for follow-up with agencies	Permission not given
Police	17*	16*	14*	2
Men's programmes				
Project A	11	11	7	4
Project B	6	6	4	2
Project C	2	2	0	2
Total	*19*	*19*	*11*	*8*
Prison				
Prison A	4	4	3	1
Prison B	7	3	1	2
Total	*11*	*7*	*4*	*3*
Probation	7*	7*	7*	0
Other welfare agencies	5	4	4	0
No agency	17	8	2	6
Total	*75*	*60*	*41*	*19*

* One man from both police and Probation.

various welfare agencies; together with a number of men who were not currently in contact with agencies at all (Table 3.1). In all cases, the men themselves clearly had to give their permission before interview. This diversity and range of sources mirrors an issue discussed by McKee and O'Brien with respect to fathers. They remark 'The first problem we encountered in our studies was the recruitment of men as *fathers*. There is no ready-made sampling frame of fathers and as a group they are less accessible and conspicuous than mothers . . .' (McKee and O'Brien, 1983: 147). Because of the nature of legal and criminal processes, there are major difficulties in constructing a satisfactory sampling frame for men who have been violent to known women. The criteria for inclusion of men in the sample were two-fold:

- whether they defined their action as constituting violence to women; and/or
- whether they were in a particular relevant agency location because of violence to women, whether alleged or admitted, or because of their status as a client of an agency working against violence to women.

Access to men has generally been via agencies that deal with men, involving two, sometimes three, four or five stages: approach at the management level, co-operation of the staff team, co-operation of the individual workers, agreement of the men, arrangement of the interviews. Interviews were always conducted outside the men's homes. On several occasions this involved being calmly assertive about the reasons for this. There were many times when men did not turn up on the first or even second arrangement, and in one case not until the eleventh. Such unreliability is, of course, frustrating for researchers; it involves a loss of valuable working time, which needed to be built into the work schedules. On the other hand, this unreliability may reflect men's ambivalence about being interviewed, and indeed about the violence itself. A policy of persisting with offering interviews however many times necessary was adopted, to ensure that we were taking the contact seriously. There were four instances when men who agreed to participate were not eventually interviewed; two of these were men who agreed with probation officers and then 'vanished'; one was a man who had agreed face to face through a men's programme and subsequently decided not to; and a fourth arranged by a social worker failed to turn up because he had changed his mind. In each of these cases, the man appeared to have agreed to please or appease professionals.

The interviews with men, first, involved the man telling his own story in his own words, using open-ended questions and prompts. In most cases the man provided an account of the violence he had done, what had happened subsequently, how he understood why he had been violent, the reactions and responses of family, friends and agencies. Not all topics were covered by the man in all interviews and topics were often addressed unevenly in different interviews. As such, this part of the interview varied considerably in style and detail. Furthermore, the main areas sometimes interconnected with or blurred into each another. This of course raises the question of to what extent men's accounts of violence stay close to the acts of violence or whether men decide to talk about other things.

The second part of the interview was organized very differently. This used a pre-coded questionnaire, which covered biographical details (class, education, housing, religion, and so on) of both the man and the woman to whom he had been violent. Following Mitchell and Hodson (1983), it also included questions on the pattern of social support the man had from friends and family, and the kinds of responses from agencies, especially the police, solicitors, social workers, counsellors. There were also measures of the man's well-being/lack of well-being; his self-esteem; his sense of control of his own future. At the end of the interview men were asked for their permission to do follow-up interviews and consulting of their case records with the agencies that had had dealings with them or their 'case'. These were then followed up in every case, that is, the 116 permissions which led to 130 agency contacts (see Table 9.1).

The combination of methods used – unstructured and semi-structured interviews, pre-coded interview and interview/case records from agency staff – meant that a more diverse, in some ways more complete, picture of men's violence could be obtained. This is particularly important as some men may not tell or may not be able to tell others about their violence. In many cases, pre-coded interviews alone would have given a very limited indication of events. The open-ended part of the interview provided many examples of detailed constructions of violence not apparent in the pre-coded questionnaire. It would be very difficult to produce a questionnaire that fully addressed the subtle meanings of many of the men's statements on their own violence. Indeed what is most difficult to code in questionnaire formats is often of most interest in qualitative analysis. The use of qualitative and quantitative methods together, and triangulation of accounts between men and agency staff, provide a sounder methodological basis than reliance upon one method alone (Brannen, 1992).

In most interviews, two hours was a reasonable time limit; beyond that men's tolerance might be exceeded. Men gave their time freely in talking of their violence; it was important not to overstretch their co-operation. There are limits of tiredness and boredom beyond about two hours, and difficulties of taking time out and relaxing, partly because of the subject matter and partly because of some of the venues. Setting a limit of about two hours at one sitting was also to reduce frustration and annoyance, and so minimize the possibility of aggression and violence towards the interviewer. Because of the difficulty of arranging interviews, it was essential to complete as much as possible in one sitting. Throughout safety had to be a prime concern, sometimes delaying the arranging of interviews, for example, to find a suitable venue. Fourteen venues were used, requiring flexibility, attention to detail, and the checking out of their local features. In some situations, notably in prison, interviews were limited to two hours by organizational rules. Repeat prison interviews involved an additional formal arrangement of a 'special visit'.

When talking to men as the doers of violence, it is far from clear what violence is to be taken to mean. For women experiencing violence, violence may be that which violates; with men who have been violent the actual definition of violence and exclusion of certain actions and behaviours is problematic. Research practice thus involves being constantly engaged with men's own definitions of violence, whilst completely open to all and any definitions not recognized by men. While in some senses each interview is unique and concerned with the telling of the unique story of a particular man, there are definite recurring themes. These were used to structure the analysis of interviews – the qualitative analysis of the qualitative interview material. Recurring themes are of two main types: those apparently consciously expressed by the interviewees; and those recognized from transcript analysis that may not be apparent to the interviewees.

Another issue is the extent to which conventionally masculine modes of behaviour are used with the men or agencies in this kind of research. Making arrangements often was done with some 'masculine firmness'; the interview process is best kept under the interviewer's *control*; obtaining assistance from agencies may involve being 'normal'. It may also mean not responding to provocative comments from agency staff, such as the prison officer who suggested jokingly that the questionnaire needed just two boxes: 'alcohol' and 'full of shit'.

Let us now look in more detail at particular issues and difficulties that have arisen in this kind of research.

On Difficulties

There is a powerful ideology and myth of clear, linear research and research methodology (see Stanley and Wise, 1983, 1993). The existence of 'social mess' in research is often perceived as a problem largely because of other expectations and assumptions. In previous research on sexuality in organizations (Hearn and Parkin, 1987, 1995), the research difficulties found took on major significance. What were at one time perceived by us as 'methodological difficulties' were rather part of the way the topic 'sexuality in organizations' was (or is). The difficulties were there for investigation, not avoidance. They were part of the substance, not just the method, of research: 'part of the way in which sexuality in organizations was obscured for us was by our perception of its study through the eyes of methodological difficulties, rather than organizational processes' (Hearn and Parkin, 1995: 48).

Similarly, in researching men's violence, there are great 'difficulties', including 'pervasiveness', 'elusiveness', 'avoidance' and 'ambivalence'. These are, however, not simply 'methodological difficulties' in research, but rather likely features of the substance of men's violences. For example, despite the fact that men's power and control is socially sanctioned, taken-for-granted, and reproduced interpersonally and structurally, it is generally not easy to contact men about men's violence to known women. Additionally, for men who have been violent to known women, such violence is both a form of power and a source of shame; indeed the stigma of being or having been violent may be a personal ascription – it may speak of the very body of the person.

While the difficulties in this research have been immense, they should be placed in the context of the difficulties of the women experiencing violence from men, and indeed of some of the men interviewed. The research problems included: the sheer volume of work in the time available; difficulties in contacting men for interview and in making arrangements with some of the agencies; administrative complexities around finance; equipment, office accommodation and personnel; several burglaries; difficulties in obtaining the questionnaire to be replicated; as well as the stress of studying violence. Some of these difficulties arose from the research directly, others indirectly; some were predictable, others not.

Research Access and the Analysis of Organizations

Research access is a standard part of 'field' research. In this project it was especially important. Not only was the access a necessary stage in the research process, it was also significant in understanding agencies. In most cases access was to *men's* organizations, that is, organizations controlled by men. Access involved different procedures, processes of co-operation of access, ethical considerations and agency constructions of violence.

Different agencies clearly relate to violence in quite distinct ways, particularly in terms of their everyday work.

Differences around the organizational constructions of violence as a component of agency tasks are reproduced both in the definition of 'clients' (in the broadest sense of the term) and in research access. Men are primarily defined in relation or not to violence. With the police, probation and men's programmes, violence is recognized explicitly, even when mediated through legal, social work, therapeutic or other discourses. There are also significant differences between such agencies in the extent to which men are understood in individual or collective terms. This is partly a question of professional and organizational ideologies and partly a question of technologies of information handling. For example, access to men through the police was possible by means of their computerized system, together with their obtaining consent. Access through men's programmes was to men as a group. Probation contacts were much more individualized, with individual office contacts, individual life histories and the (in)appropriateness of individual cases.

Whether men are seen in terms of violence explicitly or implicitly, *separately from other parts of their being or totally defined as such*, is part of what Rosengren and Lefton (1969) called the organizational orientation to clients. They noted how different medical conditions suggested different organizational arrangements, but, more importantly, how the same person could be defined differently by different medical organizations. Elaborating on their work, contrasts may be drawn between (a) violence as a very specific (separate/narrow) part of the person and (b) violence as a more diffuse (integrated/broad) part of the person. In case (a), violence is the point of contact; the organizational personnel are interested in the man in relation to his violence. This is the dominant pattern in the police/Crown Prosecution Service/court system. The 'client' is approached in a more 'segmented' way – violence is a lesser part of his being, yet, paradoxically, there is more *possibility* of resolving 'the problem' by simply stopping the violence or not bringing it to the attention of the organization. In contrast, case (b) looks at the 'client' in a more 'integrated' way – violence is seen as a greater or more integral part of his being, yet, *paradoxically, a specific focus on violence may be of more interest*, through the realization of greater difficulty in the resolution of the problem/the solution of the situation/man. This is the dominant pattern in the men's programmes. Probation seems to be placed in the tension between these two ideologies, with referral through the criminal justice system, yet drawing on its own model of social work. There may even be tensions between these modes of operation within men's programmes – between approaches emphasizing professional/client relations, mutual self-help, anger management or pro-feminism (Gondolf and Russell, 1986; Horley, 1990; Dankwort, 1992–3).

Conditions of client definition bear strongly on the facilitation or otherwise of *research access* – there are in effect many 'good organizational reasons for bad research access' (cf. Garfinkel, 1967). The reasons for the non-availability of clients for research reflect not just the reluctance of individual men to 'come out' as violent, but the organizational construction of violence and organizational reluctance to come out as centrally involved in violence, both at the policy level and at the level of the individual worker/professional/practitioner. Not surprisingly, different organizational definitions of men affected how men defined themselves in relation to agency workers, agency tasks and violence.

Preparation, Safety and Confidentiality

Then there are important issues of preparation for fieldwork, including training, the development of increased awareness around men and violence, and piloting of interviews and questionnaires. This involved repeated interviewing of each other, interviewing strangers and role plays, as well as more focused sessions on, for example, safety and danger, violence to women, and interview methods. As there were few written sources on the research issues we were facing, we had to develop our own thinking on many questions.[3] This became the basis for our own guidelines on men interviewing men about violence (Hearn et al., 1993). Other detailed questions around the conduct of interviewing and other fieldwork itself included safety, confidentiality,[4] the search for 'good data', the significance of 'denial' and the relevance of 'any account'.

A good deal of attention was given to safety, in terms of establishing control and confidence, selection of venue, assessment of possible danger, giving absolute discretion for interviewers to withdraw, telephoning in after the interview, and so on. Giving such absolute discretion to the interviewer is very important. For example, the drawing up of 'factors' to learn and watch for as indices of 'dangerousness' is no substitute for the interviewer having confidence in doing (and being given the confidence to do) whatever is appropriate in the interview. The reduction of risk and danger to lists of factors may reduce complexity to a formula and may lead to a sense of failure on the part of the person attacked or violated. Questions of safety and danger of the interviewer may parallel processes affecting victims or potential victims elsewhere. For example, there is a danger in the interviewer who experiences threat or physical violence apologizing that 'I shouldn't have riled him,' or 'I was stupid, too stupid to see it coming.'

Attention has also had to be given to confidentiality. Moreover, confidentiality is itself a social and political construction. Different versions operate in different agencies. Particular difficulties surround the possibility of men talking of (a) either their intention to be violent to women, or their intention to commit other crimes; (b) their violence or other crime in the past, both unsolved crime, ongoing crime investigations and crime which is not yet known to the police. Accordingly, while these were confidential research interviews, we informed the men that we operated within the limits of the law.

Interview Venues

Interviewing was not done in men's houses, even when men were keen to be interviewed there, and appeared safe and 'completely harmless'. We adopted this policy partly because we did not always know whom we were interviewing and partly because we did not see apparent 'niceness' as any indication of safety (or danger). Additionally, not interviewing in men's homes meant that men might be able to speak more freely away from their own home. Interviewing in their own home might mean that in some cases the women who have been violated, or other family members, might be in the next room. Meeting away from men's homes also avoids particular associations of the home, especially if the domestic scene might provoke violent feelings. Less dramatically, meeting outside the home might avoid interruptions (from television, telephone, callers), which could cause embarrassment; using another venue helped anonymity and confidentiality. Meeting outside the home also gave more control to the interviewer and enabled at least some consistency of venue.

Men Working on the Topic of Violence

For men to research on the topic of violence can be demanding: it entails the acknowledgement of our/my own violence and the potential for violence; it involves being alert to the effects of working with and on violence, the need for sympathetic and critical support, and attending to whatever 'comes up' in the work, no matter how unwanted and apparently trivial that may seem; it also brings a depth of emotional engagement that is difficult to convey on paper; it demands a personal and political commitment against violence in all its forms; it produces a continuing personal and political re-evaluation, a process of consciousness-raising. Perhaps, above all, it necessitates a constant critical relation to the material – of self, the research process, the men interviewed, the interview data, the agencies studied, as well as various kinds of totalities. We need to be ready to recognize the multiple ways in which men can re-establish forms of power, dominance and violence, even when working against violences. Most importantly, such research needs to be pro-feminist, located, where possible, in close association with feminist research.

A practical issue is the possible tension between listening, coping with listening, and critique. Listening occurs in both interviews and their subsequent analysis. It is not just a matter of being a sponge for whatever is said. Similarly, coping with what is said is a critical, not a purely reactive, process. Listening to and coping with men talking about violence can be unpleasant. It can also feed into feelings of vicarious interest, and superiority over and difference from other men, which may need attention in the research group.

Working on violence also involves constant thoughts about violence. It also challenges men who often have limited experience of negotiating non-violently and non-abusively. Not only is violence a troubling kind of thought, but it also provokes personal and political re-evaluation. This is not always upsetting or negative; it may bring a distinct uneasiness; and sometimes it may also give rise to a paradoxical positiveness. The uneasiness relates to the complexity and depth of relations and situations, the sadness and the damage; the paradoxical positiveness derives from the possibility of change to non-violence.

These processes are complex, and deserve closer specification and conceptualization. Studying violence and being against violence does not mean distancing oneself from violence. It comprises a series of different and changing relationships with the material (of violence). This may involve the recognition of some of the ways in which we have been formed by and through violence; the examination of ambivalence towards working on violence; and attention to relations between men in the research group, particularly around authority and power. While there are some dangers in working as a group of men on men's violence, particularly in terms of male bonding and collusion, on balance, a group does create the possibility of counter-voices. Because of the danger of 'group-think', stereotyping of others and scapegoating, a critical scepticism is useful.

While the subject matter of the research is very serious, this does not mean that doom and seriousness is necessarily an appropriate stance. Indeed the feelings that may arise from this kind of research can be partly dealt with by lightness and humour. At times, this may be a form of avoidance or defence; on other occasions, it may be a means of discharging emotions and distress; it may also be simply a more enjoyable way of working; sometimes the research, such as things said by men, can be funny or tragi-comic. On the other hand, there are, of course, dangers in this. The most obvious is the reduction of the seriousness and urgency of the problem of men's violence. More subtly, humour can involve stereotyping the researched and thus distancing from them. We, as researchers, may see ourselves as different from 'them' and may even place ourselves in a falsely positive, even 'heroic' light.

Men Interviewing Men

In much social research it is assumed that the interviewer is in a position of power relative to the interviewee and that it is women who are employed for interviewing women and men, on behalf of men (Platt, 1981; Warren, 1988; MacKeganey and Bloor, 1991). In this project, the interviews are not simply an encounter between an interviewer and an interviewee; they are encounters between men. This raises some novel questions compared with malestream social science, peer research and feminist research. In peer research, there may be ambiguity between the equality of peers and interviewer/ interviewee hierarchy. With women interviewing women in feminist research, attempts have been made to reduce the interviewer's power over the interviewee and develop less structured interviewing styles (Oakley, 1981, 1987; Malseed, 1987). In recent years there has been increasing attention to the complexities and dilemmas of interviewing and qualitative research within debates on feminist methodology (see, for example, Edwards, 1990; Wolf, 1996). With men interviewing men within the framework of Critical Studies on Men, the situation is even more contradictory.

In one sense, men interviewing men represents *no* challenge at all to the traditional hierarchy of the interviewer over the interviewee. On the other hand, the situation does create possibilities for a reformulation of interviewing along lines that relate to but are different from feminist debates. The interviewer is a man, rather than a woman; a man is doing what may be perceived as 'women's work'. Both know what it is to be a man. Both can relate to other men in ways seen as 'natural'; 'fraternal' relations can be employed. Peer status 'as men' may lead to taken-for-grantedness reframing/obscuring the information sought.

Such processes are in some ways contradicted and in some ways reinforced by the fact that the interview is about violence, something that it is not usual for men to discuss in detail. This may bring an unusual degree of intimacy and/or disclosure into the talk between two men who are strangers. On the other hand, the interviewer may use authority to control the interview and obtain information. More arguably, the power relations are potentially negotiable as the interviewee has information which the interviewer seeks. Talking about violence can also be a sign that the interviewee is now *changed/changing*: he is now different to the way he was; he is assumed to be now more like the interviewer.

In addition, there is the specific possibility of collusion, *conscious or unconscious*, between interviewer and interviewee, for example, in not overstating the extent of violence. An example of a collusive question is as follows: 'Was that the *only* time you've been violent to her?' (my emphasis). This question makes it easy for the man to minimize his violence. In this instance he gave the following reply: 'Well I've slapped her and that's about it.' To which he immediately added: 'She's slapped me, just a few slaps.' Let us also consider the following interview extract (Q = interviewer; A = interviewee):

Q: She's never been injured or anything like that?
A: No.
Q: You just sort of bodily held her against the wall?'

This exchange could be understood in several ways: as collusion with violence; as a means to maintain the flow of the interview; or a deliberate ploy to encourage the man to say more about his recollection of violence. Accordingly, the most detailed aspect of research has involved tensions, difficulties and decisions to be made between modes of behaving – which may or may not elicit information, reinforce or challenge current ideas and practices on violence, reinforce or challenge practices of 'masculinity'.

Social differences by class, 'race', age, sexuality, and so on, may inter-relate with the possibility of collusion in a number of ways. For example, where the interviewee is from a higher status social group to the interviewer, the interviewer may defer to him and so collude. Alternatively, where the opposite is the case, the interviewer may not wish to question the inter-viewee too firmly for fear of being thought 'oppressive'. Such processes may be more or less conscious. For men to critically interview men on violence involves attention, listening, empathy, but also critical distance and critical awareness, rather than collusion.

However, in interviewing and research in general, there is usually more than one agenda. This means that an interviewer may, more or less consciously, go along with the assumptions of the interviewee, and in that sense at least collude with him, yet in so doing may elicit much more of the interviewee's perceptions and assumptions. Thus, what may appear to be 'bad questions' or 'naive comments' can actually produce more interesting and more useful data. From the point of view of the interviewee, being interviewed by a man can mean that he makes certain assumptions about the interviewer, on the basis of how he expects a man to think and behave. This may involve bravado, putting down women, assuming heterosexuality, using drink as common knowledge, and so on. There are many examples of men using small turns of phrase with the apparent certainty of an exchange between men: 'And she had to understand, stop that and I'll stop what I'm doing. It's some for some, 50–50, do you know what I mean?' Another example concerns the man's drinking: 'When you get drink in you, sometimes you don't know what you're doing, do you? That's it, my old cock [to interviewer].' In such ways, the normality of men's exchanges with men are maintained.

All this is overlain by the possibility, for both parties, of self-reflection in the interview, and the possibility of emancipatory communication.[5] By emancipatory communication I am not just referring to the possibility of undistorted and accurate communication but communication that may assist in emancipation, in this context, of women who have suffered violence from men. This may of course lead indirectly to the man's metaphorical 'emancipation' from his own violence – violence which can certainly diminish or even ruin his life as well.

While for men to do this kind of research is breaking a taboo, it is available for reincorporation into male hegemony – through *therapeutic clinicism* (treating men interviewed as clinical cases to be understood and perhaps 'cured' by therapeutic or similar means), *abstracted scientism*, *heroism*, *collusion* and *redemption*.

The Emotions of Research

Research is conventionally represented as unemotional and rational, as about bringing an unemotional stance to the 'object' under examination.

Like executive and professional work, it is supposed to involve a 'tough-minded approach to problems' and 'a capacity to set aside personal, emotional considerations in the interest of task accomplishments' (Kanter, 1977: 22). Doing research on men's violence to known women is a process that demands an emotional response. It involves engagement and commitment; it can bring a whole range of social, physical and psychological effects, pains and aches. It can involve getting used to dealing with violence, and the possible dangers of the suppression of emotion, particularly in cutting off from the effects of violence. Violence is a potentially powerful topic to research, because it connects with other powerful experiences in researchers' own lives – men's own violence, men's experience of being violent, men's relations with women, feelings of love and hate, and so on. Then there are a wide variety of emotions that may occur within different interviews – anxiety, fear, sadness. There are also emotions in relation to the research as a whole.

Much of this was about coping with uncertainty and tension. This did not necessarily mean baring our souls at every turn or wallowing in emotion; it did, however, mean dealing with emotions. The emotion of doing this kind of research appeared to increase with the 'amount' of violence, the perception of uniqueness, unpredictability, the lessening of male hegemony, and the individual's relation to violence. However, it would be misleading to overstate the emotionality of the researching of violence. In many ways, researching violence was set in the tensions between the *routine* business of doing research and the disjunctive and coincidental elements of researching violence.

Throughout the research, I became aware that I was in a state of stress and potential alarm – stress that the research might not get done; potential alarm that something might go completely wrong, such as an interviewed man attacking or even killing the woman the day after the interview. So for much of the period I experienced a mixture of alertness and near-depression. I also several times 'accidentally' damaged myself, shortly before or going to interviews.[6] Anyone contemplating doing research on men's violence needs to be aware of the likely emotional and other effects, and to make suitable arrangements for handling them.

Often in the course of doing this research, I got very upset. One occasion was after I had had a particularly successful phone call, which I had made from home, that meant that I would be able to make contact with some more men. I cried, because of the privilege of being allowed to do what I was doing, albeit very indirectly, in connection with the pain of the women who had experienced the violence of the men concerned. Other times were when reading through transcripts: I stopped and wept at what I was reading or listening to. On occasions, when physically writing up this research, I have broken down and cried at the recollection of what this research is about. It is the *movement* from the experience of the man being violent to the experience of the woman receiving the violent blow, to the experience of the man later talking of this in interview, this then being transcribed, analysed, and now written up. Those *transfers* of medium carry with them the imagined emotions of violence and its experience.

During the research other events occurred that affected the emotional nature of the research work. These included ongoing routines at work and at home, the particular domestic and working circumstances of the researchers. All the researchers worked on the project part-time. During the research there was family illness, death, separation, the birth of a child. Difficulties in other parts of the researchers' lives *overlapped with* difficulties in researching men's violence, producing at times some special poignancy.

Dealing with researchers' own emotions also meant dealing with the emotions of the men interviewed. Not surprisingly, emotion figures in a wide variety of ways in the interviews. First, emotions are shown – in crying, laughing hilariously, shaking. Second, the man may *tell* of his own emotions, of his need to change emotionally or his general emotionality. Third, men may use *emotional language*, with or without showing emotion. Also the motivation to be interviewed may be emotional. One man inter-mingled talking about violence, talking about emotion and being emotional:

> When I'm on at her [being violent], I don't see her, do you know what I mean? I don't see Alexandra, because . . . it ain't her that I'm getting at. When I get [on at] her it's, it's hard. And then, even, like this Sunday, I'm crying, I'm like this because I've got to be like this [*crying*] else I can't *get it out*. It's then they [his parents] start on me. [His emphasis]

However, what was interesting was how easily most men talked about their violence to women *without* much apparent emotion. When men did 'get emotional' it was usually linked to their own violation – from fathers, mothers, teachers, as boys and young men, for example, describing their own abuse as a child, perhaps for the first time. Listening to a man say such things about himself, whilst at the same time hearing his accounts of his violence to a woman, is a complex experience. For this man, 'getting the emotion out' is equated with moving away from violence. Yet this hardly touches the emotion of his violence or his violation of the woman.

Doing research work in this field, the field of men's violence to women, is often very unpleasant. This is especially when dealing with information about a man who has been violent *in a whole series of ways* to a woman, and then stopping to think/feel what on earth must this be like for the woman concerned. Sometimes in listening to tapes or reading transcripts, the enormity of the *accumulation* of violence becomes a brick wall in thinking and working.

Knowledge and Writing

Researching men's violence to women raises questions not only of methods but also of the construction of knowledge. Researching violence is a very involving, at times all-consuming activity. Doing research – arranging interviews, meeting new people, hearing their stories, being surprised by them, and so on – is a process full of interest and humanity. The engagement with the process can easily lead to absorption. The absorption can itself reinforce a preoccupation with the detail of research, with case studies, with the idiographic, with the empirical – the thrill of the tell, the thrall of the tale. There are clear dangers to empiricism, especially when it is the reports of the perpetrators of violence that are being studied.

This empirical detail of research in the doing of research, in the meeting of people in interviews, is reproduced again in the *lure* of the tape and the transcript. The *particular* appeal of interviews, tapes and transcripts may divert attention from the non-empirical. The tape and the transcript can have a disconcerting, almost magical, life of their own – a curio, an 'authentic voice', data, the seduction of the text. They can appear as *the* source of knowledge, within which 'nuggets of truth' are to be discovered. Items of interest are sought. The tapes, transcript and text of research on men's violence to women have a definite lure. These place the reader as voyeur: they invite a distanced or partially distanced analysis of discourse. Items of analytical interest may override, in the act of interpretation, the mundane and the ordinary, the experiential and the violating.

Writing (up) violence is a demanding and at times almost horrendous business. It is difficult to convey thought, experience and meaning around violence on the page. There are also sometimes difficulties in actually writing about it at all. The issue of writing was also important *throughout* the research in another way. Whilst I kept a research diary, I tried to resist the temptation of constructing theories and explanations of men's violence prematurely. It was important to avoid typologizing or stereotyping men, and instead to attempt to maintain an open-mindedness to what the men were saying, why they were saying it, and what might or might not explain these violences. Thus, *not* coming to a conclusion, *not* seeking an overall pattern, and *not* trying to make overall sense of men's violence has been part of the process of knowledge formation – a process of interpretation and possibly coping within the research.

The various methods highlighted what it is that unites and separates men from each other, by class, age, race, sexuality and relation to violence. The material produced cannot be treated as 'pure' information but is mediated by power relations, particularly men's relation to women through violence. It needs to be understood in the context of an epistemology, which places women's experiences of violence from men as central, and acknowledges the silence that 'talking to men' might produce. In some cases, such as with murder, these silences are for all time.

Men's accounts of violence to women only make sense by reference to the absent 'other' – the woman who has been violated. A political and epistemological task is to avoid re-centring men as the knowers, the subjects of discourse, even though it is men speaking about their violence. These are thus complex *interrelations* between the topic and content of the research;

the research methods; the overall conceptualization of methodology; the specific experiences of doing research in practice; and epistemology. All of these are aspects of pro-feminist research and pro-feminist politics more generally.

In talking on violence, the objects of the research become temporary subjects, just as they have been the subjects of violence. Of crucial importance, men as subjects of violence are talking about themselves: in so doing, they are being reaffirmed as people (men) of interest to other men, as at the centre of things. Critical Studies on Men need to recognize such temporary re-centrings of/in discourses, and attend to their de-centring. This returns us to problematizing 'men' and relating men's accounts to women's accounts (see, for example, Dobash and Dobash, 1979, 1992; Kelly, 1988; Hester et al., 1996).

Some General Issues

Finally, all of the issues highlighted in this chapter may be of more general relevance to those doing research on sensitive topics, especially in relation to questions of gender. This applies to the sociological significance of 'difficulties', access, preparation for interviewing, venues, the gendering of interviewing, the emotions of research. There are thus a variety of lessons for future research that can drawn from this review:

- understanding the *context* of research;
- building *preparation* into the research process;
- building the analysis of *access* into the analysis of 'the topic';
- addressing *confidentiality* and *safety* as social processes;
- understanding the *gender, 'race' and other dynamics of interviews*;
- developing strategies for interviews on *problematic topics*;
- working with *multiple methods*;
- developing an understanding of the research *work process*;
- considering the relationship of *the topic, writing and knowledge*.

Part II

TALKING VIOLENCE

4

Violence and Talking About Violence

In order to stop men's violence to known women, it is probably useful to understand how men understand violence. Men may talk about their violence to known women before, during or after the violence. Men may talk to the women concerned, to relatives, friends, agency staff, interviewers. Talking about violence is assumed to be reporting past events; it is also much more and much less than that. Thus these are not 'true' explanations; rather they are part of the way in which violence is often continued, less often contradicted. Talking about violence might involve defensiveness, diversion, denial, as well as directness, even bragging. Talking about violence can be exciting, convey threat, be 'really interesting', be mundane, sometimes even be 'pleasant'.

In seeking to understand men's understandings of violence, it is necessary to do some work on conceptualizing the relationship of violence and talk about violence. Indeed as incarceration of men who are violent to women is rare, talk is the main medium of agency intervention with men; accordingly, it is necessary to ask how men 'talk violence'.[1] This chapter outlines a framework for understanding the relationship of violence and talk about violence.

Four basic models are outlined. The first two of these are premised upon the centrality of the notion of the behaviour; the third prioritizes text; the fourth speaks simultaneously of the material and the discursive. The first two are distinguished by their focus: in the first case, on both violence and talk of violence as behaviour, and, in the second, as violence as behaviour and talk of violence as representations of violence. Thus these four approaches are referred to respectively as *behavioural/realist*, *behavioural/ representational*, *textual/constructionist* and *material/discursive*. Such different perspectives on the relationship of violence and talk about violence do not apply to abstract social phenomena; they themselves relate to specific socially situated occurrences, in this context, primarily interviews and their analysis. Not surprisingly, interviews can themselves be understood in a number of ways as behaviours, as representations, as text, and as material/discursive practices.

Four Perspectives

Violence and Talk as Behaviour

As a first step, let us begin by a simple conceptualization of violence as a non-problematic behavioural phenomenon. Violence clearly has a real existence in its own right; it does not only exist through social construction. Violence is real in terms of existing within a real social context, of its specific enactment, of its effects, and of the responses to it. To put this rather differently, violence has a past, present and future. Thus a simple way of developing such a model of violence is to consider first, *its past* – What happened before the violence? What preceded it? What social circumstances led to violence? What kind of history does violence have? – second, *its present* – What happened during the violence? What form does it take? What is done by whom to whom? What actions and behaviours are involved? – and third, *its future* – What happened after the violence? What follows the violence? What effects, consequences and responses are there to the violence? These pasts, presents and futures of violence may thus be thought of respectively as: the antecedents of violence; the acts of violence themselves; the responses to violence.

In this *behavioural/realist* view (see Table 4.1) talk about violence has its own past, present and future: it too has its own contexts, its own acts of talking and its own responses. Thus, talk about violence may be most obviously thought of as *subsequent* to violence, as an effect of or a response to violence. However, talk about violence can of course also be part of the *antecedents*[2] of further violence, and may even itself constitute violence. Thus the relationship of violence and talk about violence is more complex than appears at first sight. Talk about violence may be understood as not just part of the effects of violence, of violence's future, but as the representation of violence. So let us look in more detail at the implications of such a more definite focus on *talk* about violence.

Talk as Representation of Violence as Behaviour

In the previous approach both violence and talk about violence are fundamentally understood as behaviours; a second perspective is to emphasize the way in which talk about violence can be conceptualized as *a means of representation* of the behaviour of violence. Accordingly, I call this the *behavioural/representational* approach. While talk is considered to be a

TABLE 4.1 *Four models of violence and talk about violence*

	Behavioural/realist approach		Behavioural/representational approach	Textual/constructionist approach	Material/discursive approach
Focus	(1) Violence	(2) Talk of violence	Talk of violence	Text of talk of violence	Violence, talk of violence, and violence of talk
Contexts (PAST)	Contexts of violence	Contexts of talk about violence	Representation of contexts of violence	Contexts of violence as constructed within text	Contexts as acts/ representations/texts and responses
Acts/representations/ texts (PRESENT)	Acts of violence	Acts of talk about violence	Representation of acts of violence	(1) Text of violence (2) Subtexts of violence	Acts/representations/ texts as contexts and responses
Responses (FUTURE)	Responses to violence	Responses to talk about violence	Representation of responses to violence	Responses to violence as constructed within text	Responses as contexts and acts/ representations/texts

direct representation of previous violence, it may also be granted a slightly more active role in representing that violence, *more or less fully*. Thus in this second view, which is itself an extension of the first realist approach, the violence is real and the talk on the violence is a representation, though not necessarily a complete representation, of that reality of violence. It is still the violence that *produces* the talk: the talk is the *product* of the violence. In turn of course the antecedents of violence (for example, the person and their personal history, the immediate situation, the relevant power relationships) can be hypothesized as producing the violence. Thus the antecedents of violence, as assumed in the first behavioural/realist approach, produce the violence which in turn produces the talk – the talk of violence, whether or not that refers to those antecedents.

The uncertainty about the inclusion of the antecedents of violence and talk of violence stems from at least three sources: uncertainty over the nature of those antecedents; uncertainty in the knowledge about those antecedents; and uncertainty in the 'completeness' of any account, even if there was full knowledge. These kinds of uncertainty can in effect produce gaps in talk of violence.

This second kind of model of the links between violence and talk of violence remains premised upon a relatively simple link between behaviour and representation. It is also arguably premised upon the notion of a singularly rational actor, in this case a man who has been violent. This combination seems unlikely, particularly when one considers all the reasons why men might not want to 'tell the whole truth'.

Talk of Violence as Text

The behavioural/representational model described above, while attributing some limited power to language, still presents language as a relatively passive and transparent medium for the communication of information, in this case, violence. In recent years, there has been greater attention to the more active, constructionist view of language as against a more passive, transparent view (see Grosz, 1987). This has particularly been the case within feminism, poststructuralism and postmodernism, and their various interrelated forms of knowledge. In the case of feminism, language is subject to critique as not neutral, by virtue of its domination by men in both content and process, grammar and syntax. Furthermore, it is important to acknowledge that the distinction between active and passive views of language is itself not fixed and absolute. Similarly there is an ongoing relationship between form and content in language, so that interviews, like other talk, always reconstruct to some extent.

Thus an alternative textual model to the behavioural/representational for understanding the relationship of violence and talk about violence begins from quite different assumptions. Talk about violence is not understood as the representation of behaviours but rather as *texts*; talk about violence is not understood as merely representing violence but rather as actively

TABLE 4.2 *Behavioural/representational and textual/constructionist approaches*

	Behavioural/representational approach	Textual/constructionist approach
Theoretical privileging	Behaviour	Text
Substantive privileging	Violence	Talk about violence
Temporal privileging	Prospective	Retrospective
Conceptualizations of violence	Behavioural	Textual
Conceptualizations of talk (about violence)	Representations of previous violence	Constructing of violence
Conceptualization of 'context'	Representation of contexts of acts of violence, especially antecedents	Contexts within text of violence
Conceptualizations of 'act/text'	Representations of acts of violence and their explanation	Text of violence
Conceptualization of 'subtext'	Incomplete representation	Subtexts within text of violence

constructing that violence. Not surprisingly, in this view multiple interpretations and multiple narratives may be drawn up in making sense of the material. This I therefore label the *textual/constructionist* approach. In this there is no direct one-to-one relation between violence and talk, and talk itself actively creates and re-creates the presumed reality of violence. The very reasons that make the *behavioural/representational* approach questionable lend weight to a perspective based on text and constructionism. Furthermore, the fact that my focus here is partly on *men's* violence to known *women* means that the *textual/constructionist* approach is to be taken seriously, as at the very least there are clear structural reasons why men might construct very different texts of violence to those of women.

Within the *behavioural/representational* approach social contexts of violence, the acts of violence and the responses to violence are all represented, in varying degrees of completeness, in the talk. In contrast, according to the *textual/constructionist* approach, contexts, violence 'itself' and responses are constructed within the text, as text (see Table 4.2). In addition, within this approach, talk about violence may be further interpreted in terms of possible subtexts. The concept of subtexts has been developed in psychoanalytically informed cultural studies to refer to the deeper, less conscious structures of meaning that may be present in cultural texts. The idea of subtext has also been used within more sociologically grounded analyses of gender relations.[3] The subtext does not refer to incompleteness or even inaccuracy in representation, but to the presence of structural meanings and silences in the text that are not conscious to the speaker. This is particularly significant when there are conscious attempts to produce 'objectified and objectifying models of organizing the systematic consciousness of society' (Smith, 1989: 35), as in the social sciences, but the idea of subtext also applies to more everyday talk and representations. Subtext, whether formed around class, gender, race differences or whatever, can be thought of as the articulation of the 'repressed'. The subtext of men's talk about violence includes the (hetero)sexual subtext (see Chapter 8).

In the textual model, talk does not just represent the violence, it actively intervenes in the construction of the violence, even if that entails a silence on violence. Talk does not simply construct violence through omissions but also through commissions. It is not just a partial construction but partial in its construction. This *active* character of talk can take many forms and be for many reasons. These include general questions that are not specific to violence. For example, it can be argued that the use of talk and language is a social accomplishment and that talk and language are just as much social constructions as other actions, including violence 'itself'. In this view, talk is a socially variable enactment that in part constructs social reality, including in this case violence. Thus, for example, whereas in the behavioural/representational approach the social contexts of violence are represented by talk, in the textual/constructionist approach social contexts of violence are constructed *within* the text itself.

Having said this, the textual approach does carry a number of distinct problems specifically because of the content matter of violence. At its simplest, talk of violence may involve lying, deception and denial. It may obscure rather than enlighten, justify and excuse rather than analyse. Second, talk may not just be selective from a 'complete' picture of recollections, it may *more arbitrarily invoke* aspects of the social contexts of the man's life, of his violence and indeed of the talk itself. Indeed there is always a danger in making sense of talk about violence in a way that assumes that *all* talk that includes references to violence is *simply about violence*. Men's talk about violence may also be about all sorts of other things: the weather, drinking, money, parents, football, and so on and on. Talk about violence is *not necessarily* about violence. While men may respond to questions about violence, what may be talked about may be quite different. The answers may not address violence; they may not refer to violence as a significant topic worthy of the speaker's attention. They may refer to completely different issues, be on completely different 'wavelengths'. Such talk may be analysed in its own terms – without necessary reference to violence. It is, after all, talk.

The logical conclusion of this approach is that violence itself is not strictly a form of behaviour but is itself a form of text, actively constructed and constructing of 'reality'. Acts of violence may be amenable to analysis as texts in certain specific ways just as other social actions and social accomplishments may be. Indeed in this view violence can itself be a form of communication that exists in the context of *previous* communications, including violence. However, it is necessary to record that to *reduce* violence to talk, even more so to text, is or can be dangerous – theoretically, politically and personally, metaphorically and literally. Indeed to present violence *solely* as talk or text is positively and extremely dangerous.

Violence and Talk of Violence as Material/Discursive Practices

The basic problem with the textual/constructionist approach is that violence can be reduced to representation, talk, text. This is potentially dangerous as it may obscure the material being and effects of violence. The shortcomings of the textual/constructionist approach make way for a more broadly based analysis of the relationship of violence and talk of violence. This includes the problematization of the strict distinction between and separation of violence and talk of violence. Men's violence to known women and men's talk about such violence are both separate from and intimately connected to each other. Each is a form of the other. We are not concerned just with the *impact* of representation upon action and behaviour, but with the ways in which representation and talk themselves may constitute violence.

While the focus on socially problematic behaviours as reported by the doers of those behaviours means that the textual/constructionist approach is indispensable, those reports in turn have to be placed in their own social and political contexts. Indeed a general rule is that self-reports by members of oppressor groups or social actors who are in the dominant, oppressive position in social relations need to be deconstructed as texts whilst at the same time those oppressions and texts are theorized as material and materially based. Text, and indeed discourse, becomes especially important when making sense of what the powerful say.

Thus a fourth perspective is to conceptualize violence and talk of violence as simultaneously *material/discursive*.[4] They are not just behaviours but are material, bodily happenings; they are not just texts but are set within socially produced, historical, cultural discourses – regimes of 'truth'. Men's violence to known women involves both violence and talk of violence that are simultaneously material and discursive. *It is a form of material/discursive culture practised by men rather than shared between men and women* (see Hearn, 1996b).

Similarly, the relationship between violence and talk of violence needs to be firmly understood in relation to gendered processes and powers. A dominant malestream view might suggest that language is for men an accurate means of conveying information, while for women language is a reconstruction of 'reality'. Feminist critiques of malestream perspectives have turned the tables on this, by reconstructing the malestream as itself a construction in which language is far from neutral but part of that process of construction. Meanwhile, women may be assumed to be able to convey their experiences of previous and other events through talk, language and, indeed, interview. While feminist critiques might emphasize the constructivist view of language and talk, this might be accompanied by an informational interpretation of women's own accounts within a realist epistemology, emphasizing women's oppression by men.

Such a gendered interpretation of language links very clearly with debates around the nature and significance of women's and men's subjectivity in the development of knowledge. Some Marxist accounts (for example, Lukács,

1971) emphasize the superiority of the proletariat as a source of knowledge through subjectivity, and in due course the transcendence of objectivity/ subjectivity. In this view, bourgeois knowledge is generally, characteristically or always the product of abstraction, from the experiences and realities of exploitation and oppression in the material social world. This is largely paralleled by feminist accounts which emphasize the superiority of women's subjectivity and the transcendence of objectivity/subjectivity against men's subjectivity.

The resort to men's subjectivity is no guarantee of truth, accuracy, knowledge whatsoever. It is contextualized in relations of power. Men's subjective accounts have to be examined carefully within these relations (Hearn, 1993a, 1993c). For example, an account by a man of his own experiences of being abused has to be interpreted very differently to an account by the same man of his experiences of being abusive. However, such social contexts cannot be assumed to be just read off from the usual categories of social division that are generally privileged in social analysis, for example, class, age, ethnicity. Constructions of both men's violence and men's talk about violence as material/discursive practices move beyond the limitations of narrower behavioural, representational and textual approaches. Material/discursive perspectives on men's accounts of violence involve interrogation and analysis without presumptions rather than starting from other social assumptions. For this reason, they are reported in the subsequent chapters with a minimum of information on these usual social locations, in order to avoid the imposition of pre-judgements. Paradoxically, discourse becomes significant because of the reality of men's material domination, including violence.

Alternative Perspectives and the Organization of This Text

Whereas behavioural approaches privilege the violence and analyse talk with reference to it, the textual/constructionist approach privileges the talk and analyses violence with reference to it. Thus, in one sense, the former approach is prospective, the second retrospective. On the other hand, violence can become talk, yet is not only talk. It is more accurate to see both behavioural and textual approaches to interpretation as relevant, as both relating to material and discursive processes that occur simultaneously. For this reason the next four chapters draw on both representational and textual approaches, and the tension between them that is incorporated within a focus on material/discursive practices. These chapters, on contexts, texts and subtexts, need to be read together: each is part of the others; and gains meaning through its interrelation with the others, through a process of intertextuality. The distinctions between context, text and subtext are not absolute. The material/discursive approach incorporates all three concepts (as well as problematizing their separation) within a social/political framework. Their analysis needs to draw on broader understandings of material/discursive formations.

While men's talk about violence included reports on agency responses, these were supplemented by interviews with agency staff and other contacts with agencies. The two following chapters draw on both men's self-reports and the reports from agencies. As such, the confirmation of 'events' between men and agency staff might lend some weight to a representational rather than a strictly textual approach to the accounts. However, in most cases, although men's accounts were full of gaps, confusions, minimizations and inconsistencies of detail, they were not completely incompatible with agency reports.

Throughout all the next six chapters it is important to be aware of both the informativeness and the limitations of different kinds of accounts. In particular men's violence to known women and men's talk about such violence need to be thought of as simultaneously connected to and separate from each other.

5

The Contexts of Violence

Talk in Social Positionings

Men's talk, and indeed silence, about violence is set *in contexts*. This chapter addresses the contexts of men's talk about violence to known women. These include those recognized by the men, and those observable through analysis that may not be apparent to them. Accordingly, men, in their talk and silence, are located in social positionings. Men are *positioned* by social structures in particular locations, and yet may contradict them in some way. They may also position themselves or be positioned by others, and may be in several different positionings. Men may occupy *subject positions*, which may be multiple, shifting and contradictory, within discourses.

Types of Context

Contexts usually comprise a number of disparate elements: strategic, societal, agency. Strategic contexts refer to the strategic orientation of the man or strategic response of the man speaking about his violence *in general* as a problematic activity.[1] Societal contexts refer to the social divisions and social structures that may act as contexts to violence. Agency contexts refer to the agencies that men have had contact with, sometimes affecting their societal positioning. All three are both material and discursive.

Strategic Contexts

Violence as a Strategic Context of Violence

Society is structured, divided and sometimes unified by violence. Violence is a major social division and major social structure. Thus violence itself is a social positioning of further violence and talk about violence. Yet the doing of violence, the threat of violence, the capacity (labour-power) for violence is rarely (I feel like saying never) considered to be a form of social positioning, social division or social location. Men can be differentially positioned from women in relation to violence, and different men can be differentially positioned from each other in relation to violence. First, it is men doing most violence. Second, men may be currently violent, may have been violent or may not have been violent. Third, men may use such violence more or less regularly. Fourth, men may be defined by others more or less in relation to such violence.

Agreeing to Talk

Violence is a problematic activity, as is talking about violence, especially one's own violence. A fundamental strategy for negotiating this difficulty is the agreement to talk, in this context to be interviewed in the first place. Necessarily men were always in that context of agreement and their subsequent talk, including denials and minimizations, has to be placed in that context. This *general* framework presented opportunities to talk or be silent on particular events or experiences around violence.

In some cases, the agreement to be interviewed may be a means of demonstrating change and movement away from violence. The ability to talk about *past* violences may demonstrate the *veracity* of the man's 'non-violence' claims *in the present*. This may involve confession or be a more reflective, distanced account, even with irony, self-parody, 'camp' or authentic inauthenticity.

Talking about one's own violence can of course be a way of creating *a different self*, of facing or reducing guilt, or redefining oneself as someone who has not just been violent *but moreover who has talked about it*. Accordingly, talking about violence, especially for a research interview, is a 'good investment'. The talk accumulates. It may never completely pay off the debt of the violence, but it can assist the accumulation of other resources, of positive *gifts to the self* that are *of value* to oneself and perhaps others. The agreement to be interviewed may provide support for reproducing the violence or for stopping it. Or indeed violence may be an *indifference* to the man; it may hardly warrant serious attention. It may be talked of as one might the washing up, the week's shopping or the adverts on television. These are all effective 'technologies of the self' (Foucault, 1988).

Establishing Credibility

A second major strategy for dealing with the problematic nature of talking about violence is to attempt to 'save face' through establishing credibility. This can of course apply even when violence is confessed. Accounts of violence typically include 'a complex of anticipated judgement, face-saving, and status negotiation' (Ptacek, 1985: 46).[2] Most, though not all, men attempt to portray themselves in a way that does not categorize themselves to the listener, the interviewer, as (simply) 'violent men'. This appears to be an issue even for men who later 'happily' tell of many examples of their violence. This is generally conveyed at the beginning and/or the end of the interview. It is the context in which the specific talk of violence sits.

A common way of attempting to maintain credibility with the interviewer is by asserting 'I'm not a violent man.' As two men on life sentences said, 'Well deep down I'm not a violent man,' 'I don't class myself as a violent person.' Another man who spoke at length of his considerable violence to three different women concluded: 'I don't see myself as a wife batterer at all.' A man who articulated unapologetically 25 specific examples of his violent behaviour, including the use of weapons to severely damage the woman, began by saying he was not sure if he qualified for the study – 'I'm not really the violent type,' 'It's not like I'm a bad case or anything like that, a psychopath,' 'I didn't actually think what I'd done was going to be enough for this project. I thought it might be men that, like, tortured their girlfriends.' For men who spoke of less violence, the imperative to say 'I'm not a violent man' appeared entirely unsurprising.

Many men sought to engage with the interviewer to elicit sympathy, or at least place themselves in a diminished or vulnerable position, even when they were not apologetic about their violence. This strategy was liable to re-position the man so that he could become redefined by himself and/or others, *not* as a violent man needing social condemnation but as someone needing support. In short, the man who has been violent can then believe he can be felt sorry for. In addition to this *victim* position, the man may position himself as a potential equal through pleasantness, friendliness and humour or 'straightforward' normality and reasonableness. To be strictly accurate, such contextual strategies are not maintained by the interviewee alone; rather they are *intertextual* strategies accomplished, or indeed disrupted, more or less successfully *between* interviewee and interviewer. This is not to suggest that they necessarily result from intentional collusion, although that is always possible. The achievement of reasonable pleasant-ness may be a way for the man to show his normality, his change from violence, his verbal cleverness; it may also show that both parties under-stand each other, are on the same 'wavelength', share something of a 'men's culture', *could* collude (even if they do not). This can reduce anxiety for both, avoid difficulties, silences and gaps in the interview. 'Mature pleasant-ness' can be ways of men hiding their shadows or reproducing other splits in their life within the interview. Alternatively, a dominant contextual strategy may involve bragging by the man about his violence. It reproduces his dominance over the woman, and seeks to assert dominance over the inter-viewer. This may or may not be resisted by the interviewer. Not surpris-ingly, in specific interviews these various strategies intermingled in contradictory ways.

The success with which such strategies are accomplished may assist in confirming, challenging or disrupting identity for both interviewee and inter-viewer. It is generally in the man's interest to distinguish between himself as violent actor and himself as talker about violence, to present himself as having two different subjectivities: one past–violent/potentially violent, one present–non-violent (see pp. 106–107).

Setting the Context

A third strategy is attending to the context of violence. For a man to adequately set the context for violence is problematic. If he sets the scene in what could be construed as 'excessive' detail, then he might be seen as avoiding the violence. If he gives a cursory description of the context, he might be considered glib, lacking in self-understanding and self-reflection. Thus describing the context of violence is itself a strategic context. It can also be a form of excuse-making for the violence that followed. Rather than saying, 'This is what I did, it was my responsibility, and what went before doesn't explain or excuse or justify it,' men are well able to talk at some length about what went *before* – the context of violence.

Contexts of violence provide a means of *distancing* the man from his violence. Apart from those few men who were intimidating or threatening in the interview, his violence is talked about as if it is elsewhere. The context remains in the past, in societal divisions or impersonal terms. He may refer to himself as if he were in the third person. Talk about contexts refers to matters *elsewhere*. The context of violence can also provide justifications for violence in a different sense. Men who choose to use violence may conveniently emphasize the *societal* context of their violence or argue that their societal location *justifies* or even *excuses* their violence. Some who use violence may be so imbued with a societal view of reality and/or of themselves that they fail to notice they are violent, abusive, intimidating and capable of bringing others less powerful than themselves to desperation.

Societal Contexts

The Heteropatriarchal Context

In analysing the *variety* of men's reports of their violence to known women, it is necessary to locate them within the context of men's *societal power*. Men's accounts are a means of saying and showing that power, a means of maintaining that power, directly and indirectly. To acknowledge a broad societal framework is not to argue that *all* men's statements automatically reproduce power over women. However, men's accounts reflect and reproduce men's societal power, especially in relation to violence as one means of power for men, individually and collectively. The overarching societal context to men's talk about violence is heteropatriarchal relations, structures and cultures. The social positioning of men within heteropatriarchies is the most important and pervasive form of social positioning. These questions of patriarchal context are, however, rarely explicitly addressed in men's accounts of violence and thus may be thought of as implicit societal contexts or subtexts (Chapter 8).

Societal Contexts and Personal Difficulties

While heteropatriarchal relations may be ever-present yet *implicit*, in most accounts men *explicitly* introduced societal contexts in one or more of the following other ways:

- a relatively brief account of the man's employment and family situation;
- a more extended account of the man's difficulties in the more distant past, in terms of relations with parents, own abuse, institutional living;
- a description of recent deterioration in the man's relationship with the woman concerned, usually through drink, depression, stress or some other 'extraneous' cause.

Constructions of events in time can provide the context to explanations of violence and reduced moral responsibility for violence (see Chapter 7): distant past contexts may support excuses; recent contexts may underpin justifications.

The main social divisions and social experiences through which the *societal* context of violence was described were:

- work, job, money and unemployment;
- family background and upbringing;
- institutional living (children's homes, in care, youth custody, and so on);
- drink and alcoholism;
- depression and mental illness/frailty;
- the man's relationship with the woman.

In most cases, and even when men seemed remorseful and determined to stop their violence, men set the societal context for their violence in terms of *their own* difficulties in *their own* lives. These included changes in domestic and personal life, such as separation, divorce, access to children, and changes in their work life, such as unemployment, redundancy, money problems. Men did not refer to the harm to the woman or her changing circumstances as the context to their own violence. They usually brought together references to social divisions and biographical information. Men sometimes described particularly difficult and deprived circumstances; more usual were *mundane* rather than dramatic contexts, the usual changes of work and family, perhaps mixed with 'hard times', often 'self-evident' accounts of 'life in a nutshell'.

A considerable proportion of the men interviewed were in positions of social difficulty, through unemployment, low wages and imprisonment. Those in prison are subject to that institutional regime, its restrictions, deprivations and indeed violence. For some men, there is the complex of circumstances and experiences whereby they both have a multiplicity of problems of their own and have been violent to others. Interestingly, measures of 'personal resources' (by a combination of education, income and occupation) showed only a moderate negative correlation with more and greater violence, as well as with higher self-esteem and lower levels of depression. Much more significant was the connection between referral source and social class. The men referred from the Probation Service were all unemployed, in intermittent employment or lived by crime. The men in the men's programmes were predominantly in skilled manual occupations and financially relatively better-off.

Family, Locality and Institutional Living

Descriptions of current family life did not figure as a significant aspect of societal contexts; however, for a few their 'personal difficulties' were described by them as rooted in their family background. An account of the man's family of origin which provided the major context of one man's story of violence is as follows:

> I've got me sister who loves me. But all though my childhood I've had er er . . . I accept it now because I've been abused from being a child. I've never had the love I've ever wanted and I've never been accepted in my family that I've ever wanted. . . . I got married at 19, no sorry 20, I didn't go out of the home till I were 19 and I got married at 20 to get out of the house. I got divorced because wife committed adultery. I re-married on the rebound, that's partly why it didn't work out because I re-married sort of six weeks later.

For some men, material deprivation and family background were complicated by institutional living or by living in particular localities, associated with social difficulties. Both of these two additional factors are found in the following account of a man who described extensive violence, including murder:

> You see when I was a kid, when I was 9, I stole a chocolate bar. It was a dare. . . . I ended up doing six years for it, you know what I mean. And while I was there [in approved school] I got brutalized and I mean brutalized. None of these little cases like, it was a walking stick and they bang hell out of you, you know what I mean. If you were small, the headmaster he used to stand you on a chair like and say, 'You're my size now, aren't you?' And you used to say 'Yes Sir.' And he used to punch you straight in the middle of the face and you'd go flying off the back of the chair. He used to do some terrible things to you. . . . I wasn't even violent when I got out. When I was a lad, I used to live at Robston[3]. . . . There, it was already there, my mother and father got divorced, and so my mother moved to a place called Cranburn, a little place. It was really violent, tough place. . . . I used to get bullied a bit . . . .

Drink, Depression and Stress

Whilst drinking was mentioned in most of the accounts, in a small number of cases drink and alcoholism were seen as the primary context of the violence. One man began as follows:

> I drink a very lot. If I have a bad day, I'm in a bad mood, I take it out on my girlfriend. Shouldn't do but I do. I bray [hit] her. She leaves me for eight week, comes back, stays a while. I go back on drink heavy again. I'll come home, no tea [meal] so I give her a good hiding. . . . I do drink a lot. Anyway, drinking – all the time. Can't stop drinking. Think I'm alcoholic. I'm a registered alcoholic but I still do it and I'll keep on doing it until I probably die, I just can't stop drinking.

Some men specifically constructed the context of their violence through mental health difficulties, sometimes linked to addiction, drink and drugs. However, more usually, their own mental ill health was portrayed either as a relatively more independent factor or as linked to isolation and lack of prospects:

> *A*: I've been pretty bad, although things have been pretty bad for a long time.
> *Q*: What do you mean by bad?
> *A*: Depressed. Not seeing any hope for future.

Agency Contexts

The third major social positioning derives from the agency context in which the men are placed. The major groups of men in terms of agency locations were:

- not in contact with agencies (including those interviewed but not arrested by police);
- arrested by the police;
- on probation;
- in prison;
- in men's programmes;
- in contact with mental health agencies.

These groupings often overlap, with men's involvement with more than one agency. Men in different agency locations tend to talk about their violence in different ways and with different emphases. Agency location also affected the process of referral to the research, the interview arrangements, the interview process, the conditions (for example, comfort or discomfort) and the length of interviews, the general framing of the talk, and other matters of detail.

Differences by agency can be distinguished in a number of ways. Men who came via the police often reported their violence as an aberration. In half the cases they said they had been violent once or twice. Most had not been involved with the police before or for other reasons. In contrast, men referred from Probation had often been involved in a variety of crime. Violence to women was often understood as incidental to their other criminal activities, including violence to men in some cases. The men in prison were of two quite different types. One group conformed to the pattern described in relation to the probation referrals; the other men were imprisoned for murder or attempted murder of women. For these, the crime and the imprisonment had transformed their life. Men in men's programmes often talked of many examples of violence, sometimes over many years. They had clearly told their story before. Men who did not come via a formal agency did not generally see violence as a problem in their lives. In addition, there were men who were referred via other welfare agencies, and talked of long-term violence. A number of men had been involved with psychiatric services; for them, violence was often interconnected with other psychological difficulties.

Agency context often affected where and how the topic of the man's own violence fitted into the whole interview. For example, where men were referred from agencies where their violence defined them, they were often able to begin the interview with the topic of their own violence. This applied particularly with men in prison following conviction for murder and men in men's programmes. In focusing on agency location, there is a clear danger that the man in question is defined simply and solely through the agency's relationship to his specific violence. Thus man A is an attempted murderer and man B is a man who has committed assault occasioning actual bodily harm. Such assessments need to be used with caution, not least because other men may have completed similar violence but are not similarly labelled. The remainder of this section considers the main groups of men according to their source of referral.

No Agency

The eight men who had had no contact with agencies or whose contact with the research was not through agencies that deal with violence did not generally define violence as a major theme in their lives. Having said that, they were often very willing to talk of violence at length and in some depth. The extent of damage to the women reported by these men was considerably less than most of the other men contacted via agencies. Interestingly, this group self-reported a higher level of violence than those men referred from the police. The descriptions referred primarily to particular incidents of physical violence, relatively simple sequences of events, and a small number of physical blows.

Reactions to the men's violence from other family members and from friends did not figure strongly in these accounts. Men often reported that parents or other family and friends did not know; when they did, they did not generally intervene. Where agencies are not involved it may be difficult to intervene against the violence. It remains private. Making violence more public through agency intervention may facilitate intervention from family and friends.

The most obvious common characteristic of these eight men was that to *their* mind violence did not figure prominently in their lives. In this, they shared something with most of the men referred from police contact. For men not involved with agencies, the violence was *described* as relatively limited in extent and effect, incidental to the rest of their lives, *and not disruptive* for them and their lives.

Police Referrals

The men who were police referrals were inevitably self-selected. While they cannot be said to be representative of men who have relevant police contact, they provide information on one particular grouping of men involved in the criminal justice system in relation to men's violence to known women. Those men who had been arrested or detained by the police certainly recalled their violence in relation to that experience, even if the outcome was inconclusive. Of the 16 referrals from the police, eight claimed that there had been only one or two instances of violence. A typical example that was treated with relative unconcern by the man follows:

Q: Was there a particular incident or what?
A: A domestic. I had a big argument with my wife.
Q: When was this?
A: I can't remember. It were a bit ago. Her sister locked me out of my own flat, so I broke door down you know what I mean. Police came and arrested me. I went to court. I were fined £225 criminal damage. That were it.

Men who had been arrested by the police generally gave a different perspective on violence to those who had not been. Their involvement with the police appeared to structure their perception and definition of their violence. Most chose to describe their violence in terms of its effects for them, particularly their arrest, and in some cases the subsequent impacts on family life. They also saw themselves as *exceptions* from the usual kind of man arrested by the police. In two cases this was clearly explained by references to the sustained violence that they alleged against the woman. Their perceived *exceptional* retaliation to the woman had, in their view, then led to their own arrest. Others described the events as their responsibility and fault, and as something that had happened when they had snapped: it was 'out of character', a 'one-off'. Police referrals, above all others, demonstrate the tendency for men to decentre themselves in relation to violence – to place themselves away from the centre of violence. This insistence on *exceptionality* is opposed to some other men's tendency to see violence as completely normal and therefore *unexceptional*.

Probation Referrals

Seven men were interviewed from Probation Service referrals, often following special efforts by individual probation officers. At times the referral had, from the officer's point of view, to conform to specific criteria. If the man's violence was current, it was often thought to be too risky to refer him to the research. If the man's violence was too far in the past and was thought to be 'resolved', then it was also thought to be too risky to refer him to the research, in case this somehow reactivated his violence or resurrected other difficulties. Officers sometimes referred men to the research because they thought it might be helpful to the man in addressing his violence because previous probation work had not done so. One probation referral contextualized his talk about his violence strictly in terms of his agency location:

> He [the probation officer] wrote me a letter. Asked if I was interested because I'd spoken to him previously, with him being my probation officer, regarding my ex-girlfriend. She was my girlfriend regarding the past few bouts of violence, as to whether when we got out, would we continue. When we split up earlier this year, I think it was about May, he seemed more interested to see whether I'd get out. . . . While I'm in prison and I just wrote off, I read the little piece of paper [about the research] and I thought about it and it couldn't do me no harm.

The most blatant, unrepentant, one could say naive, accounts of violence were given by those men in contact with Probation, particularly those *not* in prison. Here were found the clearest statements of the man's assumed 'right' to be violent to the woman concerned. Some such accounts were repudiations of violence: the violence was talked about as if it was not violence; for some men, it was rather like 'going out' with a girlfriend, or 'having a night-cap' before bed. It was normalized and naturalized within the fabric of what was taken to be the way he, or men, or men like him, lived, particularly in the heterosexual company of women. In another sense, such blatant statements were confessions of violence, but confession without remorse. These confessions without remorse can easily slip into repudiations. Men's acceptance of responsibility and blame for violence *without remorse* can in effect mean that violence becomes normalized as 'normal life' rather than violence.

Definition, responsibility, blame and repudiation may be interconnected so that if all are recognized, the phenomenon becomes normalized, *not in need* of justification and excuse. This shift is a rather complicated and paradoxical process. Violence can be normalized, be understood as not (really) violence, even though it has been talked about as such. On the other hand, redefinition and repudiation are only involved because of the problematic nature of violence, whatever the man's consciousness or lack thereof. To put this another way, confession and repudiation only become necessary if something, in this case violence, is problematic. Normalization of this specific problematic behaviour can be achieved, but the general problematization of that general category of behaviour, violence, remains. Moreover, that general problematization of violence continues *irrespective* of the consciousness of the individual (man) of the status of their particular behaviour as problematic or not.

Men in Prison

It is very unusual for men to receive a custodial sentence for violence to women, and thus the violent offences to women for which men are generally imprisoned represent a rather limited range, specifically, murder, manslaughter, sexual offences and rape. For men in prison, there are a number of possible motives for being interviewed. These include avoiding the usual prison routine; doing favours for staff; going along with what staff say; wishing to understand their violence, to reform themselves, and stop being violent; wishing to talk to someone new, to tell a story, to brag; and, most important of all, to do what they perceive as assisting them in getting out earlier. As one man in prison put it 'Will it [doing the interview] help me get out?' While the interviewer immediately answered, 'No, no, because this is a purely voluntary interview, I'm afraid. As I said, it's nothing to do with the prison service,' this may not be the whole story. At the very least agreeing to be interviewed shows the man is a co-operative prisoner; and it may also show he is willing to talk about his offences and/or violence.

For those convicted of murder and sentenced to life imprisonment, the murder figured centrally in their construction of their life, their subsequent life in prison, and their understanding (or lack of understanding) of their violence to women. In particular, the notion of the *accident* of murder or the murderous *accident* recurred. It was sometimes possible to discern a subjectivity before the murder, when the man was not violent, and a subjectivity after the murder, when he was no longer murdering, and so also was not violent. One of the men who had murdered began his account in a more uncertain way:

> We're here in Oldwood Prison. My name is Bill. I'm in for killing Shirley, who I lived with. . . . I've been here 10 months now, in this prison, But I've been in prison now nearly two years, one year eleven months sort of thing. . . . You know, it's a case of there are some things in your life where you can't come to terms with what's happened and things like that. Because I know basically I'm not a violent person, but it's just happened to be that every now and again sort of thing, and there does seem to be a pattern where every couple of years, that something crops up. And bump! I seem to explode.

In the case of men imprisoned for reasons other than violence to known women, their violence to women was not central to their understanding of their lives. Some embraced a criminal self-definition but not one that related specifically to violence to women. Usually for them, the violence they described was some combination of what they defined as 'minor' incidents of physical violence, verbal violence and violence to property. Such violences were generally seen by such men as incidental to daily life. The prison of course also provided the venue for the interviews. Prison rules and procedures were the interview context – not least in limiting the interview to two hours. The referral process and access were also affected by the prison context, such as in observing security. These interviews had to be conducted at definite times by strict appointment. Cigarettes were expected and appreciated, and sometimes soft drinks. In this situation, it was in the man's interest to fill the full two hours. One man was wise enough to not finish the interview in the two hours so a second interview was arranged.

Men's Programme Referrals

For men to initiate some public action on their violence is unusual. To join a men's anti-violence programme is an unusual course of action for a man who has been violent. Most of the men from these programmes structured their accounts around 'serious incidents'. Thus joining a programme involves motivation that is out of the ordinary. For some, it is only when they are at 'rock bottom', when their marriage appears near to ending, or they have been given an ultimatum by the woman concerned, that they do this:

> . . . my wife, or my ex-wife's, family are beginning to . . . I mean at the moment they're not speaking to me, because they still haven't forgiven me for what happened in the past, but they're actually beginning to realize that what I'm doing with [the programme], I'm serious, you know, it's not just a passing thing. I mean I've been coming here ever since it opened. . . . And they're beginning to realise that I'm not joking. I'm not messing about, and that's good for me, that's going to win me a lot of house points with her family. That's about it.

Two of the three men's programmes were run mainly by women. And in some interviews there were repeated references to these women. The men clearly saw them as significant figures in their lives, often as saviours – of the man, their marriage or similar long-term relationship. In a small number of instances, the societal context of talking about violence was couched positively in terms of personal 'success' rather than personal difficulties. These men were by far the most articulate in talking about their violence.

The Research Project as an Agency Context

In this study the agency context and the research interview were linked through the co-operation of agency staff and managers. In addition, the research project itself constituted an agency, and thus an agency context. The research project was an organization with which the men had contact. The agreement to be interviewed for research purposes, however ambivalent or even reluctant, involved entering a new agency context. Records were kept on and knowledge was developed in relation to each man. Six men sought additional information from the research project – one about services in relation to his own sexual abuse; three about services around men's violence to women; and two about the research itself. Furthermore, several men had been referred to the project by agencies because the staff had thought it would be useful for the men. This might be because they did not see themselves having time to focus on the man's violence or because this was not part of the agency's formal brief. The conceptualization of the research as an agency and an agency context was especially important for those men who sought to use the interview as a form of agency intervention *for themselves*. This could occur either in the interview itself, through disclosures of their violence or violence to them, with discharge, crying and in one case being sick, or at the end of the interview in seeking information or access to other agencies. Several men commented on how useful the interview had been for them in reviewing their situation and thinking about ways of stopping their violence. Research projects may become agencies that may disrupt, challenge, confirm or bolster the identity of men who have been violent.

Two Forms of Otherness: The Atypical Man and the Absent Woman

Men 'reporting' their violence, violent events and experiences around violence always involves reconstruction. Such talk, in interviews and elsewhere, involves the invoking of the other or others – as that which is apparently peripheral to, even absent from, the account yet is fundamental to the structuring of the account – of how the account *works*. Talk is produced 'just about itself' with great difficulty, if at all.

Throughout these contexts – strategic, societal and agency – two major forms of otherness recur. First, men are at pains to present themselves as not typical violent men – men present themselves as other than, separate from *some supposed centre of violence or violent men*. This may be attempted by portraying their violence or violent self as distinct from their self in the interview. Second, the woman to whom the violence had been done is also strangely other and absent from *men's discourse* that is *centred*, but quite differently, *on violence*.

Men in different agency contexts are well able to define themselves as not typical 'men who are violent to women' or 'wife batterers'. They are (almost) always exceptions. They may define their violence as occasional, infrequent, 'one-off', as a response to 'the relationship', or a reaction to alleged provocation (by the woman). In a few cases they refer to their retaliation to the woman's violence or forcible attempts to control her 'for her own sake', for example, to stop her drinking. If they have not been prosecuted or convicted, they may define their violence as 'not serious', not 'real violence'. If, however, they are prosecuted and convicted, this may register as significant, but it may not be defined as a typical criminal act (Godenzi, 1994).

Another possibility is that the man may define his major problems as lying elsewhere than with the violence to the woman – in depression, addiction, his upbringing, career through care institutions, and so on. Whatever way, he can then define *his* problem in these terms, so that his violence is the mere effect of his 'real problem'. This is particularly popular for men in contact with psychiatric or counselling agencies. The violence is not usually presented by them as the, their, central problem. Even if men do admit to a more consistent and continuous pattern of violence, this can also be redefined so that they do not see themselves as typical 'wife batterers', in three main ways:

1 The violence can become taken-for-granted, raising the threshold of what counts as violence.
2 If the man is also violent to men, he can define that as the 'real violence', in which he may use or threaten greater physical force than with the woman concerned.
3 If he has been involved in *other* criminal activities, particularly if that meant contact with criminal justice agencies, he can define these as the major or sole crime. He may see himself as an offender or a criminal, but limit that definition to offences and crimes other than violence to known women.

Men who have murdered, and in some cases been convicted of attempted murder, are able to define themselves in relation to the *specific* event of the murder rather than in relation to their violence to women or as 'wife batterers'. The act of murder can provide a strange 'rebeginning' for some men, in that they can begin to define that particular form of their violence as 'one-off', with all that that entails. What is usually not one-off is the man's history of power, control and violence in relation to women. In such ways, men decentre themselves quite willingly to become other than men who are violent to known women.

The second other, which is more or less implicit, is the woman/women to whom the man has been violent. In men's accounts the woman is usually absent, except as the *receiver* of his violence, or occasionally as the doer of violence or misconduct *to him*. Either way, a *very limited, empty* portrayal of the woman is made. It is rare for a man to refer to the violence in terms of the experience of the woman, the violated. That would involve taking the position or at least attempting to imagine or empathize with the position of the other person. To do violence is not to take the position of the other, not to be interested in the experience of the other. Violence involves dismissing the other. To be interested in the experience of violence of the woman/other/violated might be a contradiction in terms, certainly so at the time of the violence. As time goes on, it may be more possible for a man to reflect on his violence and re-understand it in terms of the woman's experience.

However, the passing of time may mean that he is less concerned with past violences or less likely to recall the woman's specific experiences. Indeed to take the position of the other might mean opposing violence. The woman is constructed, if at all, implicitly and peripherally, and then by virtue of the *effects* of men's violence. The known woman is in most men's accounts an effect of men and men's violence.

Furthermore, the fact that the accounts are only the man's accounts (apart from two when the woman sat in on the interview) is likely to become a central facet in the interview when the woman is dead (as was the case in three interviews through murder and one interview through illness). One man who had murdered summed up this methodological, indeed epistemological, issue:

> . . . the thing is now, or the worst part about it, is now, you'd only get one version of it sort of thing. You'd only get mine. So whether or not you'd take my word for that is a different matter altogether, so no matter what I say, well it's guarded anyway. You know yourself, when you're looking at things well whatever he says, I can't fully believe the man . . .

Talk can be a defence, psychological and social, against the other, the woman effected by men's violence.

6

The Text of Violence: (1) How Men Describe Their Violence

Men enjoy many possible alternatives for talking about violence, not least because the repercussions of talking in different ways may *not* be so very different for the men concerned. Even so, talking about violence provides the means for disclosing violence, or at least a process of talk and silence constructed as 'self-disclosure'. Paradoxically, for most men, talking of violence – the construction of the text of violence – is a powerful way of *distancing* themselves from their violence. Indeed the man usually presents himself as *at least two* selves – the *violent self* who did the violence; and the *talking self* being interviewed.

The text of violence is that which speaks (of) violence directly. It is not background information. The text of violence has two main elements: the *description* of violence; and the *accounting* for violence. While these two elements may be analytically distinct, they are in practice very closely bound up with each other. First, the way violence is described can also carry with it the indications of accounting for that violence. For example, if a man says 'I just hit her', the insertion of the word 'just' can, depending on the context of the statement, convey minimization of the violence, a lack of responsibility on his part, a justification. Second, some accounts of violence themselves constitute forms of violence, for example, possible 'justifications' might include 'because I didn't like her mixing with those friends'. These are themselves violence when reframed as 'control of the woman's patterns of friendship' and 'control of where the woman goes'.

Rather surprisingly, most studies of men who have been violent to women say little about how men actually describe their violence. This chapter catalogues those descriptions; the next examines how the various forms of accounts of the violence are structured. I should add that I write this chapter with some trepidation and on the assumption that you, the reader, can always put the book down.

The Time and Place of the Violent 'Incident'

Men usually describe their violence as a *specific* incident, or less often a series of incidents, happening at a certain time and place. Violence is rarely seen as a general social relation even when it is extremely extensive. The violence was often presented as 'incidental' to the man's life. The idea of the incident is so widespread and dominant in both lay and professional accounts that one might reasonably speak of its hegemony. The word 'incident' is itself a convenient reduction, fitting neatly into, and perhaps between, several discourses, including those of medicine, law and social work. In medical discourse, violence may be of interest as the antecedent of bodily traces; in legal discourse, as the antecedent of the alleged offence and the decision of the court; in social work discourse, as part of the antecedents of future welfare. In each case, there is a possible circumscription of the violence.

The incident is distant from *its own* context, even though the incident provides a context to subsequent incidents. The foregrounded incident is different from the background; it may be portrayed as *an exception* to the non-violent rule. Violent incidents may be described as occurring throughout a relationship, or they may literally mark its beginning, middle or end, or aftermath. One man described his violence at the end of the relationship in a very matter of fact way: '. . . yes, there was some violence. The day she left I hit her. I think it was a bit late. It was the booze. There was no dispute.' Splitting up can be a particularly dangerous time for women as some men respond to this with increased anger, control and violence. Some men will attempt to maintain control of women after separation by returning to physical violence. One man interviewed used physical violence after he had separated because he knew this would appear out of character and be especially hurtful to her. He also explained how he hit the woman in the street hard enough to hurt her but not to drop their child she was holding.

Men's violence may be described as concentrated at certain times, on certain days of the week or at certain times of the year. Some men reported Friday nights being a particularly likely time for their violence, so much so that reference to this particular evening carried a special fear within their family. As one man put it: 'The kids used to call it nightmare night.' A few men spoke of the additional tensions of Christmas and New Year. Such times may involve men and women spending more time together, extra demands from family and friends, public or semi-public displays and expectations, and the use of large amounts of alcohol.

Some men specifically chronicled an evolving, often escalating, personal history of violence. One such man recalled: 'I think one of the first times would have been a slap or a twisted wrist or something daft.' This was explained in a rather dismissive way as a prelude to what he himself perceived as 'more serious' violence. Thus men's construction of the timing of violence, or rather the location of violence in time, includes references to different kinds of time and *meanings* of time. The perceived timing of violence may also have significance in relation to the man's perception of the development of the relationship with the woman.

Similarly, men's violence may be described in different places. Most obviously, men's violence to women occurs when the particular man and woman are physically, spatially together, even if that involves seeking the other out, as, for example, when the man tracks down the woman after separation. Most of the men's violence to known women is done in houses and homes: hers, his or theirs. However, it is important not to forget violence elsewhere, in the street, outside pubs, clubs and shops. Men described their violence in pubs, clubs and town centres, but not inside shops. As Coveney et al. (1984) note, men do not suddenly 'lose control' and commit sexual violence inside Woolworths. The enactment of perceived 'loss of control' is spatially contingent.

Textual Devices for 'Talking Violence'

There are three main devices that men use in describing their violence. The most common type is the *subject/object relation* – 'I hit her.' The man is the subject, the woman the object; the violence connects them, done by him to her. The second form is the description of violence as a *reciprocal process* – 'We were fighting each other,' 'It was 50–50.' Violence is constructed as operating in both directions: from the man to the woman, and vice versa. The supposed 'reciprocity' may or may not be described as equal. It goes without saying that descriptions of equality in violence have to be treated with very great caution, even suspicion. The third device involves the construction of violence as having *an abstract life of its own* – 'It just happened,' 'It boiled up.' Here the violence is an 'it' that is constructed as having an active agency that then *affects the man*, the doer of the violence, and the woman, the receiver of the violence. A fourth, much less frequent way is describing violence as a *totality* of destruction and dominance from the man to the woman. While this could be understood as a development of the subject/object relation, its comprehensiveness tends to reduce a sense of agency so that it may be presented as if it has a life of its own.

These devices may be intertwined with each other. For example, one man switched easily between the first two kinds:

> I slapped her and I said 'Oh shit', then I was torn to pieces. . . . She freaked out and I was covered in scratches and the next day I hit her once more, ran out of the room and that was it.

He continued:

> *A*: I hit Thelma I would say total of four times, but it wasn't very nice.
> *Q*: When you say hit, I mean what . . .?
> *A*: Well once I slapped her face very hard, and it nearly knocked her head off. She kicked me back. She did karate . . . .

Such intertwining of devices may be particularly prevalent when combinations of violence are described or more than two people are involved (see pp. 102–104). These four devices may also interconnect with different forms of accounting. For example, the construction of violence as a reciprocal process may be a means of minimizing and denying violence. Treating violence as having a life of its own may be a way of excusing violence, and referring to subject/object relations may be compatible with justifications and confessions. However, it would be inaccurate to equate forms of descriptions and forms of accounting too deterministically.

Types of Violence

The concept of 'violence' can be used in diverse ways. Men interviewed defined violence in their own ways. While this generally meant physical violence, verbal, emotional and other violences were also described. The violences described here vary from the ordinary to the extraordinary. Such definitions may well contrast with definitions from women who have experienced violence. There is a need for a multi-faceted and contextualized approach to what is meant by violence. Definitions, where used or referred to at all, are contingent, not absolute, and may indeed be inconsistent and fleeting.

The remainder of this chapter details the main types of violence as described by men. This classification is derived from men's accounts and should not be taken as indicative of the impact or effects of those violences.

Non-Physical Violence

Violence in the Head   Very few men referred to violent thoughts, to violence in their heads. The men generally took violence to mean violent behaviour. Men were generally much more able or willing to talk about *violent behaviour* than *violent thoughts*. Interestingly, those who spoke most of violent thoughts were of two contrasting types: men who had not had agency context in relation to violence to women; and men in prison. The first group did not define their violence by agency definitions of the specific behavioural incident. The second group had had time to 'go through' their violence in their heads time and again. Their violence may have come to the attention of agencies by way of specific behavioural incidents but that agency intervention may have come to dominate their total situation, including their thoughts. One man who had no agency contact but disclosed more than ten violent episodes described his past as follows: 'We [he and his ex-partner] weren't equal [in his previous marriage], no, I was more violent in my head than anything else.' Another man reported on his violent speculations:

> . . . I remember she were thumping me, lying on the settee, and I were just like laughing and I thought I could just like thump her like and that would be the end

of that. It were like that floated through my mind. One good thump and she's quiet. Not that I wanted to thump her I just thought how ridiculous it was at the time.

The retraction is hardly reassuring. Two of the lifers spoke of their violent thoughts: one described his feeling that he wanted to 'kick her head in', another said: 'I used to feel myself wanting to give her a slap, shake her up or whatever' and 'knew I was going to kill . . . if I'd stayed [in the relationship]'.

Verbal, Emotional, Mental and Psychological Violence Verbal and emotional violence were also explicitly reported mainly by men not in contact with agencies, and men in prison. Typical examples are: 'I used to shout at her and argue on numerous occasions,' 'I've just blown up and said all sorts,' 'I was calling her all the names.' However, even in these three examples there are questions raised. The use of the word 'argue' can imply a reciprocal process of arguing, back and forth. To say 'I've just blown up' might suggest minimizing and a lack of intention on the part of the man. Even saying 'calling her all the names' is euphemistic. Typical examples of supposed reciprocal processes are references to 'a real blazing row', 'real bad slanging matches', 'another big argument'. Indeed the movement from the verb 'shout' to the verb 'argue' to the *noun* 'argument' is a progressive distancing of the man through a move to reciprocity or the abstraction of violence.

An even more ambiguous instance is: 'The violence with my current wife it isn't often, it's mainly words.' The reference to the 'words' obscures; it remains unclear whether words are part of or distinct from the (other, physical?) violence. Men who saw their violence as normal might include verbal violence within that but in a dismissive way: 'just normal, I were shouting and bawling . . .'.

One of the most powerful and violating forms of violence does not include direct physical violence at the time, although it may follow and rest on physical violence, and indeed may have direct physical effects. This is men's control of women's definition of their situation and reality. This may include the woman's definition of how she dresses, appears, defines herself, sees herself, monitors her behaviour or potential behaviour, stops doing things that might bring an adverse reaction from the man and all manner of apparently 'trivial' ways to change his preferences to her actions and then to her preferences: 'It weren't so much the physical side of it, it were more the constant mental sort of putting her down, sort of thing, you know what I mean.' Such psychological violence is particularly profound in heterosexual relationships, in which gendered power differentials are constantly reinforced by societal gendered power relations between women and men (cf. Mann, 1993). It is rarely recognized explicitly by men.

One man charted his ability to use verbal abuse, his greater age, his demeaning, and in particular his total domination of his partner through determining when she could and could not visit him in prison as a means of his further demeaning of her:

A: [I said] 'Don't push me.' Cos I used to call her a silly girl. 'You're just a young girl and there's four years between us, just remember that all the time. What you're going through now, I've gone through four years ago.'

Q: You like used your seniority over her?

A: Yes, I did it all the time. I used it all the time. I used to tell her that she looked like shit. I used to tell her, 'You're not attractive and nobody will fancy you' and I could get better than her, and what did I need her for.

. . . It was so that she wouldn't think she was interesting to anybody else, so I had like a hold. It's a crazy little thing. It feels a bit embarrassing actually even though I don't know you, but it's got to be said. I've just wrote her a letter saying that it'll be alright for you to bring t'youngster up to see me [in prison], which I'd not previously wanted because she actually wrote to me about a couple of months ago saying I'll bring Kenny [their child]. And I said 'No.' I'd rather see you outside [prison] you see I don't want to be behind a table where she can say what she wants and I'm restricted, because there's officers watching me you see. And I can't say what I want, not because I'm wanting to be violent, and then she leaves, but I've said 'Yes' now and she's actually wrote me a letter saying think about it because a lot of people are going to see me. As if to say I've been on a visit and she's going to walk in all tired and haggard with big spots on her face, and people are going to look at me because my girlfriend's whatever. I suppose that's because of what I've put in her mind. I've made her think that way. I've dominated her all the time.

Anger   The idea of 'anger' and 'anger management' has attracted considerable attention in recent years in cognitive-behavioural intervention on men's violence. However, the concept of anger was invoked only occasionally by the men in this study. The word 'anger' can distance the man and give his violence some independent life of its own. Its use in accounting can be a form of interpersonal and linguistic violence, and be a prelude to other violences. Anger, or temper, can also be euphemisms for direct physical violence:

I used to vent my anger onto Freda.

And it wasn't just a screaming match, it was complete madness. When I say madness, I nearly lost my voice, you know with screaming in sheer anger and sheer frustration.

Another man related his anger to physically not facing the woman:

I didn't actually face her, I had my back to her. I wasn't shouting, but it was definitely stern tones. It was like making my anger felt there was no doubt about that. . . . I've got into that type of frame of mind, where I've got angry, I've had my back to my wife, and that's quite a significant part of it, actually turning my back, not wanting to confront the other person with it, turning away from the other person.

This turning away from the woman is a physical way of not attending to her (experience). It is also ambiguous in both ignoring her, not communicating with her, doing violence to her, and not facing her in such a way that he might use physical violence on her.

Non-Physical and Physical Violence

While both lay and professional discourses usually distinguish physical and non-physical violence, there was a range of descriptions that transcended any clear separation.

Threats   A few men described the specific threats that may or may not precede physical violence. For example, one man said how he had 'chased her [the woman] with a big whisky bottle we had'. He also threatened her that if she turned the electricity for the television off he was going to hit her: she did, he did.

A more unusual example was the description of written threats:

> Because I wrote to her saying, 'You've got so much doubt, do you doubt you're gonna live till you're 34?' And she's obviously took it that I'm going to . . . kill her before she gets to 34.

Another man who had never been prosecuted for violence to women but had a variety of other convictions explained: 'I might say I'll do it [violence], but that's probably just to put the frighteners on.' He went on to say that he had said to his wife that if he found out that his suspicions of her relationship with another man were true then 'there's going to be some violence'. He added that 'I'm sort of saying that in such a way where it's directed at both of them sort of thing. . . . she knows me, if I say something, I usually go and do it.'

Threatening Violence from Another Woman   An unusual form of threat was planned by one particular man on the woman via another woman:

> . . . I was going to get this girl [woman friend of man] to beat her [the woman] up, you know, because of some of the little things she'd said to somebody. Not about me. About somebody else. And I said to her [the woman], 'I hope you can fight.'

Goading   Three men mentioned goading.[1] The general pattern comprised several steps or stages: initial verbal provocation; spiral of verbal abuse; the threat of physical violence or physical restraint or other physical violence this in turn constitutes further 'goading'.

A: . . . we sort of came together and run into sort of various clashes of how we expected the house to be run. Sort of resentment perhaps that I spent more time playing rugby or something like that than she would have liked. And there again I suppose a spiral of picking on each other for one thing and another, it would gradually get more heated, in terms of the discussion and gradually raise the stakes as it were.

Q: What sort of things?

A: I suppose for me it was very much goading and once I knew Lucy was upset, not letting it drop and just sort of pushing a little bit farther and a little bit farther until she lost her temper. And I suppose the opposite way round would be that Marlene would insist on doing something despite that she knew I didn't want it done or whatever, and she'd carry on, getting to the point where I would say, 'You are not going to do that,' and physically stop her, sort of restrain her.

Q: When you say physically restrain her, what do you actually mean by that?

A: Holding basically, or sort of sitting by the door and saying you're not going out there and doing that or whatever! Which again is part of the goading sort of treatment.

Interestingly, this description also carries an explanation of the development of (physical) violence. Like harassment,[2] goading crosses the boundary of description and explanation, and the distinction between physical and non-physical violence.

The Use of Things: Violence to Things Some men described how they used things to do violence to women. Things may be used without having direct contact with the woman, that is, physical damage may be done to things. The damage may become part of the material form of the house in which the people live:

A: I know there are times when I've been wound up and I've hit the wall or summat [something], or kicked the door. I've damaged the door sometimes. So I channel my anger and aggression by hitting furniture and things.

Q: So has that been intimidating for her?

A: I think it was intimidating for anyone who was around, yes. It also embarrassed me afterwards when I've realised I've damaged the door and I'm thinking, 'What have I done now?', you know, I've got to fix that.

Others described not just the damage to fixed objects like walls and doors but damage to moveable objects: 'I ripped some of her dresses up and then she went quiet and I'm ranting and raving . . .'; 'I'd throw some ornaments or I'd smash summat up . . .'; 'Like I blew up many a time, when I smashed the house up, thrown ornaments.' Sometimes this damage was followed by an aftermath that solidified the violence upon the house: '. . . I threw a plastic jar of body cream at her. And it went down the wall. That was a week and a half on the wall.'

Breaking or throwing of objects was sometimes contrasted with direct hitting:

She came in, carrying on with me, but I wouldn't hit her, I'd break stuff. . . . I'd pick a load of pots up, just through madness.

I remember one time I'd smashed a litre bottle of rum to show her how angry I was, as opposed to being violent towards her. . . . I thought, 'a litre bottle of rum'. We had a phrase [i.e. phase] when there was a lot of little arguments like that.

Control of the Woman and her Movement   Verbal, emotional and psychological violence all contribute to the control of the woman and her movements. Such control is thus an indirect form of *physical* violence. A simple example is: 'I'd sent her out of the nightclub and sent her home.' 'Sending someone home', especially when backed by threat of violence, is an indirect form of physical violence; it produces a physical violation of the woman's body, in this case, where she is, how she moves, where she goes. Similarly, after attacking his ex-wife in the street, a man commented:

As far as I know she was like, for a while she was quite worried about going into the centre [of the town] on her own in case she bumped into me again.

Interestingly, he said this even though there was a six-month injunction prohibiting him from going to the town centre, meaning that he 'was supposed to avoid seeing her'. A still more dramatic example of the control of movement which is clear physical violation is the following:

We'd starting arguing, we lived in some high rise flats then. I'd locked her out on the eighth floor, I'd locked her out all night.

Progression from Control to Physical Violence   While men tend to describe violence as particular incidents, it is important to recognize that there are often forms of 'progression' in men's accounts. This is illustrated in the following statement of developing violence from the control of the woman's movement to direct physical violence:

. . . there's been times when I've been a bit cruel and I've said, 'Listen, you're not going anywhere, stand in the corner.' I've made her stand in a corner for perhaps a few minutes or perhaps even half an hour at times, I don't know exactly. At other times I've made her go upstairs. I've said, 'Go upstairs, I don't want to talk to you Barbara.' And there's times when I've gone up myself, she's asked me to come upstairs and provoked me, with things like, 'You don't want to talk it out. How do you expect to sort it out if you don't talk it out Terry?' And I'm getting mad, so I can't talk it out. I know for a fact that I'll just end up hitting her or something. So I'll just stay in bedroom and she comes and gets me more [angry]. And eventually it's either giving a slap to her or pulling her hair. I have hit with a stick before. I've cut her head with a stick before, when I was ready to go to a nightclub, and she was screaming.

In this example the control of the woman's movement is clearly and intimately bound up with both the threat and enactment of physical violence. The 'progression' can be understood as a description of violence transcending the physical/non-physical distinction.

Letting the Woman Go: Not Being Violent as Violence   A rather different example of the intersection of physical and non-physical violence was in the demonstration of the *capability* to be physically violent but the decision not to be. One man reported:

> I mean sometimes I know I've got to the point and I've got hold [of the woman ready to be violent] and I've thought 'No' and let her go.

In this statement, the 'No' refers to his *decision* not to be violent *on this occasion*. It paradoxically asserts his ability, even right, to be violent in the future, and to *choose* to be violent or not. For him, the 'letting her go' is constructed as a way out of the 'holding', and thus his (potential) violence. For the woman, the meaning may be different. 'Letting her go' can be a form of violence, the power to release the woman from being held.

Children and Violence   Almost all the men interviewed did not appear to see violence to women as child abuse, or vice versa. Children witnessing men's violence to women (often their mother) is both child abuse and violence to women. Two unusual examples of reference to children witnessing violence are as follows:

> No. It wasn't as though he sat on his bouncy chair or something like that, when I used to jump up and go wild. It used to be perhaps late at night or if he wasn't there. There's been times when obviously I've pulled her hair or slapped her or something while he has been there. Because there's been a number of times when I can actually remember when he's had a little cry over it. He's been too confused. He's probably hugged me, or hugged his mother. Like if I hit her, he'd probably hug me because he didn't understand.

> So I grabbed the baby off her, threw her [the woman] on the floor [street]. I sort of flung her on the floor and I walked off with the baby. Not intending stealing the baby, just walked off, and she's screaming, 'He's got my baby, he's got my baby.'

These were both mentioned very much in passing, rather than as what was considered by the men to constitute violence to women.

Violence to the Woman's Pet   Physical violence to the woman can also be enacted by direct violence to the living possessions of the woman or that which is valued highly by the woman. One man described his decision to be violent to the woman's pet:

I was going to stab her with the knife. I'd just had enough then. I thought, 'No, she's so fond of the dog.' I just done the dog . . . I killed the dog. I stabbed the dog, cut his throat, broke its neck.

Physical violence to the pet is a form of violence to the woman.

Physical Violence

Physical Intimidation: Pinning, Holding, Pushing, Shoving, Prodding, Throwing There are many ways men can be physically intimidating and which use physical, sometimes momentary, contact:

Just pushing and shoving.

Holding, or sort of sitting by the door and saying you're not going out.

I think it were a bit of pushing and prodding and verbal abuse.

I pinned her against a wall, like I said, you know, 'You'll do as you're told, because you're being so stupid', it were half eleven on a Saturday night and nowhere else for her to go anyway. After that I pushed her towards home and went home. That were it really. . . . I didn't like pin her against and hold her against, I just stood in front of her. It must have been quite intimidating for her. After I just pulled her the way, pushed her the direction we should be walking to go home.

These may also be interpreted as pre-emptive warnings to the woman that further violence is available. Throwing the woman was also described:

So she starts tanking off . . . starts carrying on, so she starts [telling the man off]. So I just picked her up and threw her against wall.

So I said, 'That's it', and I've got her, and threw her into the passage. I said 'Get your shoes and your coat, you're off out.' And I threw her out, thinking she'd go somewhere, cool off a bit and come back.

I propelled her out the house mainly to prevent any more [argument/violence].

Violence to the Supporters of the Woman Another form of violence to the woman can be physical violence to her friends and supporters. These might be people, usually men, who have had or are having an intimate relationship with her, or they might be supporters of a less intimate kind. Either way, such violence is intimidating and damaging to the woman:

Well I come in one night and he [his mother's boyfriend] were there, my mam were there, and . . . started having a go at me. And he come in, and starting shouting his mouth off, and we ended up us two sort of having a bit of a scuffle. So I went for him, and hit him. That's about it.

We [the man and his male friend] barged into his house . . . not terrorizing him [the male friend of the man's partner] just sort of like picking little things up and saying 'Is this valuable?' and actually it might have been a bit callous at the time because some of it were obviously his late wife's stuff, but it didn't matter it was his late wife's, 'cos he was not giving them booze and cigarettes for nothing, and my girlfriend had actually told me that he'd said to one of the girls something rude like.

A neighbour tried to intervene . . . saying, 'You can't leave her out there [outside the house]' and I chased him off with a hammer.

One man with a long history of violence to women reported two major additional attacks on men who were the woman's supporters:

. . . she had her brother come round to have a go at me . . . I weighed them in. I used a hammer on him.

. . . she . . . kicked off [left him] in real good style. This geezer came round and that was it. I done him in. Got three years for that one. . . . This guy come round . . . interfering, so I weighed him in. Cut throat, cut his ear off, five skull fractures, stabbed him . . . grievous bodily harm.

What is lacking from these accounts are descriptions of the man being interviewed coming off worse from attacks from other men. This silence conveys the man's sense of being a man.

Grabbing and Tugging Hair   One particular interviewee had a special preference to grab the woman's hair and other parts of her body, as well as hitting with force:

You know at first it would end up like tugging her hair to show her if she doesn't pack it up I will be violent towards her.

This suggests that he distinguished 'tugging her hair' and 'violence', and does not see tugging the woman's hair as violence. He continued:

So I grabbed her by the back of the hair to show that if she didn't shut up [from screaming] I'd shut her up, and it must have been hurting, because she's screaming her head off.

It appears here that the grabbing of her hair is used to threaten her to stop screaming, yet the man recognized this grabbing contributed to her screaming. On a third occasion, he described:

I bent her over the railings, and I think at one point I grabbed her by the hair and banged her head into the shop window . . . .

Strangling and Throttling   For some men, distinctions were made around the use of violence on the woman's neck – 'strangling' or 'throttling':

> I literally hit the girl and was strangling her. . . . I wanted to strangle her and I literally were strangling her but not self-consciously realizing it.

Another man distanced himself from this, rather hesitantly, by the phrase 'not like throttling':

> I grabbed her by the back of the, her head, or her neck, I could actually put my fingers round a little bit and it would bruise. Do you know what I mean? And it's not like throttling, as in some Dracula, like his victim, more of a restraining, holding her, but it would bruise her neck.

Hitting   The basic generic term men tend to use for the placing of one part of his body – usually hand, arm, foot, head – with force onto the woman's body is 'hitting': 'Physically I hit her three times in my life, that's all.' Hitting is the term that is used to describe most, though not all, direct physical violence. It incorporates slapping, clipping, backhanding, clouting, lashing, punching, beating up, and so on.

Slapping, Clipping, Backhanding   There is a wide variety of different kinds of assaults. Some men distinguished 'slapping', 'clipping' and 'backhanding' from what they saw as more serious assaults, such as 'beating up'. Slapping usually means the use of the palm of the hand in one individual action rather than the back of the hand or the clenched fist or some other combination of actions:

> So I hit her. It was only a slap.

> . . . it just blew up . . . and I just hit her . . . a slap.

> . . . so eventually what I did, I slapped her in the face, and she fell on the settee.

Clipping is similar, though it can suggest use of greater force, sometimes with the back of the hand:

> *A*: It was coming out of a nightclub . . . and my mate was with a girlfriend and he pushed her. Two girls was involved in the situation again. Now luckily I gave the girl a clip. It wasn't nowt [nothing = anything] else, just a clip. Anyway . . .
> *Q*: What do you mean by gave her a clip?
> *A*: Backhanded her. Anyway, she went flying and cut her lip or something like that.

> And I've tried to assault her then clipped her a few times . . . .

Backhanding uses the back of the hand:

> I'd cracked her . . . just backhanded her a couple of times, but nothing serious or anything like that.

The ideas of slapping, clipping and backhanding seem to rest on their instant, unpremeditated and 'minimal' use of force *as perceived by the man*, and their assessment by the man as 'less serious' than other violences.

Kicking, Clouting, Thumping, Lacing, Lashing, Punching, Headbutting   The next 'more serious' kind of assault distinguished by men includes clouting, thumping, lashing and punching. Clouting can mean 'slapping hard' or it can be a more generic term for various kinds of hitting. A key issue is that, even with clouting, lashing and punching, the blows are individual actions:

> I thumped her hard enough to hurt her . . . .

> *A*: And I turned to face her and I think I got hold of her at one side and hit her sort of against the face sort of that way.
> *Q*: Hit her with a fist against the face?
> *A*: Yes, with a fist, yes.
> *A*: I just kicked her and I don't usually kick her.
> *Q*: When you say kicked her . . .
> *A*: I kicked her in the legs and she went down on the floor and I just banged her like that.
> *Q*: You say you punched her?
> *A*: Yes.
> *Q*: Whereabouts did you punch her?
> *A*: On the side of her head there. Because she got up and starting hacking [kicking] me.

> When she was pregnant, I think I'd punched her a few times, I was really worried at the time, because blood started coming out of her ears. . . . A couple of times, on the side of her head.

> . . . she'd nag and nag and nag until I just explode . . . headbutt her or something.

The notions of 'lashing' and 'lacing' were more ambiguous – sometimes referring to individual acts of force, sometimes to 'letting go' with a combination of violences.

> *A*: I gave her a good clout a fortnight ago I think. She's just aggravating me all time, and she can't take it in, when she gets in a state like this.
> *Q*: So can you tell me what happened?
> *A*: I let go at her!
> *Q*: You hit her?

A: Yes.
Q: With?
A: Fists. Oh yes, I lashed into her.

A: . . . and I started lacing into her and then I realised what were happening
Q: When you say you realised what was happening, what was happening?
A: Well I were hitting her in face and sort of like looked at her, and I thought, shit, and I just got up and said I'm off out. Next thing I knew I were arrested.

A Good Punching, Cracking Her a Few Times, Knocking Her about a Bit   In men's accounts, a 'progression' can be recognized from individual acts of clouting, punching, and so on, to a clear sequence of attacks. These are described as 'a *good* punching' rather than 'punching'; 'cracking her *a few times*' rather than 'cracking'; 'knocked her about *a bit*' (i.e. a lot) rather than 'knocked her about':

> That got me grievous bodily harm. There was no broken bones or anything like that, I just give her a good punching sort of more or less. . . . I hit her more than once like, but I went a bit too far this time. I hurt her bad.

This quote is very unusual in that it actually refers, however briefly, to the effect of the violence in that he 'hurt her bad'.

A: Yes, I cracked her a few times. I hit her a few times, backhanded her, punched her, hit her in the head. Not mostly to face but to body, you know, it was like fuck her. She couldn't do nowt about it sort of thing.
Q: Sorry, she . . .?
A: No this is how I were thinking when I hit her. Like to toss her like. Like I can hit her where she couldn't do nowt about it like she were hit, she stood for it.

This illustrates the way that a man can become aware of his ability to be violent and the woman's to stand for it. It is also an account that is close to a perceived 'beating up'.

Beating Up, Battering, Hitting Anywhere, Going Berserk   'Beating up' and 'battering' describe the *combination* of several direct violences. They also convey an additional intensity, seriousness or ferocity, often with a clear intentionality:

> I hit her anywhere.

> . . . got fed up and battered her.

> I used to beat her up. Punch her. Punch her silly so she couldn't stand up. Kick her all the base of her spine . . . she couldn't go out for a few weeks one time. She couldn't walk . . . she went down and I just started kicking her in the spine . . . all bruised on her back, just punched inside her thighs.

In some cases, the notion of 'going berserk' is introduced:

One day I just went berserk and broke her nose and her teeth. . . . Punched her in the nose. Broke it. Hit her again. Lost all her teeth at the front.

Went berserk. Then I started beating up. I had her on the floor [street] and was going to kick her in and she had her hand up so I broke her arm with kicking her arm. I was aiming for her head and she got her arm up to defend her head.

Being Out of Control? Beating Up Bad, Battering Her Silly, Wading Into, Laying Into, Knocking from one End of the House to the Other, Going Out of My Head, Nearly Killing, Attempted Murder   In some accounts, the line between what is described as controlled, deliberate violence and what is described as being out of control becomes unclear. Such descriptions usually recall violences understood by the man as *more* than 'beating up' and 'battering'. They are sometimes described as still further force or greater combinations of violent acts, in terms of effects, damage, and perhaps 'losing control'. The result can be nearly killing the woman:

And I beat her up pretty bad, facially, bodily . . . .

. . . I was quite worried because I practically left her in a pool of blood. I nearly killed her.

I didn't just hit that girl, I laid into her like a man shouldn't be allowed to. I deserved to be sent to prison for it. It would be attempted murder basically on both accounts I would say. But I was pushed at the time, where I felt I were pushed on to the edge you know.

I were sat watching telly and she came in. She was in a mood or something and she said something to me and I just . . . she said summat criticizing towards me about my home, or as a kid, or what she knew about me, and I just blew up out of the chair, and I just knocked her from one end of house to other sort of thing. And I mean I laid into her tremendously. I mean a grown man punching a girl it was bang out of order. It were just like I couldn't stop, you know, once I started, I was out of control. And I waded into her pretty heavy. Her nose, her face, her ribs. I mean I thought I'd killed her Christ's sake. And then I just stopped dead. You know, like it seemed 10 minutes, 20 minutes, but it wasn't, it were so quick. And I was upset, crying. I actually broke up, I was a mess. Laid her on the sofa, stopped the bleeding from her nose and her lip and stuff, and her eye. But I mean the facial damage what I did to her, alright the swelling went down . . . .

Even though I felt I was in control and I had reasonable intelligence to understand what was going on, I was losing it myself, like not interested or not bothered because the other person wasn't bothered as well. Like they was encouraging . . . like I felt they were encouraging it in some daft way. That's how it seemed to me and yet there really wasn't obviously . . . nobody was encouraging to get their head beaten in as I hit Theresa in the head. I mean I just dived out of that chair and I laid into her, and I just thought, stuff it, and I just battered her silly, and I mean silly. And I wouldn't stop, I had her face to the floor and I were punching her and punching her, then stop dead, thank God. By then she was a mess and whatever and I felt . . . I was shaking, I was frightened, I was sweating and I lifted her on sofa and I put her there like a little rag doll. If I'm truthful with you, there was a certain kind of buzz from it, like . . . you know, for them few minutes or whatever. I can't explain it, it is hard to explain, there was a kind of thrill to it.

Use of Household Objects as Weapons A variety of violences may be accomplished with the use of household objects as weapons. Parts of the house/ home, of the living environment of the woman and/or man, may be used upon the woman. The home/house becomes a resource for enacting violence: objects that have domestic, functional, aesthetic and sentimental value may be redefined as violators of the woman's body. They are de-valued in one set of meanings and re-valued in another set:

> . . . I don't know if I actually caused it but, I think I hit her with a brush. . . . I don't think it broke a bone in her leg but she actually had some pain in her leg, and months later, when she went to the doctors, and they said you've fractured your ankle or something. . . . But I don't think it was from me. It's always in my mind this. I'd been watching TV and we got into this silly argument like it's my house, it were her house you see, her flat, but all the stuff was mine you see. She said, 'It's my flat' so I said, 'Well get off my bed, get off my furniture, get off my carpet,' you know, childish sorts of things. So she said, 'Well it's my electric and you're watching the TV, so I'm going to switch the electric off.' So she went to the passage and I said, leave the electric alone and I turned it back on again. And straightaway as soon as I turned it back on again, she turned it off again. So I turned it on again and I said, 'If you turn it back off again' I said, 'I'm going to hit you.' And she turned it off again, so I just picked the brush up, and whacked her on the leg. I don't know if I did break her leg, or fractured her leg, but it was fixed back wrong.

> . . . the brush had got a bit of a nail in it, and the nail hit her on the eyebrow, and cut her eyebrow.

> I went daft and got one of those bamboo canes that you have with a plant. I just whipped her with that really bad and cut her up with it. All the back of her buttocks.

Stabbing and Murder Four of the men interviewed were on life sentences for murder. Two had stabbed the woman they were in a long-term relationship with, and one had murdered and allegedly raped a friend of his wife. The fourth had murdered his ex-wife's partner and attempted to murder her. One man also described a previous stabbing of a woman for which he had been convicted, imprisoned and released, before a second stabbing which had killed a second woman:

. . . one day I just flipped and stabbed her. I never killed her or anything, but I stabbed her. . . . she said, 'You're never, ever going to see the children again.' And when she said that, I just snapped and that was it, I stabbed her with a penknife . . . it was just one of those things, my mind just exploded.

He continued regarding the subsequent murder:

A: . . . we'd had an argument one night. I had belted her one. Nothing serious, but then a few weeks later, I killed her, it was as simple as that . . . she started arguing in the garden. Anyway, we'd gone into the house, she's arguing in the house, and I grabbed her. And all I grabbed her for was just to shut her up, but I grabbed her by the throat. . . . I'd gone upstairs to the bathroom. I come out of the bathroom, she's on the landing, still going. . . . She started screaming and shouting. I grabbed her again to shut her up. I pushed her away . . . I got changed and as I'm coming out [of the bathroom] she's back upstairs waving a carving knife like that at me . . . a 12 inch blade on it. Prodding me with the knife and that. She cut me twice on the hand. Next thing she's laid at my feet, dead, I've stabbed her in the throat.
Q: You grabbed hold of her?
A: Yes, we had a bit of a struggle and that and I've stabbed her in the throat with a knife.

Other descriptions of murder included:

. . . we were just arguing for about three hours. And I ended up stabbing her. The thing is where I stabbed her like, you know, I stabbed her in the shoulder, I got into the cavity and that. Really she bled to death. I didn't even realise I'd stabbed her, it just happened in a split second. . . . I just didn't realise I'd stabbed her. . . . I'm jabbing the knife at her, do you know what I mean, and you know just saying, 'I'll stab you, you bastard,' like, you know what I mean. . . .

And like I jumped up and I grabbed her, which I didn't mean to and I just took a blackout, and I just can't explain it . . . when I finally came round she was laying on floor, dead. . . .

Torture   In addition to immediate and direct violence to the woman's body, there was at least one case of deliberate torture though restraint and incarceration:

It just started off with a normal good hiding. Just hitting and then I completely flipped. I tied her up in the bathroom to the cistern. I gagged her and fucked off and didn't come back for three or four days.

When he did, he took the woman to Casualty for dehydration and injuries. He was not prosecuted.

Kidnapping   Another man described how he had abducted the woman, who at the time was in a refuge:

. . . she'd . . . told my mum that she'd meet me in town at a set time. So when I went into town, it was like she was there with the young 'un, you see as soon as I'd seen her I was in a mood with her, and I actually kidnapped her, you know, I said, 'You're coming with me.' I took her back to my mum's.

Another man gave a vague account of an abduction which had included assaults on the woman, partly through the use of an animal trap to restrain her.

Sexual Assaults Sexual violence or, more accurately, 'sexual sexual violence' (see pp. 148–150), did not appear to be considered to be 'violence' by almost all of the men in this study. The main exceptions to this were the small number of instances of prosecution and convictions for crimes of sexual violence, sexual assault and rape. Sexual violence that did not lead to prosecution did not figure; neither did other sexual violences, such as coercive sex, pressurized sex, sexual harassment and pornography.

> *Q*: And the other incident was indecent assault?
> *A*: Yes.
> *Q*: Can you tell me what happened there?
> *A*: I'm supposed to have, what is it, touched her breasts and said to her, I want to take you to bed.
> *Q*: Touched her?
> *A*: Her breasts. And I turned round to her and said, 'I want to take you to bed.' I don't even remember nowt like that.

> I can remember ripping her clothes off, but not the raping bit. . . . I can't remember.

Multiplicity of Acts and People A number of combinations of violent acts have been described, particularly 'beating up', 'battering' and 'going berserk'. Needless to say, it is possible for all forms of violence to be combined together in multiple violences, either to the same woman or to a number of women. To some extent the construction of *multiplicity* of acts depends upon how violences are understood within particular time frames. While the hegemony of the incident (see pp. 84–86) tends to segment multiple violences, multiplicity of violences is recognized in some men's accounts, particularly those with a long history of violence. More will be said of the hybrid accounts in the next chapter (see pp. 142–144).

Multiplicity exists in those accounts that involve more than one woman and/or man:

> *A*: Maisie was a friend of my mate who'd . . . had a child to her, . . . and it were just in from the pub where I'd met Maisie. Funnily enough I actually fancied the girl and I think she knew it as well, and I wasn't going out of my way to try to get off with her, and it was just that she was just a bloody argumentative person anyway. . . . It were just really through Tony, when we got in

the car she started spouting off, mouthing off, . . . and she started pushing me
to edge, like winding me up, you know, making me actually encouraging it.
Like encouraging me like she wanted a fight, if you know what I'm saying.
And when I did she's laugh . . . at me, you know like . . . is that the best you
can do sort of thing. And then when Johnny [Tony's relative] was encouraging
the situation or down this ginnel [alley], this is where it all came out, she was
going overboard and she was saying, 'I'm going to get you, I'm going to get
you' . . . and I just went completely off my trolley sort of thing. And got up
and battered her, you know strangling her with belt and I didn't give a toss
you know what I mean? I thought I'll teach you bitch, you know like . . . and
I literally were pounding her, not punching her as such, but holding her over
and I had a belt there and I throttled her and she went kind of unconscious
and this girl, her mate, were trying to keep me off. I can't remember as such,
but I remember picking her up and just lobbing her [the woman's friend] over
wall, just said, 'Fuck off.' And I felt quite chuffed about it, I wasn't feeling no
emotion at the time, but maybe an hour, two hours later, I thought fucking
hell, realised. You know what I mean? I realised then when it was completely
over, but I wasn't bothered if you know what I mean. It was like I actually
thought, good God, if they knew this, I'd get locked up for life like, they'd
throw key away on me. But I wasn't prepared to tell anybody about the
situation what happened, so it just blew over sort of thing, thank God. I
mean, I was in a sense if she would have died, I wouldn't have give myself up
to police or nothing like that, because I felt that I were justified. You know
she provoked me enough, though she didn't if you know what I mean. She
wasn't assaulting me or trying to take my life away, but I would have
probably tried to look for justification for what happened in the situation.
Though I feel that I wasn't cold blooded, cold-blooded murder, to murder
somebody, it wasn't like that. I don't know, I know maybe this sounds crazy
but it was like a cry for help, or despair or total grief or sadness. I know them
feelings came in, why I'm saying it, because them feelings came into me, you
know the despair and sadness and the emotion I felt totally isolated, alone.
And I felt totally broken up, literally was broken up inside, and then I just
snapped out of it.

Q: . . . I mean, that time [when you attacked] Maisie you said she had a mate
there. What did the mate do while you were . . .?

A: Oh, as I were doing that she did hit me, with a stiletto shoe she had on. Tried
to push me off, and I just threw her. She fell against the wall so she couldn't
get near me but she were trying to hit me with a bag or something. Johnny
were saying nothing. . . . He were just standing there encouraging me more
than owt [anything]. I realise that now. He were there saying, like, 'Go on, go
on,' you know, like encouraging me. And it excited me as he were encouraging me. He said, 'Go on, do it, do it, do her in,' you know like that. Not
sort of saying kill her, not saying them words, but he was saying like you, do
it. And that in a sense made me even go worser. . . . I can't remember totally
off-hand now, but it were like right to the edge, but I stopped, summat
stopped me. Thank God it did, you know.

This description provides several possible constructions of explanations of
and excuses for the violence by and for the man. Specific descriptions

of violence are usually set within narratives and broader discourses of accounting for violence.

Destruction and Dominance   While the above descriptions of violence clearly involve degrees of destruction and dominance, a few men explicitly articulated a specific notion of destruction of and dominance over the woman in a more total way:

> I didn't stop at a punch or owt like that, I literally just like sort of saw red. I wanted to lay into her, just destroy her. Literally if I could have disintegrated her like I would have done. You know, at that peak. But just on that peak where I just realised what I . . . this is what you know, shaking and frightened and really freaked me out basically afterwards.

> But at the time it was like, it was like summat triggered off inside me and I just . . . it was just like, I wanted to destroy, literally destroy.

> But it were like I had a kind of dominance.

> Because them angers when they come up in my throat, my chest, it's still there in the sense where I want to actually . . . actually if I'm really pushed like I want to rip it out. It's not just a rip or till you're sweating, I just want to destroy it, you know completely destroy the object in front of me. It isn't like seeing blood, I actually wanted it, I wanted to wipe it out completely.

Concluding Remarks

In this chapter, I have focused on the specific ways in which men describe their violences to known women. Most of these descriptions are located within the framework of the incident rather than that of a more general social relation. The incident is usually described through a subject/object relation, sometimes through a reciprocal process of violence or the violence having a life of itself, and occasionally as a totality of destruction and dominance. Whilst there is a strong tendency to isolate violence in the incident, complications may be introduced in combinations of violence, as, for example, in 'beating up', and the involvement of more than one man and/or woman. Furthermore, isolated descriptions of violences are themselves usually set within narratives and discourses of accounting for violence. Sometimes these are constructed so that violence itself is presented as a relatively insignificant part of the story; on other occasions, the man develops a more explicit account of his violence. In these alternative discourses men articulate 'men', 'women' and 'men and women'. Throughout, there is a continuing relationship between the incident, narrative and bodily, material discourse.

7

The Text of Violence: (2) How Men Account for Their Violence

When men account for violence, they are often both giving an explanation and constructing a rationale for that violence. Sometimes explicitly, often inadvertently, these interviews, like other talk about violence, provided the opportunity for men to justify and/or excuse their violence to women. The means of doing this are varied and at times extremely convoluted; they often draw on several different modes of accounting, within one interview, or even one statement or sentence.

All of the men interviewed were able to give some kind of account of their violence, an account that was of varying credibility. In giving an account of his violence the man may (a) recognize and name his violence; (b) refer to his intention to do harm; (c) refer to his production of harm; (d) accept blame and/or responsibility for his violence; (e) explain or attempt to explain those elements. In most accounts only some of these elements are present; if none are present, there is no account.

However, to isolate such explanations from the whole of the interview might be misleading. Whatever the man says prior to 'the saying of' his violence or whatever he says preceded the doing of his violence is also part of an explanation. All matters, however 'trivial', are relevant:

Just silly things, you know. The arguments would start, being really trivial, they just went on and got more progressive [leading to his violence], you know both sides. We were both as bad as each other.

A key issue is the contrast between presenting violence as ordinary or as extraordinary (see pp. 75–82). In the first case, violence is described as part of the usual fabric of life; in the second, violence is described as an unusual, exceptional and more dramatic part of life. When violence is presented as ordinary, the account may be about 'other things', and violence may hardly warrant or be worthy of explanation; when violence is presented as extra-ordinary, the explanation can be in terms of the extraordinary – how the man felt, what the woman did, or did not do, what others did or did not do, and so on.

When men account for their violence, they usually refer to specific incidents rather than some general social relation of violence. Incidents are, however, usually placed within more extended narratives. Violence is both specifically described and told through its location within stories – 'this is what happened'. These different accounts, including descriptions of incidents within narratives, can be understood as examples of both particular *tactical* orientations to violence and wider *discourses* of men's relations to violence, women and gender more generally.

The Double Self of the Man

I have already discussed how for many men talking is problematic (Chapter 5) and how this may be managed through a man's own construction of himself as atypical (see pp. 81–82). In most of the accounts, 'men' appear (at least) twice over, while women appear little, if at all. Men generally appear, that is, are represented, as two differential selves usually a violent one in the past, whether recent or distant, and a non-violent one in the present, in the interview. There are two subjectivities, two narrative selves[1] (Wetherell and Potter, 1989). There may also be, for some men, who are more self-conscious, reflective or ironic, a third self, that is, that which refers to the other two. In contrast, the woman was usually absent, except as an object of the man's violence. In some accounts there is a reference to how the man and the woman 'get on', or how she has offended him by the way she has brought up the children or related to other adults.

This basic situation is extremely important in understanding the structure of most men's accounts of and for their violence. In the text of violence, men (apart from a deliberately threatening minority) generally locate their *violent self* as *somewhere else*. This is usually in the past, often in relation to particular incidents, and sometimes in relation to particular difficulties, conflicts, 'things they can't control' or even simply their mood swings. To construct a different subjectivity for themselves is for men one way of making sense of their violence. This may be in the *planning of* or *intention to do* violence, the *specific enactment* of violence or very occasionally in remorse or other effects afterwards.

For one man this separation of selves was not just a central part of his account but was also crucial in his explanation, justification and rationale for the violence. He explained that acting violently would be seen by his ex-wife as *out of character*, thus adding an extra shock to the effect:

> I mean other women who I know have been hit, and it's like, they've been hit and that's it, they suffered physical damage and no long-term effects but I feel that because I hit her and *it was out of character* and *in the context where it was*, it's like . . . who is this person who was like *a completely different alien person* to who she lived with years ago? [my emphases]

He also commented on his planning of the attack:

And that's one thing I never got involved with and that's violence. We had arguments but I never got violent to her, aggressive or whatever. And so I felt that if I could hit her, she would be shocked, because it would be me hitting her. . . .

Then again *the shock* became physical and literal in the violence itself, when he said:

And like she sort of staggered back, sort of sat down against a window of the shop, *literally stunned*, and I just walked away. [my emphasis]

Forms of Accounts

Self-disclosive accounts differ in a number of ways: in the *form*, for example, excuses, justifications; and the *content* of these forms and structures, for example, behaviours of the woman, other people, past events, drink. Form and content are not separate. Rather there are common patterns of interconnections between them. For example, drink tends to be used as an excuse (abdication of responsibility), while the behaviour of the woman tends to be used as a justification (abdication of blame?).

Different forms of accounts are not mutually exclusive. On the contrary, different ways of accounting sit quite easily alongside each other within one interview, even when they follow quite different 'logics'. Indeed arguably each kind of account is necessarily incomplete: it has its own narrative and its own suppression of the other, the excluded, usually the woman. Such specific incompleteness can be supplemented by the incompleteness of other accounts. Different kinds of accounts may be found within one particular interview or talk, particularly when this is relatively extended.

Men's accounts of their violence frequently draw on 'vocabularies of motives' (Mills, 1940; Gerth and Mills, 1953; Matza, 1964). These refer to means of explaining away or justifying actions that are illegal or perceived as deviant. The structure of accounts has been explored through the distinction between excuses and justification (Austin, 1961; Scott and Lyman, 1968; Lyman and Scott, 1970). This has been an important theme in work on violence, particularly sexual violence. Taylor's (1972) interviews with sex offenders distinguished the use of justifications during the event and the use of excuses after the event. Scully (1990) also found the distinction between users of excuses and uses of justifications helpful in her analysis of interviews with rapists. Research by Fuller (1995) on child sexual abusers found a more flexible pattern – namely the invoking of justification before, during and after the abuse.

Ptacek (1988) has applied the excuse/justification distinction directly in the accounts of men who have battered women. Drawing primarily on Scott and Lyman (1968), he has used this as a *comprehensive* framework to categorize these accounts. Accordingly, excuses are defined as 'those

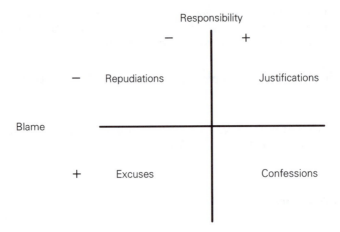

FIGURE 7.1 *Repudiations, excuses, justifications, confessions (after Bull and Shaw, 1992)*

accounts in which the abuser denies full responsibility for his actions', while justifications are 'those accounts in which the batterer may accept some responsibility but denies or trivializes the wrongness of his violence' (Ptacek, 1988: 141). These forms of accounts are rationalized within cultures as 'socially approved vocabularies' (Scott and Lyman, 1968: 46, 52). Drawing on Bandura (1973), Ganley (1989: 215–16) refers to accounts of the *origins* of aggression, the *implications* of aggression, and the *maintaining conditions/ regulators* of aggression. Bandura describes the processes used by individuals to neutralize self-condemnation as follows: justification by higher principles, palliative comparison, displacement of responsibility, diffusion of responsibility, dehumanizing the victim, attributing of blame to the victim, minimization and selective forgetting of the consequences in terms of the presence or absence of blame and responsibility.

While this is a useful framework, it is still too rigid for my present purposes. Instead I prefer to consider forms of account in overlapping clusters; and to see excuses and justifications as much more closely related than suggested above (Figure 7.1).

Five broad clusters of accounts have been identified in this research (Figure 7.2).

1   *Repudiations* include either the whole or parts of the violence being repudiated, denied or in some way absent. Repudiations comprise full denials; removal of the self and of intention; and diversions.
2   *Quasi-repudiations* are similar in that they include an important element of repudiation, but in this case it is coupled with an important element of recognition of certain types of violence. Quasi-repudiations include not knowing; minimization, reduction and relativization; distinction and debate; and naturalization.

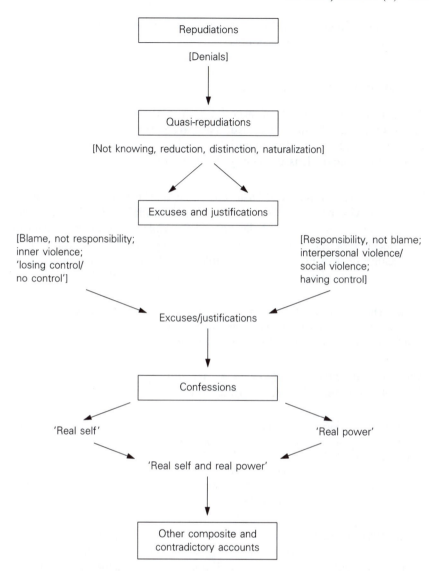

FIGURE 7.2 *Repudiations, quasi-repudiations, excuses and justifications, confessions, and other composite accounts*

3 *Excuses and justifications* involve the recognition of the violence but the denial of either responsibility (excuses) or blame (justifications). Whilst in some senses excuses and justifications are conceptual opposites, they are in practice sometimes closely interlinked.
4 *Confessions* in their complete state include the recognition of violence and the acceptance of both blame and responsibility. In practice, this may be rare.

5 *Composite and contradictory accounts* comprise combinations of the previous four forms of accounts.

Repudiations: Varieties of Denial

Repudiations are a form of account that make violence absent. Both responsibility and blame are denied. They are part of a discourse of denial and detachment. Within this material discourse, violence becomes invisible, as does the woman. It is the bodily discourse of the male(stream).

Full Denials A first and most basic way to account for violence, and indeed to continue violence, is to deny it. This may be denial of the violence itself; of particular types, aspects or elements of the violence; or of the impact or consequences of the violence; and so on. Only one man in the sample specifically denied his violence completely. He had been convicted of murder of the woman and murder of a man. Accordingly, he said:

> I was charged on murder, an attempt, which they say I could have done it, but coulds and ifs are no good, unless they are positive, and I have been pleading my innocence since they brought me [to the prison].

Another man gave the following rather unreassuring, even threatening claim of his non-involvement in violence to women:

> Like it sounds sort of corny, but I've never taken my hand to my wife, and I don't think I ever could. Its not the sort of thing . . . I mean I'm 6 foot 2, and my wife is sort of 5 foot 3, 7 stone wet through, so I mean I've nothing to prove by hitting her. You know I could knock her from next week. . . . We're both pretty short tempered, but that's about as far as we goes, shouting at each other. We don't ever come to blows, not yet anyway!

An attractive form of denial was of the link between the violence used and the 'self' of the man. Within an explicit account of violent assaults, one man commented about himself: '. . . I'm certainly not using her as a punch bag because that isn't my nature.' This implies that other kinds of violence are in his 'nature', his 'self'.

A particularly common form of denial, especially for men who have used extensive violence or whose violence has led to extensive damage of the woman, was to disclaim being violent. One man who was nearly charged with attempted murder and reported numerous assaults said throughout the interview:

> No, I'm not a violent person. I have to be really, really provoked. I'm just so placid. It takes me a long time to wind up, a long time. Somebody has to really hurt me before I'm wound up. Anybody will tell you, I'm not a violent person.

I'm not violent. I mean I've never been in court for violence [this was untrue] or anything. . . . I can look after myself, don't get me wrong, but I'll try and avoid it. I really do.

Another man, interviewed in prison, following self-reported major assaults on women, reported the following throughout his interview:

I'm not really the violent type.

It's not like I'm a bad case or anything like that, a psychopath. This is all in seven years. . . . There'd be times or months, like, when I've not done anything. Even a year perhaps I'd not done anything.

I didn't actually think what I'd done was going to be enough for this project. I thought it might have to be men that, like, tortured their girlfriends. . . . More attacks than . . . not attacks, I shouldn't say attack, because that sounds bad.

This is despite his description of numerous violences, and the fact the woman eventually left for a battered women's hostel to hide from him.

Denial may also extend to whether violence contributes to the end of relationships:

We've not split up through violence, you see. We've split up through [her] obviously getting bored of waiting [with him in prison for violence].

Removal of the Self and of Intention   A small number of men attempted to break the connection between the self and the actions. Violence may be spoken of as if it happens (or 'just happens') without one's intention, as if it has an independent existence:

. . . well I kicked a tin in the kitchen and she got a bruise under eye there, but that were just pure accident. I just kicked the tin and she happened to be, down and as it come up it hit her, because she's only short.

Some men spoke of the *lack* of a connection between their intention and the damage resulting. One man said the woman ducked down and so received a blow in her face rather than on her body which would have caused less damage; another man disclaimed the effects of the woman falling down steps even though that was preceded by his pushing her. He explained this in the following way:

Q: So sometimes you have hit her in the face?
A: Oh yes, I'm not saying I haven't hit her in face. I've blackened her eyes, yes. She says broke her jaw. She says that I broke her jaw. It was wired up and that, but truth about, I didn't break her jaw. I clouted her, but she fell down the steps, bashed her head against the wall, or her jaw or whatever. But I looked after her while she was in hospital. But I know, what is it I know on my children's life I didn't break it. But she always accused me of it. She doesn't now, but she did accuse me.

This statement has two key features. First, the man's ability to redefine the effects of his violence as not caused by him. He describes:

(a) Clouting → (b) Fell down steps → (c) Banged head/jaw → (d) Broke jaw.

He acknowledges the clouting, falling, banging of head or jaw, but not their connection. The second key feature concerns truth claims. He says twice that 'she says I broke her jaw', follows this by 'but truth about . . .', and then asserts his ability to redefine *her truth claims*: '. . . she always accused me of it [breaking her jaw]. She doesn't now, but she did accuse me.'

The circle is completed. *He has coped* with the situation by redefining it, avoiding it and removing intention. The same man also referred to another occasion as follows:

> I never punch her in face or owt like that. But if it happens she bends down and it's coming towards her, obviously she going to cop for it isn't she? She can't move out of way of it can she because it's already gone then.

Here the fact that a punch he has already thrown (already 'gone') removes his intention if it 'happens' to come into contact with a part of the woman's body not intended, in this case her face. This cuts a causal connection. These cuttings of causal connections are partial repudiations.

A particularly gruesome example of the attempt to cut the causal connections was from a man who had murdered the woman:

> . . . as I went to jab forward [with a knife], she was sat on the bed you see, and she'd gone to get up, as I went forward the knife had gone in.

He suggests, first, the knife that has 'gone in' is given agency rather than him controlling the knife; second, that 'she'd gone to get up', implying it is *her* action that produces the outcome of the death. Later, he adds:

> there was no intention of doing it, like, it was just something that happened.

Diversions   Finally, in this section, there are occasional examples of men's use of clear diversions in the accounts. An explanation is given but in such a way that it obscures other explanations that are implicit or explicit elsewhere in the account. For example:

> . . . after she left me, I just went to pot. What is it, I were out drinking all time. I were just torturing myself and that's when the violence come out.

This statement ignores his violence that had been going on for up to ten years and certainly for the previous six months, with the man himself admitting the police being called on five or six times in that latter period.

Quasi-Repudiations: Admitting by Not Admitting

These are similar to full 'repudiations' but their structure is such that the attempt is made to not define the violence as violence. The violence is admitted through a process of partial denial. This is often done by devices that take attention away from the violence to something or someone else. Quasi-repudiations can also introduce a measure of uncertainty into the mind of a generous listener. Such accounts can often be characterized as 'patchy' and uneven: they may be clearly inconsistent and have significant gaps and empty spaces, that may be filled by the listener. Four bodily (sub-)discourses of this type were available: not knowing; minimization, reduction and relativization; distinction and debate; and naturalization.

Not Knowing and Other Forms of Ignorance   First, violence may be admitted by not knowing (fully) about it. While denial involves a positive reference to an absence (violence), forgetting, blanking out and not knowing involve a negative reference to a presence (violence). In the latter, violence is acknowledged and *not* specifically denied, but description of it is absent. Thus the refrain 'I can't remember' is *not* a simple absence but is a way of describing a (possible) presence, of constructing and accounting, however minimally, for violence. The clearest case of such gaps and empty spaces is forgetting and blanking out. Such devices carry an ambiguity: they might be deliberate lies and avoidances or they might be genuine lapses in memory. Indeed in some cases admitting to not knowing might be the most honest response. In this uncertainty lies their power.

Forgetting and blanking out may be linked by the man to drink and/or drugs, but not necessarily so. One man described the process *without* any drink or drugs as 'I just took a blackout.' A rather contradictory account from one man specifically addressed the way his violence had the effects of reducing his own consciousness of what was happening:

Q: Did you worry about violence in a way that made you stop you doing what you'd normally be doing?
A: Well violence does it doesn't it? It blanks you out.

A man who was attending a men's programme was able to recall much of his violence and give an explanation of its cause, yet unable to describe his first violence and instead made a linguistic slip by confusing the programme leader with the violated woman:

Q: Can you tell me what you did the first time?
A: I can't really go into detail because I just can't remember it all.
Q: Right.
A: No, I mean like Joanne [group leader] says, I did more to Sally. I can't remember it all. I can't see Joanne, I can't see Sally when I'm doing it.

Q: Do you remember anything at all what you did?

A: No, I remember, remember getting hold of her but when it come into details I just don't.

Much less common were men who 'admitted' not knowing how to explain their violence. One man mused on how to explain his long history of multiple assaults on women, and could find no answer:

> I've got to try and explain to you why men are violent to women, when women say, 'Come on, I know you're going to hit me, do it now, don't just do it when people are here. You're not going to be happy till you've done it, so just do it.' I can't explain that to you because that's how it goes. . . . I love her somewhere, so I thought to myself, 'Well, why have I been doing this all this time?' but there's no answer, so I'm trying to find an answer, I've just shut the book. . . .

Another man who reported 'loads' of times of physical violence found difficulty when it came down to specifics:

> I can't think back to incidents. . . . I can't seem to remember the cause what actually led me to behaving like that.

Sometimes this process is further elaborated so the man has a well-developed theory of *not knowing* how to account for his violence. This can be especially important for men with long 'careers' of violence to women or serving long prison sentences. Such not knowing may be combined with detailed, sophisticated accounts of their behaviour, particularly where they have taken on professionalized accounts as their autobiographical accounts.

Minimizing, Reducing, Relativizing In a second sub-discourse, violence is not fully denied but is reduced in scope or impact.

MINIMIZATION Minimization can refer to a range of processes: of definition, extent, frequency and effects of violence (cf. Semin and Manstead, 1983). In some cases, this is clear and blatant. A 10-minute attack including punching the woman's face, grabbing hold of her neck and pushing her on the floor was described by the man as:

> It was just sort of like a little incident that went wrong.

The same man continued:

A: I don't see slapping as being really violent.

Q: Well say how many times have you slapped her and how many times have you been 'really violent'?

A: I don't know how many times I slapped her.

Q: Are you saying every couple of weeks or something like that?

A: No, every two and a half months. I've only been violent to her twice . . . never really violent. The last one was really, really violent.

A man who described a long history of different forms of violence to women, summed up one relationship as follows: '. . . I used to be a little bit violent to my girlfriend.' In other cases, the minimization is more complex. One man seemed to suggest a distinction between 'blows' and 'violence':

A: . . . the violence isn't getting worse but I mean the blows are getting worse.
Q: Are you hitting harder?
A: Yes, and what is it, they're showing off more, you know. . . .

This man distinguished 'blows' that may be more or less hard and 'violence'. Presumably the violence might refer to (a) the use of differential forms of attack, for example, for violence to be 'getting worse' could mean punching the face or the use of implements rather than the use of the open hand, or (b) the frequency of attacks. In contrast, *particular kinds of* the blows are understood as not worse or less worse (better) according to the hardness with which they are delivered. Through this 'logic', there is a separation of violence and the *mode* of violence. This is like saying, 'I'm not exercising more but I am running faster.' This suggests a possible (but unlikely) further interpretation of the original statement, that is, the blows are getting harder but the man is decreasing his violence in some other respect, so that for him 'violence' is not getting worse.

VIOLENCE THAT IS NOT DONE An occasional form of 'admitting by not admitting' was for the man to explain the form of violence he had not done. A man attending a men's programme and reporting a considerable history of violence was at pains to explain what he had not done:

I was never violent to Tessa [i.e. before that occasion]. The first time that I became violent to Tessa was when I took Tessa home to meet my parents, sort of to try and be right with the family. . . . I never fisted her or pushed her. Never pushed her. . . . I've never hit her with anything, never punched her.

FAVOURABLE COMPARISON WITH ANOTHER MAN Another form of quasi-repudiation involves the man's comparison of himself with other men. One man who had been violent to a woman over an extended period saw himself as not as bad as another particular man:

Even now she's at it ['winding men up']. Because she's suffering violence now with this boyfriend now. Physical violence. Hell of a lot more than she ever got with me. My daughter's told me this you see.

This statement neatly: (a) affirms that the woman 'winds men up'; (b) affirms that he is better than the other man; (c) affirms his relationship with his daughter, who was a source of difficulty in the marriage.

WOMAN WANTING VIOLENCE FROM ANOTHER MAN   Another man neatly linked minimization of his violence with his assertion that the woman wanted (perhaps unconsciously?) to suffer violence from another man:

> She must love violence, she must love it. She must love it. She's been in hospital twice through him [another partner]. Through him, not me. . . . She said in statements that she started it all. She were the one who started provoking me.

Distinction and Debate   A third sub-discourse is that of distinction and debate, argumentation and dispute, inclusion and exclusion. Violence is not specifically excused or justified but reframed in the words (world) of supposedly rational argument. Violence becomes a topic to be put in its place, to be debated and argued over. It is subordinated to the supposedly rational, which is 'above and beyond' violence. Violence is simultaneously admitted, made present *and* discounted, excluded or in some other way made absent.

The process of defining violence, of excluding from and including in certain actions what counts as violence, is itself a way of accounting for violence. If something is not *counted* as violence, then it does not need to be *accounted* for. As such, men define and contribute to violence. For example, the distinction between verbal violence and physical violence may be related to official definitions of 'breach of the peace' and 'violence': 'they've [the police] been involved a couple of times with Susan [the woman] but *not in terms of violence*, it was breach of the peace. . . . So the police have been involved and what they've done is lock me up for the night and let me out at 6 the next morning.' Also the *discounting* of certain forms of violence as violence can carry powerful implications for those forms that are counted as violence. For example, if sexual(ized) violence is discounted, then sexual explanations of other kinds of violence may also be discounted.

Women's views and definitions of men's violence are wide-ranging and include emotional, sexual and physical elements, including threat (see Hanmer, 1996). They also encompass women's experience of 'being unable to avoid becoming involved in situations and once involved being unable to control the process and outcome' (Hanmer and Saunders, 1984). Women's views of violence include an awareness of the uncertainty and potential of men's violence (Stanko, 1994). Such definitions are not necessarily specifically or exclusively related to the law or direct bodily damage.

Men generally define violence in much narrower terms than do women. The paradigm form of violence for men is physical violence. But even here certain kinds of physical violence are often excluded or referred to in passing. Thus, for men (who are violent to women), the construction of what is meant by violence is itself part of the problem. Features of physical violence that are often excluded include pushing, holding, blocking, the use of weight or bulk, throwing things (like food or furniture or crockery) and damaging property (like doors). Physical violence itself is often reduced to the use of force of a part of the man's body (especially the hand or foot) or an object (weapon) held by the hand in a relatively fleeting way onto a part of the woman's body. Holding or blocking, or even throwing the woman, is not necessarily constructed as (physical) violence.

Physical violence is included when the extent of the violence is greater than the exclusions described above, when there is visible damage, when the damage is relatively lasting, when police arrest and courts convict. Thus men's violence to women is for men a combination of physical force, legal effects and personal effects, usually visible, and at least verifiable.

Sometimes definitions and ways of talking about violence involve very complicated, contorted logic on the man's part. For example, one man explained:

> I wasn't violent, but she used to do my head in that much. I picked her up twice and threw her against the wall, and said 'Just leave it'. That's the only violence I've put towards her. I've never struck a woman, never, and I never will. . . . When I held her I did bruise her somewhere on the shoulder, and she tried making out that I'd punched her, but I never did. I never to this day touched a woman.

Thus in this account, 'throwing against a wall', 'holding', 'bruising' do not appear to be constructed as violence; while 'striking', 'punching' and 'touching' do.

There are two other important forms of violence that are usually talked about by men only indirectly, in terms of violence to known women. First, there is '(sexual) sexual violence'. Men generally separate violence from sex/sexuality. For most men, what is usually called 'sexual violence' is not included in accounts of violence to known women. Visual violence, including pornography, is excluded from men's talk about violence to known women. Apart from legal rape following arrest and charging, men rarely define coercive sex and pressurized sex as violence. However, 'sex' and 'sexuality' do figure strongly in men's accounts of violence to women, but more usually as a 'reason' for their violence (see Chapter 8).

Second, there is violence to children as a form of violence to women. While some men do acknowledge that children witnessing violence to women, usually their mothers, is relevant, it is more usual for the men not to see this as part of the violence. Indeed violence to women and violence to children seem generally to be seen by men as unconnected. This is to some extent reinforced by the way agency responses to child abuse are separated, through the child protection system, from those to violence to women (see Chapter 9). No men described their violence to children and young people as a form of violence to women.

Men's generally narrower definitions of violence are partly a product of men's generally structurally dominant social position and partly a consequence of the particular form of the particular social relationship with the woman in question. Namings and definitions of violence are themselves a social not a natural process (see Chapter 2).

Varieties of Naturalization A fourth form of quasi-repudiation itself operates through resort to some kind of supposedly natural process. The violence may be portrayed as natural. A man who was on probation following both multiple assaults and other offences saw his violence as part of an everyday naturalized process:

> You know, everybody has arguments, everybody has a bit of a smashing time every now and again, you know, pots and pans and what have you. I didn't think nowt about it.

The 'natural process' is sometimes portrayed at a deep rather than surface level:

> We used to talk it through and argue and scream and shout, and we would throw something at each other. Curse each other. And that just went [came to an end] then. It was just a waste of time because at the end of that you come to blows.

Men more often construct with violence as a supposedly natural process *between* people than with men as naturally or biologically violent or potentially violent. Much more usual were vague references to an underlying propensity to violence, often between men and women, that is reciprocal, could have been worse, not to do with gender, mundane, 'just happens'. These are more accurately forms of social naturalization, not biological naturalizations.

NATURAL INSTINCT A rare example of a man's reference to his own 'natural instinct' was as follows:

> You see owt agitates me. It isn't if things go wrong, it's the matter if they try to clinch me into a tight corner, you know I must bust out of that corner before they try to get me penned in there. It's just. I don't know, *it's natural instinct I think*. I won't be told by anybody, put it that way. And the violence starts like that. If anybody starts to be funny or be clever with me I react straight away, you know what I mean. Because I just can't take it because for the simple reason you know, they're nobody to me. I might never see them again, whatever. You know what I mean. I mean I just stick up for myself, and I don't see no violence in it actually. I think it's straightforward. [my emphasis]

However, even here his 'natural instinct' is not unfettered, but is portrayed as a reaction to being 'penned in' (like an animal presumably). Interestingly, he extends his naturalization of his violence to argue that 'I don't see no violence in it', that is, he does not see it as violence.

GENDERED NORMALIZATION One man specifically distinguished *slapping*, *hitting* and *punching*, and in turn related these distinctions in the violence used to his construction of 'women' and 'men':

Q: You start to hit her?

A: Oh yes. But it isn't like a boxing match you know. I just slap her. . . . It isn't like a man, you put a fellow down, I more or less slap her than hit her. But if I hit her, I never, what is it, I never punch her in the face or owt like that.

Whereas men see violence *with* other men as a serious *fight*, violence *to* women is understood as something requiring less force, less effort. It is constructed gender difference.

Another saw his verbal abuse, throwing things (jar, ashtray) and ripping up the woman's dresses as 'just normal', 'no more than rows'. He did not feel he had to explain this away. He considered it was appropriate to 'treat them [women] quite equally, and as the gentler sex . . . they're not built like a man, they've not got muscles or owt, so they're weaker . . . you just don't hit women.'

NOMINALIZATION Closely linked to minimization and other quasi-repudiations are processes of *nominalization* (Kress and Hodge, 1979; Trew, 1979): the reduction of complex social phenomena, in this case complex violent actions, to the status of a noun, a word, a name, or to a natural process. The very reduction of such complexities to the word 'violence' or to verbs like 'hit' or nouns like 'slap' is part of this process. Many such words – like hit, slap, punch, kick, knock, and so on – are simultaneously and sometimes ambiguously verbs and nouns.

Perhaps the most significant single word in men's accounts is a very small one – 'just'. The word 'just' is used very frequently in men's accounts of violence to known women. It perfectly brings together at least four meanings: as *only*, suggesting that the violence was not greater in extent or quantity; as *exactly*, suggesting that the violence was just that as described; as *justified*, suggesting that the violence was just, a form of justice; as *instant* and *spontaneous*. The idea of 'just' can imply that the violence is an active subject that 'just happens'. This can convey a sense of *naturalness*, and naturalizing of violence.

> . . . up to the last couple of years, I wouldn't have thought that were a violent incident when I pinned her to the wall, *just something that happened all the time.* . . .

> *Just a slap* you know.

> So I *just* picked her up and threw her against wall.

A: Well that's what's supposed to have happened. I'm supposed to have hit her with a broom. But I don't see why I would have wanted to hit her with a broom.

Q: And I mean do you know if she suffered any injuries from that?

A: She *just* had some bruising.' [my emphases]

The significance of violence can also be reduced by referring to *just one action* within a given attack or an attack that could have been more severe: '. . . I could have hit her a lot harder, and it was just the once as well.' This statement also makes a 'favourable' comparison with violence he *could* have used. The actual is reduced in relation to the potential.

RECIPROCITY A common means of reducing the man's sense of agency was to account for his violence as the outcome of a 'mutual', 'reciprocal' or '50–50' process between the woman and the man. Often these kinds of accounts were strongly naturalized – so that arguments 'just escalated' into physical or other violence. This *process* was often described as if it had a life of its own. Physical violences can be constructed as the 'natural' outcome of reciprocal anger and arguments. Such accounts sometimes reproduced a modified version of family systems explanations in lay terms. For example, two men who were on probation orders following multiple assaults on women accounted for their violence using this 'reciprocal' model. The first man, explained:

> *A*: Not really no, just a few little arguments, just slaps, where she's digged [hit/punched] me and I've digged her back.
> *Q*: When you say you've digged her and she's digged you back, at the end of that. . . .
> *A*: Do we get back together?
> *Q*: No I was just thinking if you slap her is she upset by that?
> *A*: No she slaps me back [*laughs*].
>
> *A*: Well I've slapped her and that's about it. She's slapped me, just a few slaps.
> *Q*: What does a few slaps mean?
> *A*: If we're arguing I'd just shove her like that, back of her head, or her ears.
> *Q*: You mean you hit her with your palm across the back of her head?
> *A*: Yes. She does it to me [*nervous laughter*].

The second man saw the situation as one of equality of violence:

> *A*: Oh she, what is it, *she could punch back, so we were on equal terms*. The harder she punched, the more she got, you know what I mean. Oh we've had stand up battles and that, don't worry about that. I mean we had every reason to do it like, you know.
> *Q*: Were the police ever involved in the violence between you and your first wife?
> *A*: No, no, because she could stand her corner [i.e. she could fight back], you see. She could stand her corner. [my emphasis]

These kinds of accounts give both a *description* of violence and an *explanation*. The reference to 'reciprocity' and even 'equality' (re)constructs the actions and the process of those actions. Accordingly, the violence that he does or that is *part of* or *follows* such a process may be seen as 'just happening'. He thus removes his agency wholly or partly.

DE-GENDERING An example of generalization across women and men is found in the following account of verbal violence. Here the man does not account for any specific violence towards the woman:

> I think verbal violence is much crueller [than physical violence]. She's said that to me. She's said that – that I'm really brutal. . . . She makes me hurt and angry and really resentful and all this crap, but she never says anything that really gets inside me . . . insulting, I do a lot, yes. Therefore I'm running her down. That's the way I definitely oppress her. It isn't a sexist thing, but I can do that with anybody . . . swearing, well I swear a lot anyway. I say 'Fuck this, fuck that.'

A more complex example is from a man who first distinguished hitting a person as a woman, and then stepping back to note that he happened to be married to her:

> Julie was the first woman I hit *as a woman, I happened to be married to her.* [my emphasis]

MUNDANENESS After punching his ex-wife in the face in the street, a man reported:

> . . . and then I just walked away . . . we just walked away and went into this café for a cup of tea and talked about it with my girlfriend.

Excuses and Justifications: Moral Discourses

Both excuses and justifications are material and moral discourses: they seek to allocate blame or responsibility – in the man, in his past, in the woman or wherever. With excuses, the man accepts the blame but not the responsibility; with justifications, the reverse is the case. The content of these moral discourses, the definition of the sources of blame and responsibility varied by class, locality, culture and other social divisions. However, the prime form of excuses is the construction of *the man as a victimized, potentially violent self, arising from forces beyond his individual self.* With justifications, the prime discourse is the construction of *the man as a holder of rights of possession of the woman.* In both cases, his violence is constructed as a reaction to something else.

Within these discourses there are necessarily further alternative emphases. Excuses tended to be founded on either the notion of *exception* (whereby violence is constructed as exceptional to normal behaviour) or *normality* (whereby violence is constructed as normal behaviour available for enacting). Justifications may emphasize the (positive) *ownership* of the woman (whereby violence is constructed as the demonstration of or the means of reinforcing that ownership) or the (negative) *correction* of the woman (whereby violence is constructed as the means of correcting the woman's exceptional behaviour or behaviour that is contrary to that expected by the man).

Excuses construct the man as the object of other forces – social, psychological, chemical – that are beyond him and beyond his control. They are often elaborated through the narrative of (supposedly) 'losing control'. Similarly, the woman is granted little, if any, agency. She is in turn an object, sometimes a rather random one, of the objectified self of the man, who has temporarily become a subject in relation to her. Excuses do not provide much potential for change, except perhaps through an interrogation of this process whereby the man, constructed as object, becomes a subject for his violence. Further focus on his violent subjectivity, however temporarily it is assumed, might lay the foundation for either a resort to justifications or a more grounded acceptance of responsibility in some form of confession.

In contrast, with justifications the man takes the position of an active subject, albeit one who is assumed to be responding to the active subjectivity of the woman. The man presents himself as being in control or partly in control – in this case, in control of the woman, who is herself given at least some agency in his account. Thus justifications provide the *potential* for a different form of account in which the woman is recognized as an active agent in her own right and the man recognizes his own responsibility, and perhaps power. This potential should not of course be overstated and should not be seen as any kind of justification for justifications.

It has to be an open question as to what extent men are able to identify their excuses for and justifications of violence in a fully *self-conscious* way. This may well be much more likely in men's programmes and perhaps individual counselling. In other words, the process of conscious self-reflection on violence also makes way for the *self-conscious* allocation of excuses and justifications. Having done that, they can then be either maintained and reinforced or interrogated, challenged and changed.

Excuses   Excuses involve accepting blame but not responsibility. They place the responsibility firmly *elsewhere* in time or place or person. The people who or things that are usually seen as responsible are:

- in the past (mothers, sexual abusers, school);
- in drink or drugs (including being violent when 'off' them);
- inside the man himself (psychiatric disturbance).

With excuses, something elsewhere (in the past, in drink, in another person, even in the man himself) is understood as the potential for violence *inside* the man. This is then seen as 'triggered' by something in his immediate life (Figure 7.3).

Accordingly, in this kind of account, although the sources of the violence, or more accurately the potential violence, are seen to lie elsewhere, the

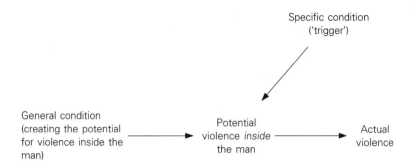

FIGURE 7.3 *Internal/excuse-based account of violence*

violence/potential violence resides *inside* the man. The bodily discourse of inner violence may reproduce a social learning model of violence. In this frame of meanings, violence is to be excused; it is not the responsibility of the man but is the result of past social, psychological and even biological events or factors, the effects of which are embedded in his body. The woman is the receiver of the effects (his violence) of these effects (his past). Violence may be presented as having a 'life of its own':

I think things what I have done [his violence] stem from my childhood.

Typical statements of this internally located violence are:

I seem to explode.

It all boils up like a volcano, it's waiting.

It's like somebody else what's inside me controlling me to do them things, and it hurts, you know. And I keep saying no, and I keep pressing it down, saying, 'No, I don't want it to come out in me.' Or, 'Leave me alone.' You know, like as though they were bad dreams and that, and I still think about a lot to do with my childhood. You know, it's like haunting me and I can't get rid of it. Some of it I dump in the dustbin, I still sort of put my mother on a pedestal. I've made her larger than life, you know. Same with my father, great man.

It was just like something came over me. It's hard to explain. All the emotions and all the anger just came out. Anyway I beated Angie up pretty bad. . . .

. . . and it just came up again, that kind of anger, you know.

I hit her anywhere, as long as I just get my temper out of me.

Men who use these internal excuse-based accounts often generalize, first, by conflating anger/temper/violence; and, second, by applying this logic to situations regardless of the people involved. In other words, internally driven anger is often generalized from specific violence to a woman, and then to people more generally: the account is not usually explicitly gendered.

A lengthy explanation of this kind was given by a man on probation but not for violence to women. He described six assaults in detail and referred to many others in passing. His account was based around his anger from childhood and his wish to harm his mother and father:

> . . . well briefly, it's been in . . . since I was a 3 year old kid, I've been into children's homes for 16 years. All my life into basically nearly every institution you could possibly be in, prison. Altogether, I've spent about 25 years in and out of prison, like a life sentence in a sense. I think some of my anger or things what I have done towards two women in particular stems from my childhood. Basically gone through the system in more ways than one. Been an unhappy child, not a very good childhood, broken home. Haven't found a mother in 30 years, just found her recently.
>
> I don't rightly know where my anger came from. I believe it's from me, as a kid. I know I've got a difficulty with it in the sense that for no apparent reason I just snap, or my anger goes over the top. . . .
>
> Personally because I think because of my . . . I don't know really where the violence really stems from me, but when I look back from a child, to do with the children's home. You see a lot of anger, a lot of bad things were pressed down, we didn't know how to express ourselves to be allowed to express ourselves. Or to get it out of usselves or to open up to anybody. I was frightened . . . as a kid I was timid, frightened. Just a kid what were basically I supposed at the time wanted my own mother and father. And I was so . . . I mean it's easy to say now that it was from that, and the life I started to lead.

> Violence stemmed up many times with lads' fights. I was in a gang with bikers. There were many times when I welcomed my own death, very much so. I wasn't bothered if I died or lived. . . . I didn't look on the quality of life for what it is around us. Now I appreciate it and I love it. Even then, some of the fights I were having, not just with women in certain situations but men as well. . . . I wasn't bothered sort of thing is they hurt me, or who I hurt, who or what. . . . you can hurt somebody but it was a hurt where I wanted to hurt and hurt. I wanted to smash them bad, . . . now I think back, some of it I feel because of my inadequacies, my own pains and my own self pity, call it what you like.

> . . . I feel it was actually from my childhood and from the way society had dealt me a short straw or call it what you want. And I felt that they was responsible for probably all my hangs ups and problems, yes. I was taking drugs, not heavy drugs, blow maybe. I were drinking. That may have some tribute to it but I don't think so. . . . I was a back street kid, street-wise and all that so I can't really give that as an excuse. Not totally.
>
> I feel it's from childhood where I was sexually messed about a bit. I don't think it is that, I've tried to self-consciously dig into my mind to see if it is that. The bit that's in society, and what they did to me, from the children's home and then they took me from there when I was 16. Sent me to approved school. There were no

need to send me there. I was in under the Care Act. They found out eight months later that I wasn't meant to be there. And I didn't deserve this, that society shouldn't have put me through this. When I went to Northampton I hadn't seen my mother in 30 years, yet I felt so much anger and I literally wanted to you know get over the table and beat her up. I felt that straightaway, as soon as she come in. Though I felt happy and joy because I hadn't seen her in 30 years, I'd put her on a pedestal, I literally . . . I never told her all this, I literally felt ashamed and I wanted to literally hurt her, take her by the neck and strangle her for Christ's sake. But I didn't, and yet I forgive her at end of it all. I said I forgive her. You know like it was nothing. So I felt good about that and yet afterwards I felt like I should have punished her for what she'd done to me. The same with me father but in another particular way. I even actually planned . . . I was so messed up . . . to kill my own father.

As far as he could see, it was the transfer of the 'anger' onto a particular woman that was the cause of his violence. This man also made an unusually frequent use of the word 'literally', perhaps conveying some unconscious reference to the ambiguity of 'litter' as 'offspring' and 'rubbish'.

The most common form of excuse, however, was reference to mood-changing substances – usually drink, occasionally drugs. This was generally constructed not in terms of 'addiction', although of course that could have been relevant, but more through the specific effects of being drunk. Typical statements are:

I think at the time it [his violence] was something to do with drugs or to do with drink.

I'm only violent because of the drink. If I get drink in me, it doubles my violence up, doesn't it.

Another man who had a much greater involvement with drink and drugs explained his violence both from being drunk and from being off drugs:

Q: Was there any other reason why you think you were violent at that time?
A: Well I were drunk and I've had a past record, I'd been violent as well, so it could be owt like that. I were either high on glue or on drink, when I were younger, when I was getting violent.
Q: When you say you were drunk when you beat up Wanda that time, what did the drink do to you that made it the reason you were violent to her?
A: I don't know really, just because I was drunk I had some sort of spark inside me.

A: I used to [slap her] if I were on acid you know, LSD and ecstasy tablets, speed, amphetamines, valium, I were on everything.
Q: So how did that relate to you slapping her?
A: What?
Q: Being on the drugs?

A: What it were is when I were taking the drugs I were OK, you know when I were actually on the drugs, but when I were off, I was a totally different person altogether. I were just moody, violent, you know a violent nature but not actually showing it, just felt sort of like shit. You know, I were trying to get off them and I had a few bottles of pills. And then she started on men and I were drunk at the time so, I just realised what I were doing.

Justifications Justifications involve the acceptance of responsibility but not the blame. Whereas excuses may tend to locate violence *within the man* so that something done 'outside' triggers the violence from inside, justifications tend to have a more *conscious* and yet *interpersonal* or even *social* focus. Justifications are constructed mainly as a *response* to something else in the present or recent past, particularly something *not* done bringing forth an internalized response in the form of his violence to fill the gap/the lack. This is usually directed to that which is not done by the woman. In this sense violence, like pornography in particular, is gendered speech. These justifications include the woman:

- not being sexually faithful, actual, assumed or expected;
- not doing housework;
- not doing childcare;
- not maintaining her appearance, for example, through *her* drinking too much;
- not restricting herself in terms of movement, autonomy, use of the house, her access to her friends.

These justifications hinge around the woman *not* doing certain things. With justifications something that is *not* done or is *not* happening is understood as leading to or even creating the violence (less so potential violence). Violence is not seen as inside the man but coming into existence between the people from the man to the woman. In justifications an absence is filled and instrumentally 'corrected' by the man's intervention as violence (Figure 7.4).

In such accounts violence is presumed to exist for men as a general assumption. It is then brought into effect by a social absence: it is an interpersonal intervention rather than the result of the trigger of an internal presence or potential.

Justifications are much less common than excuses, perhaps because they necessitate the man developing at least some minimal sense of agency and an understanding of the significance of his relationship to the woman in explaining his violence. On the other hand, the seeking of justifications for his violence may simultaneously remove that potential agency or under-standing by firmly placing the blame on the woman. Justifications by men of the decision to be violent usually rest on a bodily discourse of (a man's) social ownership of a woman. Justifications are made on the basis of the man's right and/or ability to do violence in order to correct the woman in

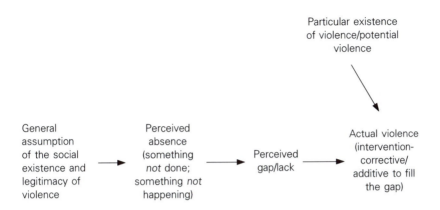

FIGURE 7.4   *Interpersonal justification-based account of violence*

the context of *his* relationship with her – a relationship of having, holding, owning and subordinating a woman. This may involve the reproduction of 'marital rights' in particular and men's social subordination of women in general. As such, women are blamed for the violence. This discourse operates most obviously in the use of subject/object statements – the woman is the object of the man's violent agency:

> I wasn't violent to anyone. Except her. In all my life. I don't know why. I don't feel motivated towards violence towards anyone else. I think it were a feeling that I owned her. I owned this particular person and she were my property, and that's why I were motivated towards her. I haven't ever felt violent towards anyone else, just her . . . I've never felt violent towards any other woman at all. I felt she was a possession of mine, that I owned her. That's why I felt motivated to be violent towards her and not to anyone.

The two most common forms of justifications were response to the woman's relations with others, particularly actual, potential, assumed or suspected sexual relations; and the woman's perceived 'provocation' of the man through her not conforming to being a deferential and passive marriage partner.

In the first case, men may use violence to punish or correct the woman's 'messing about':

> . . . she started carrying on with this friend of mine who she knew from previous, she went out with him. She started carrying on. And she were, bitching me up. Anyway, I attacked her.

A man who, unusually, was imprisoned for kidnapping and actual bodily harm put it as follows:

I mean there's a run up to it . . . all it stems from is when I found out my wife was messing about [having sexual relations with another man]. . . . I'd found out she'd been messing about about eight years before. She'd told me herself. . . . I'm not a violent person.

Sometimes such accounts were supplemented by a degree of reflection. For example, one man explained his physical and verbal threats as the result of him 'getting far too possessive'. Another centred his on jealousy:

. . . it was a form of jealousy, that's what initially sparked a few things [his violence] off . . . so if I saw her talking to somebody that I didn't know, I used to be suspicious and I used to think, 'Well how can she possibly get to know him?' Especially if it was somebody male and somebody young. . . . I used to be not jealous of them but jealous in general. . . .

and this jealousy for him explained and to an extent justified his violence.

For one man there was no need of evidence or proof of the woman's infidelity, merely gossip:

I think I'd just been released from prison [for his violence] and I'd heard some gossip, you know my head had started going crazy. There was this old fella that used to live in the next flat to us, my friend [the interviewer] . . . he used to give them [his girlfriend and his own girlfriend] drinks and tobacco . . . even though I knew in my mind he's never done anything, I could not accept why she's gone there. And that's why the violence happened.

Such disapproval by the man of the woman's sexual-social relations at times merged into disapproval of her friends and friendship patterns more generally. For example, following a dispute between a man and a woman's friend, he said that he did not want the friend in the house any more. When his wishes (i.e. threats) were ignored, and the woman partner objected to some of his friends being in the house, he attacked her. This kind of dispute and perceived justification for his violence based on his disapproval of the woman's friends blurs into more general disapproval of the woman's way of behaving towards him, either her verbal behaviour or other actions.

A simple example is that of the woman's verbal behaviour 'winding up' the man, which he perceived as justifying his violence:

. . . she came in, carrying on with me . . . she'd wind me up that much, really getting to me for nothing at all. . . . I can remember them. She just wound me up so much and obviously I knew she was messing about but I couldn't prove it at that time. I knew it, I just knew it, but I just couldn't prove it. I didn't want to believe. She wound me up so much – I didn't physically beat her up or owt, I just gave her a slap. I never you know, blacked her eyes or anything like that. . . . She's very . . . how can I put it, she winds you up, really winds people up. She's admitted to winding people up. Causing a lot of arguments all the time. . . . A lot of provocation and a lot of pressure. That's all it was. She said in statements that she started it all. She were the one who started provoking me.

This kind of justification can be understood as developing and escalating over time, so that it is women's provocation that is seen as 'explaining' men's violence:

> They're the ones that . . . they don't have to be goody goody, but you see if they didn't provoke you and push you and taunt you, then you wouldn't feel as much, if you're a wild thing you'd slap them perhaps once and that would be it. But it isn't. It recurs and slowly it's like three times a week, and the next time it's four times a week, like that for four weeks and then the next thing you know, it's every day.

> It wasn't like I'd wake up, and just take out my anger on her, a lot of it like she provoked you a lot. Like now even when I see her at home, I know she's seeing somebody now, this lad that I actually know, and she mentioned something to me that she said to the same lad, that I provoke people, do you know, like that. So she's saying that she provokes people. She provoked me, like a number of times I'd come home, say I'd met my friend in town and I'd planned with her to stay in, say my friend had said to me 'do you fancy coming out tonight?' and all the way home in my mind I had to plot how I could introduce this new scheme of going out instead of staying in you see. I'd get home and I'd go in, and she'd be watching telly and videos and then I'm bored. And then she'd jump straight down and being a bit wise and she'd say, 'you want to go out, don't you?' and I'd say, 'I'm off out.' And she'd say, 'Why didn't you just say that in the first place?' and then it'd come in a little confrontation, then she'd just jump on me and start arguing and screaming and the next thing I'd know I'd leave the house and at times she'd actually scream down the street. You know, 'I hate you.' She used to shout at me and I used to say, listen, don't be carrying on. She used to say, I know you're going to hit me, you want to hit me, so you might as well just do it now, do it now and get it over with, and things like that you see. And at times I'd just leave and other times I just couldn't leave. You know at first it would end up like just tugging her hair to show her that if she doesn't pack up I will be violent towards her. But she just . . . I asked her before, 'Do you get a thrill out of it?' She said, 'I thought you got a thrill', that's what she said to me. And I was shocked. I think at the time I slapped her actually, for saying it to me.

Less dramatically, one man explained his violence in the following matter of fact way:

> *Q*: What made you violent towards her?
> *A*: . . . what led to it, was her being clever and cocky with me.

The specific justification used by a few men was that it was their 'appropriate' response to the drinking of the woman. One man saw his attack as 'knocking it into her to stop her drinking':

> *Q*: And then what leads you to hit her in the first place?
> *A*: *Well straight off, she's only to say summat and then that's it.* I'm away. I'll just say to her, I'll say, 'Don't you think you've had bleeding enough of this?' and

it starts to get me agitated you know. And then I'll make some food and she won't eat it. All she wants to do is drink and flop about. Turn fire on and flop about and go to sleep. Then as soon as she comes out of her sleep, she wants drink. I can't rest, I can't rest over it, because if I rest and she wakes up half cockeyed [drunk] I wake, it's spoilt my sleep. Then it's starting to get me bad tempered. And then you hear the bottle or whatever and then you hear it going. Well that starts winding me up straight away because I've already told her, she's so stupid that she can't, what is it, take 'no' for an answer. She deserves what she gets. She really deserves it. I'm trying to knock it into her to stop it.

Q: So what is . . . why do you hit her in the first place? You're getting angry but what actually brings you to hit her?

A: Well, I've lost, well my day's work . . . I've lost some respectability for her in one sense, for her begging off the neighbours and that. I hate it because I don't want it off neighbours, when I've already got it. So she's had a belly full but she won't leave it at that. And all this starts getting on top of me. You know what I mean. She's no pity for me and she knows I'm poorly. I should be in hospital but I can't be hospital because she wants to drink. So it's all these kinds of things that, you know, agitate me. So as I say, I just see red and I go straight at it. [his emphasis]

This illustrates one man's explicit *justification* based on the logic that his violence will assist the woman in stopping drinking. He continues:

Q: You say you try to knock it into her that she shouldn't drink?

A: Oh yes, my way out of it, that's the only way. If she won't listen to any doctors, or any hospitals, you have to put it some way and try to frighten her off. Try and frighten her off but you're just clouting her. I don't mean punching her but clouting her. You know [saying], 'Idiot' and that, you know. That kind of stuff.

Q: Do you think it has any effect?

A: Well I don't know. I'm getting to realize I don't think it does actually. And I'm certainly not using her as a punch bag because that isn't my nature. I just want her to stop drinking and that's it.

Rather contradictorily, he concludes with the following answers:

Q: So when you hit her, have you normally been drinking before that?

A: Yes.

Q: Have you ever hit her when you've not been drinking?

A: No.

At another point in the interview, the same man linked his opposition to the woman's drinking to her friendship with a younger man:

Only if she'd stop drinking it wouldn't bring the violence out. Like just a recent occurrence, like when I was in hospital, a week ago, this lad that were helping on the house, on my house, I went to hospital, run out of hospital, went home. There was drink all over the place, just drink, empty cans, bottles, he, what is it, he provokes her to drink, but it were her idea to let him stop while I'm in hospital, so they had a good old drinking party, you know what I mean? But when I returned home to find this out, well that flares me up.

He blames the woman for her drinking alcohol which in turn brings the violence out of him. So violence is in him while drink is in her. Her having drink in her brings his violence out of him. Thus while a justificatory structure is dominant here, violence is still assumed to be within her, in a manner more reminiscent of the production of excuses. He goes on to refer to her wanting a 'lad' to stay to do the house up whilst he was in hospital. They had a drinking party, which in turn 'flared him up'. Again her behaviour is seen by him as the object of blame.

What triggered it [the violence] off, when I think about it now, was because she started to drink. She started to get bitchy towards me, and started giving me a load of verbal abuse. 'Why have you been doing this?' or 'Why don't you do as normal men would do? Why aren't you doing this?' and it actually may have been money matters at the time. And outside the family, and this other lad what called in what used to know her was annoying me, and I was losing my rag slightly. She was maybe a bit offensive, but she was drinking quite a bit herself and that kind of started to trigger me off and maybe halfway through the relationship, after a few months I started to get to know her ways and she knows mine. She was very caring and understanding, and she could be a very passionate person, you know, but she was getting to be very lazy and dirty and scruffy and not bothered about her appearance, stuff like that. And it affected me. I started to think, 'Well, what the hell am I doing this for?' And when she were pregnant and she did what she did . . . I mean I think that's what just triggered me off because she started kind of like, – 'Why bother if you're not going to bother sort of thing.' So then I started giving her abuse.

Again the man constructs the woman's behaviour as leading to difficulties between them and then violence. Perhaps the logical conclusion of the justificatory account is where the man constructs the woman as not just causing his violence, but wanting to cause it, and *her* seeing that as a victory. Thus one man specifically described how he thought the woman wanted him to lose control. And that this gave her some satisfaction or even control over him.

It was if I was giving her something [violence], you know what I mean, the satisfaction I got out of it . . . you know sort of alleviate the feelings I was feeling . . . it didn't last long . . . afterwards I felt you know, she's won again. She's got me to make an idiot of myself again. She's got what she wanted, you know.

According to this logic:

A: When you resort to violence . . . you've lost really . . . you've been provoked into it. It's sort of like you've been forced into doing something. If you had your way of living you wouldn't want to hurt people for no reason at all, you know what I mean, or even for whatever. It's only that people *won't let you live the way you want to live*. They're sort of *controlling* your life, aren't they. They're sort of making you do things that you don't really want to do.

Q: And how do you think she was controlling your life?

A: She'd provoke something, you know. An incident. Or she'd make out she'd provoked an incident so in the end I'd have to react in the way she'd expected. She'd expected me to react in a certain way. I don't know whether it was bravery on her part, you know what I mean, but she'd just carry on with it until she got the reaction she wanted. And I'd feel good about it initially then afterwards I'd feel bad, I'd get all churned up inside and then that'd start me off again, just resentment all the time, and yet I couldn't walk away from the situation for some reason. They were feelings but very mixed up and confused. [his emphasis]

This man also charted an escalating 'progression' in his self and in his relationship with the woman. First,

> . . . there developed an attitude towards women, I thought if they're big enough to wind me up or upset me or threaten me in any way then they're big enough to stand the consequences. I thought I'd treat them like I'd treat any man. In fact there's no difference. She's only a few pounds lighter than me, they're as tall as you, they're human beings same as you. If they want to live a life like that then fair enough, then . . . I ain't going to take no shit off them or anybody for that matter. I don't understand women. I don't think women understand themselves. They're just totally beyond me.

Second, he described how

> . . . you know when you're in a relationship, they're trying to make you feel small for some reason or other. You feel humiliated by summat they do or degraded and then you can't stand it – you got to do something, you've got to react.

Third,

> There's a whole complex mixture, humiliation, I suppose, anger, making you feel inadequate, you know what I mean, 'cos in some way, they're taking something away from you, you don't feel comfortable with your own image as a man, you know, they've put you in a situation and they're threatening your er . . . self-identity. You know you've got this image of yourself and they're doing summat to take it away and you can't handle that. You know you can't handle that. You know that you've got to do summat in order to live with yourself otherwise, you know, you just give up. You're not the same person you think you are.

Fourth, he went on to say:

> . . . it got so you used to enjoy it. You provoke incidents yourself, you know you get wound up over something, then you calm down and you'd have some sort of resentment building up so you provoke an argument so you could respond like that, you know what I mean, to justify what you're doing [including violence].

Excuses/Justifications   Even though excuses and justifications are in some sense opposites, as already seen, it is not unusual for men's accounts to include both excuses and justifications. For example, the propensity for a man to be violent that lies 'inside' the man is understood by him to be stimulated by the woman's action or inaction: 'only if she'd stop drinking it wouldn't bring the violence out'. The set of experiences provide the *conditions* and *general legitimacy* for his violence; another set gave him the *specific* justifications to use that violence:

> . . . but it were like she's triggered you off to go further. In my particular cases for me they [the women he had been violent to] triggered me off into a state where I wanted to physically do them in, you know kill them. Obviously I practically thought I had, thank God I didn't. And on both occasions I were very fortunate where both girls forgive me for what happened. I know that sounds hard to believe but its true. But I was even prepared, with Deborah, in particular, I felt she'd given me a raw deal, I did everything possible, I tried to make it work the relationship. She destroyed me baby [she had had an abortion].

Here the man is explicitly saying it is the woman who is 'triggering' him, to go further, to hurt her, even to kill her.

Other men described slightly different combinations: of the woman 'messing about' with another man as the general justification and drink and drugs as the specific excuse; or of brutalization in his youth as a general excuse and the woman's neglect of childcare as a specific justification. Furthermore, appeals to blame (excuses) and responsibility (justifications) are not clear logics; instead they carry their own internal contradictions and paradoxes. With excuses, violence is constructed with the man as subject. Violence is either *exceptional* or *normal* to men, or indeed both. Either way, men are constructed as acceptors of blame but only by dint of previous circumstances that 'explain' their violence and remove responsibility. This can be explained as either 'normal' or 'exceptional'. There is thus a paradox here in the sense that *blame* is accepted but on the condition that there is *something else* to explain the source that accounts for that blame.

With justifications violence is constructed with women as the object. Violence is received by women who are either *possessed* by men and/or there to be *corrected* by men. Either way men are constructed as acceptors of responsibility but only by dint of the circumstances of the actions of the woman that 'explain' the men's violence. These violences can be explained as *stemming* from actions of others (women) who are constructed as possessed by men and/or whose actions are constructed as needing correction. Thus there is also a paradox here in the sense that responsibility is accepted but on the condition that there are actions of others (women) to act as the source that accounts for that responsibility. To put this more crudely, resort to 'responsibility' as above is a form of victim-blaming.

These paradoxical constructions are thus not necessarily what they seem. The self-attribution of blame or responsibility is part of material discourses. This raises the question of the possibility of moving beyond the blame/responsibility dichotomy, either by the construction of blame *and* responsibility by men or their transcendence to some other discursive construction. The possibility of other discursive constructions needs elaboration. These might include understanding 'violence' through not separating violence from the other parts of men's actions and lives; locating violence as part of men's structural power.

Confessions

Confessions involve the inclusion or at least partial acceptance of *both* responsibility and blame by the man. They are also characterized by a relatively high degree of consciousness, completeness, accuracy or revelation. They can also be differentiated in terms of the presence or absence of remorse. Some of the most explicit statements of violence were made without remorse. Such confessions may become normalized as part of an acceptance of violence in the man's life; the violence can be taken-for-granted, repudiated and denied. Confessions delivered without remorse can bring us back full circle to denial. Such a characterization is relative not absolute. For example, what is counted more or less as remorseful is itself socially constructed between a speaker and a listener or reader. Similarly, to ascribe consciousness, completeness or accuracy to an account is a social accomplishment. The speaker (the man) may define his account as conscious, complete or accurate, while the listener or reader may not, or vice versa. While there is a good deal of room for negotiation on the various meanings of possible confessions, the common feature is some assumption of 'honesty' even when remorse is absent.

Because of these attributions of completeness, honesty, and so on, many confessions are constructed around the relationship of totality and detail. Totality refers to the tendency to seek an overriding logic to the violence; detail refers to the tendency to precision and particularities. These two features may appear as opposites but in practice they can operate together in a partial tension.

Most confessions are centred on one of two main themes: the 'real self' of the man; the 'real power' of the man. The focus on the real self is in some respects a development of the inner-located account of violence found with excuses; while the focus on the real power of the man is a development of the interpersonal, or relationship-based, account of violence found with justifications. The difference is that whereas excuses and justifications are presented as accounts, with confessions an additional effort is made to 'make it clear' that it is the way it really is or was – by involving either the 'real self' or the 'real power' of the man or both. Sometimes this is achieved through statements of extremity.

Real Power: Misogyny and Control

> I can't imagine a life without violence.

> A: I just can't, what is it, I can't handle a woman arguing with me. . .
> Q: Any woman arguing with you?
> A: Well, there isn't a lot in my life. There's only my missis and my mam and my sister. Other than that I just take the mickey out of them. I've really no time for them. I haven't, honest. They're a waste of time to me.

Such total statements describe the totality of the man's relationship to the woman or women. With such an account, no further 'explanation' may be given or needed. This is made explicit in the following account where the man specifically makes the point that he did not seek reasons to be violent before his violence:

> I used to attack or hit her, and then afterwards I'd find out what's wrong. But I couldn't go up to her and say, 'Oh I was wrong.' I'd just leave it as it was, cos perhaps months had passed since then.

The same man also used a different logic for his violence by drawing on the notion of 'equality' between men and women:

> . . . because of this equal rights now, I do believe between women and men, so I do believe that if a woman throws a drink at you, she should be able to get a punch in the face like the next guy.

More unusual still was the use of power analysis within the context of remorse. This account was given by a man who had joined a men's programme to deal with violence following separation:

> Q: Why do you think you've been violent? Have you got any reflections on that?
> A: I don't know. I've always liked to dominate, get everything my own way. I might be sort of tempted to say familiarity, you know, sort of, I know you're not going to leave me, so I can crack you as much as I want sort of thing. But having said that I did feel very scared she would leave me a lot of the time. Because she had done. So that sort of outweighs itself. The majority of the time it was sort of final straw, I can't take any more of this argument sort of thing, you know. I don't think it was so much of a question of who was winning the argument, but just the sort of verbal abuse going on. I knew that if I gave her a crack it would shut her up. Shut me up. Which of course it didn't always because she'd disappeared out the door and it would carry on in a different form sometimes.

Q: But there's nothing else that you can sort of put it down to?

A: I think *basically, it's power*. I have had enough of this argument, I have had enough of this argument, I want to stop it now. Which, that's my problem, if I want to stop it I should just walk out the door. If I don't want to shout back, why do I shout back, you know? Put the Walkman on downstairs and sort of ignore it sort of thing, for an hour. It would have been a lot better way. Which I tried sometimes towards the end. I did try that, but . . . what I used to do was go downstairs and have a couple of pints of homebrew, thinking, oh yes, that will make me sleep. Then I'll go back upstairs and go to sleep. But it didn't. It didn't work. [his emphasis]

Several men translated the question of power into the language of control, and the confession of having nearly complete control:

Like I had total control of that [violence to women].

But that, you're in so much control, obviously the girl were weaker, and a man, I'm a big bloke. Obviously I didn't really think of it at the time then, because she were fighting back and clawing and doing whatever.

Interestingly, in some accounts even references to 'losing control', the hallmark of many excuse-based accounts, are incorporated within an account of conscious control:

We tend to have disagreements over lots of small things . . . I would like to dismiss it as 'something snapped' or whatever, it wasn't, I think it was a conscious thing to the end that I was chasing her both physically and verbally round the house. She then went and locked herself in the bathroom and I wasn't content with that. I ended up kicking the door in, or down, just so that I could talk to her.

A man who freely talked of his 'lashing into her' and use of his fists said:

I control it, not like a fella laying into a fella you know what I mean, but it gets to stages when it's nearly there but summat tells you to keep back, keep back. I don't know what it is.

This quote also raises the complex interplay of legitimacy and illegitimacy in men's use of violence. It is difficult to say if the reference 'keeping back' is simply a question of inhibition and restraint. In context, it appears that the references to 'keeping back' and 'control' are linked to the *distinction* between women and men.

In many of these confessions of power and control the specific events or disagreement that precede the violence are often described as 'trivial':

A: I think I hit her twice when she was pregnant. I think they were the two worse ones.

Q: Can you tell me a bit about it?

A: Just the usual. Started arguing over nothing. Got worked up and just lose my temper.

Q: When you say you argue over nothing . . .

A: Just over virtually nothing. Well, I say nothing, it's not nothing to Georgia.

Q: And what was the actual violence then?

A: I picked her up and threw her across the living room.

Q: Can you remember what happened, roughly?

A: Yes, it was about two weeks before I came here wasn't it? Two weeks before I started coming here.

Q: And what was the lead up to the violence?

A: I honestly can't remember.

Q: Would I be right in thinking from what you said basically, your memories about the violence . . . you don't really remember what the argument was about or . . .?

A: I don't remember what they're about because they're so trivial.

Q: I see.

A: It's just that we argue, and I don't let it lie, because I always want to have the last word, so the argument carries on. I suppose if I'm not getting the last word then the violence starts. You know because I think it's going to get me it . . . that's the way I can get her to shut up.

Q: What precipitated it?

A: Difficult to put your finger on one particular thing. It was a lot of little things [*sighs*]. It was just a build-up of little niggling things which at the time you say, 'It doesn't matter, it's OK,' but then when it all come to a head, suddenly they all matter and you're dragging them all out.

The Real Self: 'Weakness' and Reflection[2] There were two main ways for men to demonstrate what they might understand as their 'real self' – through weakness and reflection. In the first case, violence is presented as an *effect* of the state of the man's self. An example of this kind of self-analysis is as follows:

Q: Why do you think you've been violent?

A: I suppose it's a breakdown on my part in not being able to cope in certain situations and, how can I put it, just a weakness in my character during that period of time. And maybe it's a question of being a little bit insecure and feeling that I needed somebody to be as honest with me as probably I was with them, and I couldn't understand that and I just saw that as a reason for . . . I mean, it was never a question of being done in a blackout situation and I couldn't remember doing it. I was well aware of what I was doing all the time, but felt once I'd got onto the cycle of getting so angry that I was going to use violence, there was no way back. I would actually follow through either the slap or the pulling of the hair and . . . it's, I don't know really, it's . . . I'm not saying that it would never happen again, but I think Beth just had an ability to bring out the worst in me, which may be unfair, but there was never any question of it, once we got back together, once I knew she was being fully open with me and I don't know, future relationships involving the same thing, I don't know how I'd react, to be honest. Like I say, I've never used violence, up to that point, in any relationship, so I don't know, I'm not really pointing the finger at Beth in any way whatsoever. It was purely a weakness on my part.

The second major way of demonstrating the real self in confession was through remorseful reflection on the process of violence and accounting for violence. In a mundane way, the single expression of guilt and shame is one such demonstration:

. . . afterwards I'd feel a lot of guilt, a lot of self-pity, all the normal emotions maybe that comes through something like that.

I felt really rotten and guilty about it and try to make it up.

. . . no matter how things went with violence, I felt ashamed.

Nevertheless, immediate remorse in itself does not produce a convincing confession, not least because guilt and shame can easily be part of the process of continuing violence (see Gondolf, 1985). More dramatically, some men and particularly some of those who had attended men's programmes spoke of their re-evaluation of their lives:

I've learnt to redefine what misplaced values and ideals that I had before.

However, not all pronouncements of the 'real self' took this form. One man who was in the process of attending a men's programme brought together the themes of weakness and reflection through an unusual emphasis on independent self-assertions mixed with remorse. He saw his violence as primarily the result of his personal weakness arising from his perceived mistreatment by his parents. His current project was to 'get the violence out' of him by talking about it all and expressing his distress, particularly through crying: 'I feel better for talking about it [his upbringing and his violence], it's coming out. But when I don't talk it's coming in . . .'. He concluded that 'from now on I'm me, just me. I'm not doing anything any more to please anybody [he was alluding to his parent's control here] or whatever. I'm me. And I'm looking after my life. . . . I'm doing what I think is right for me. I've done wrong [to the woman], I have to repair the damage.'

The Real Self and Real Power: Ambiguities of Control   A few men brought together both of these confessional strategies within the same account. They announced what they saw as both their 'real' power and control, and their 'real' self and lack of control. In this kind of account, a profound ambiguity was thus left around the question of control, and specifically to what extent they took responsibility for deciding or choosing not to maintain control and instead to 'lose control'. This ambiguity was complicated by the presence of at least a degree of self-reflection; so that their present 'real self' was at least in part able to see their previous 'loss of control' as actively constructed by them themselves, their previous self.

One of the most explicit confessional accounts that brought together elements of power, control, 'no control' and the self was given by a man who had been a long-term member of a men's programme and who reported a large number (at least thirty) examples of his violence. In particular he highlighted how some men may refer to 'losing control' when they choose to have the control to be free of control:

A: I just seemed to lose all control, and I jumped on top of her, and just lashed out . . . basically, we'd had a row again over nothing. I couldn't even tell you what the row was about. . . . Yes, well it's like I say, it's just, to me I wasn't winning. I wasn't winning this argument. We were having an argument and I'm not winning right. And I thought well, you know, I've got to win this argument. How am I going to win it? You know.

Q: So I mean, do you remember that, do you remember thinking that at the time, or is it the way which you understand it now looking back, do you see what I mean?

A: Well, I've looked back on it. At the time, no. At the time it was . . . I mean, I'm totally against men hitting their partners, I always have been, even though I've done it myself, and I always will be.

Q: . . . having gone through a couple of hours arguing, you know, like, what happened next? Did you, like, decide then to settle the argument do you think? Or . . . was it not as clear as that?

A: Well looking back on it . . . no it wasn't as clear as that. I mean since we've been sort of separated, I've given it a lot of thought. You know, the incidents that have happened, and really sort of gone deep into it to try and find out what I was thinking at the time. At the time, I think, whatever bloke you talk to will say, he didn't remember, he couldn't remember what he'd done, you know, it happened in a blur and all this. And that's just a way of covering it up. And that's what I used to do. I used to cover it up, you know, and convince myself that, I just completely lost control when actually you're not losing control. So I went back into it, and yes, that is what I've come up with.

Q: So at the time it felt as if you didn't know what was happening?

A: Oh I didn't know what was happening . . .

Q: That's how it felt?

A: But looking back on it, I knew exactly what I was doing.

Q: Right.

A: I mean it was my decision to hit her, nobody else's. Nobody else made me do it.

Q: Those times when you were pinning her or pushing her, do you see any pattern to that at all? Do you see any pattern of when they occurred, or why they occurred?

A: Yes. Yes. They always seemed to be when I felt that I was losing this argument.

Q: So it was something similar?

A: Yes. When I was losing. Or thought I was losing, put it that way. . . . I'd say, 'If you don't shut up, I'm going to hit you,' you know. And she didn't know, you know, whether I was going to or whether I was just frightening her, trying to frighten her or whether I actually meant it.

Q: How would you, I mean how would you see that yourself, how did you see that yourself at the time?

A: I was just trying to frighten her.

Q: Right.

A: Just trying to frighten her.

Q: I mean at the time, I'm trying to generalize across different occasions, but were you generally just trying to frighten her?

A: Yes.

Q: You weren't thinking of doing that?

A: I wasn't thinking of doing it. I was saying it because I knew she'd be frightened. I now knew the reaction. I knew what the reaction would be and I knew she'd sort of cower because she knew that I was capable of doing it. And I used to use that. That was a big weapon for me.

Q: Right. So it's partly around just, say, threatening physical violence?

A: Yes.

Q: I mean, any other things?

A: I think that was the major, that, the main thing.

One man who reported five 'major' assaults talked of violence 'coming over him' like some wave of emotion that he could not or could hardly control. Elsewhere in his interview he talked of his being able to control his violence to women and the situation in which that took place in a way that was very different to violence to or between men, when there was far less control and predictability in the situation. Thus regarding violence to women he said: 'Like I had total control of that.' The same man spoke ambiguously about whom his violence was directed at:

. . . I wasn't bothered who I was starting to hurt, but I realised in a funny way I were.

Sometimes I was in control of it and other times I totally lost it.

An even more complex example is of a man who had attended a men's programme and as such was able to both give 'explanations' of his violence, as he had previously seen it, and reflect on those explanations in the form of confession. This account ranges across possession, love, insecurity, oppression, loss, alcohol as an excuse, jealousy, control:

Q: You said you felt you owned her, felt you were in charge.

A: No, I think that is the reason why I felt violent towards her, because I felt that she were a possession of mine, that I owned her. That's why I felt motivated to be violent towards her and not to anyone, because I didn't care about anyone else as much as I cared about her. Like sort of, I love you so much, I'm going to smother you, you know what I mean. That's what it were. And then I were motivated to hit her because I were frightened of her leaving.

Through all that period of time, but eventually I were pushing her that much she obviously were going to leave.

Q: So there was something about her leaving throughout the relationship?

A: Yes, yes. There was always a possibility that she was going to find someone else and go, which eventually she did. My constant promptings instead of just letting her get on with her life. I smothered her. Because I cared that much about her. I know it's a stupid thing to say, but I did. I tried to protect her yet I smothered her. I wouldn't let her have any space of her own, you know. I strangled her. I think that's why I don't feel violence towards anyone else, I didn't care that much for anyone else.

Q: When you were doing it, was that the way you felt?

A: I felt insecure about things. I know now looking back that the reasons I were doing it were yes, because I were frightened that she were going to run off. But at the time I think I was more possessive of her, you know what I mean. I think it were like a jealousy type of thing. But I were frightened that she were going to go.

Q: So before she did leave you didn't really have anything to base that on?

A: No. Very irrational . . . I oppressed her that much over t'years and I realise that it were my fault, that part of it. And end of the day, I lost out a great deal I think, because I lost more than she lost. Or kids lost, you know.

Q: Do you think things would have been different if you hadn't been violent?

A: Yes. If I hadn't been violent. If I'd been like I feel now, more tolerant, not tolerant, just maybe easier going than I were at the time. Because the kids were fine with me. I thought, you know, I'd lose summat on the way with me contact being a lot more limited than it were before. I thought I'd lose something but it's been two years, and it's still as close. So I haven't lost out emotionally on that side, they still love me as much as I love them. And that part hasn't changed. The only thing that's changed is that I lost her love, you know what I mean. She did say that, in that last fight we had, she said, 'I do love you but I can't stand to be hit any more. I must go.' And then she were off. Well she were off a fortnight later. I can believe that she were that frightened.

Q: Sorry, you can't believe . . .?

A: I can believe that she were that frightened. I mean that night, I were really fired up. I were really motivated – I could have killed her the state I were in.

Q: You can't remember what brought you down from that?

A: No, I can't remember what stopped it. Probably the fact that I were hurting her. I don't know. But I did use alcohol as an excuse, like a vehicle, so that I could do it. To give me an excuse in my own head, saying, 'Oh, I've had a drink.' But it were an excuse for me to do it that's all. And I mean I do go out now, and I drink, but not to excess at all, and I'm fine. I don't feel violent at all. I haven't felt violent towards anyone since. But I think it were that sort of raging jealousy like when I'd had alcohol let me motivate meself to do these things. I'm quite convinced, I know it sounds daft, but the reason that I hit her was because I cared more about her than anyone else. And I were frightened of losing her, but I wanted to possess and control her you know in a strange kind of way.

Q: You wanted to be in charge.

A: Yes, not love at all. Well I loved her, but I wanted to own her, you know. I were that worried that she were going to leave me. It was like a self-fulfilling prophecy, if you tell someone often enough they'll do it anyway, because if they're getting blamed for it they might as well do it.

Composite and Contradictory Accounts

Finally, these various ways of talking, or not talking, about violence are not of course mutually exclusive; they often overlap with each other in the same accounts. As men proceed through a 'career' of violence, they tend to both accumulate methods of violence and increase their repertoire of ways of accounting, even if inconsistent. I have already discussed how excuses and justifications, though opposites, can often occur in a strange harmony, two sides of the same coin – each side in effect leaving blame or responsibility open. Some composite accounts included even more contradictory elements.

A combination of quasi-repudiations, excuses, justifications and confessions was given by a man who linked his violence to both the woman and children to his own sexual abuse from his father:

Q: Shall we move on now to the subject that we're primarily here for . . . well I assume that you're here because you've been violent to a woman?

A: Yes.

Q: Would that be your wife?

A: Yes it would. And my kids, I'm sorry to say. It's mainly against the wife.

Q: OK, tell me a bit about what happened.

A: As I say I've only just come to terms with what happened to me by my father. Unfortunately it's been bottled up inside me for too many years, and it's just started coming out. And now I've been taking it out on the wife and kids. I've slapped my wife, I've literally beaten my wife near to death. I've slapped my kids a few times. I've tried killing my wife. I know for definite one of these days if I don't get help, which I am trying to, I could kill her. I could kill her because what it is, is when I'm beating the wife, I don't know what I'm doing. My mind just goes blank, I go berserk. As I say, I've tried strangling my wife. I've beaten her over the head with a few things a few times. It's just got out of hand. As I say, if I don't get help soon, I am trying at quite a few places. I know for definite that one of these days, I'll kill her.

Q: How long has this sort of thing been going on?

A: For about two year now.

Q: In that time, is there perhaps a worst incident that sticks out?

A: Yes there is. It's when . . . first of all it just starts out as an argument between me and the wife. And then she turns round and brings up what my father did to me, and saying that I enjoyed it and one thing and another. I asked him to do it to me. That just gets to me. So then I just see red. I just go berserk then. If the kids are around the kids cop it. But mostly it's the wife, the kids will have been in bed. Most of the time it's been my wife that's copped it.

Q: I mean, obviously, we don't need to talk about that if it's too difficult, but what was it that your father did do?

A: He sexually abused me. I just feel bitter against him. I've told a few people.

Q: OK. Just take a few minutes, OK?

A: I've told a few people that one of these days I'll stick a knife in him. Because I've just recently found out he's doing it to my sister, and I have reason to believe he's doing it to my nephew. I've been to the police about it. The police have said that I've no evidence that he's doing it to my nephew. Because I've come . . . because I've taken too long to tell anybody that he'd done it to me, there's no evidence.

Q: Is there one incident when you've been particularly violent or anything that sticks out in your mind? You say you threatened her with a knife and you've beaten her close to killing her. Can you remember was that the incident with the knife?

A: Yes, the knife one, just after I came out of prison.

Q: What was that then?

A: Three year ago. I found out that the wife had had an affair with somebody and that she was still seeing him. So that were just by accident that I found out. My sister told me. I confronted the wife about it. First of all she denied it, and then she admitted to it. She said that he were better than me. That hurt. So I walked out of room, she comes following me saying it and saying it again. I were in kitchen and I just saw this knife. I just picked it up and she kept on saying it. So I says, 'If you don't fucking shut it, you'll get this stuck in you.' She kept saying it, so I stuck it in her arm. When I saw all the blood coming out I realised what I'd done. That's when I stopped. After I stabbed her I was just literally beating into her.

This account was particularly significant as it combined the confession of a large amount of recent violence with a keenness to deal with both his own sexual abuse as a boy and his current violence. It was unusual in the *urgency* of the articulations of both the enactment of violence ('real power') and desire to stop the violence ('real self'). This double urgency convincingly pervaded the interview. To say this is neither to pathologize the man's violence nor to argue that his sexual abuse somehow caused his violence, but rather it is to recognize the complexity of some men's accounts and situations at a particular time of their life.

In other cases, contradictions and inconsistencies were even more blatant. A man who reported intense violence to two women and one man with whom one of the women had had a sexual relationship spoke of his ex-partner as follows:

I'm not bothered about her now. She can get run over and be dead. I'm not bothered. If I lose her I'm not bothered. I don't care about her no more. I've still got feelings. Supposing she did get killed I would be upset. If I see her with another guy. Somebody'd have to be there to stop me cos I'd rip his head off. I'd kill him and do the same to her.

Men who had murdered or attempted murder and were on 'life' sentences were able to present particularly varied and intricate composite and sometimes contradictory accounts. For example, one such man explained his violence by first his brutalization in his youth with a range of other 'causes' in his adult relationship with his wife. These included her neglect of childcare, his frustration with her, her violence to the child, her egging him on (she was saying 'Go on then, big man'), drink. Another described himself as a 'traditionalist' who had witnessed violence but not received it as a child, and who in adult life was physically violent 'every few years'. His explanation of his violence ranged from 'not knowing' to 'bad blood' and his 'volatile nature' via his addiction to Ativan, his exclusion from seeing his children, the woman's alcoholism, retaliation to her scratching him. A third man did not see his upbringing as particularly relevant but referred to his own psychopathic or sadistic psychiatric diagnosis, the woman's assumed sexual infidelity, her more general 'provocation', his attraction of woman who 'provoke' and his rather confusing confession that 'I just walked out of the [previous] relationship cos if I stayed I knew I was going to kill her. The desire was there all the time . . . I didn't want to hurt her . . . I wanted to be violent . . . but she didn't deserve it . . . I just needed the violence or I needed the woman to provoke it. . . .'

Conclusion

It is important in making sense of these 'explanations' of men not to understand them as strictly distinct and discrete types of accounts. While some can be characterized primarily as denials, excuses or justifications, it is more usual for accounts to bring together several diverse elements. Discourses of, for example, inner violence, social ownership, confession, and so on, intermingle and recur throughout different accounts, as chosen by the man.

Furthermore, while the events described as preceding violence are often, though not always, mundane, everyday, apparently 'trivial' and men's accounts of them are individually constructed, these 'explanations' of violence are also forms of social talk. Men's accounts and explanations of violence take place in the context of men's power and generally reflect, indeed *reproduce*, these power relations. Not only may acts of violence be understood in terms of power and control, but so too may accounts and explanations given by men in interviews, conversations and other forms of talk. Men's account of violence are themselves usually both *within* and *examples* of patriarchal domination and male domination. Justifications given are part of the way in which women are talked about generally by men. The general ways in which women are constructed by men are reproduced, referred back to and invoked by the individual man, as, for example, when he sees those constructions *not* being conformed to by the woman. Much of this is therefore about what is taken-for-granted about relations between women and men; dominant constructions of femininity and masculinity; sexism and sexist attitudes; and heteropatriarchal structures and systems more generally. Perhaps the most pervasive taken-for-granted feature of these interviews has been heterosexuality. For almost all the men interviewed, heterosexuality was taken-for-granted (see Chapter 8). In all these and no doubt other ways men talk about their violence, maintain power and a sense of being a man, and 'do' masculinity. Developing an analysis of men necessitates detailed attention to describing and analysing these taken-for-granted ways of doing and being. This is necessary and important in order to stop men's violence to women and contribute to social, political and personal change.

8

The Sexual Subtexts of Talk About Violence[1]

Subtexts

When men talk about violence, many things are not said. This is even so when men appear to be fully co-operative in disclosing violence. Those contexts that are not explicitly referred to – gender, sexuality, age, race, family life, and so on – do not disappear; they remain within the text but as subtexts, scarcely spoken. Indeed it could be argued that subtexts are implicit contexts. The subtext is hidden, not known, not fully conscious. It is not a mere surface. It might be 'repressed', 'omitted', 'forgotten'. It is silence. Thus possible contexts – such as 'adulthood', 'whiteness', 'heterosexuality', 'family life' – may all be unspoken, forgotten, unnoticed and unnamed.

These conversions of contexts to subtexts are all examples of the abstraction of violence from the rest of social life. Indeed one of the problems of violence is its abstraction from other parts of social life. For example, men rarely portray themselves as embedded in a web of family or communal relationships the way that women may do (Hanmer, 1996). Men do sometimes, however, refer to such a web as part of a reaction to their violence, where, for example, other family members may become involved condoning or condemning them. Family life, and indeed communal life with neighbours, friends or acquaintances, is generally taken-for-granted. There are two main explanations for this abstraction. One is that it is in the interests of the dominant not to make the conditions of that dominance explicit. The other is that men, or some men, are simply not much involved in a web of family relations in the first place.

The Heterosexual Subtext

This chapter is, however, primarily concerned with a subtext that is widely taken-for-granted by most men – that of heterosexuality. It is concerned with the absence and presence of (references to) 'sex' in men's accounts of violence to known women – the pervasive but often unspoken heterosexual subtext. Indeed what is remarkable on first hearing/listening to/reading of these interviews with men is the absence of talk about sex, sexuality and (sexual) sexual violence. However, on closer examination these in fact constitute a significant presence in the interviews. Sometimes these references are direct, sometimes 'oblique and disconnected'; the boundary between the social and the sexual is often precarious (Holland et al., 1994: 24). This chapter details these several absences and presences of sex in men's account of violence to known women.

Debates around the interrelations of sexuality and violence, and specifically in the context of heterosexuality, have been intense. They have usually focused on different forms of what has been labelled 'sexual violence', a term which, as I shall discuss, is problematic in a number of ways. These forms of sexual violence that have been the focus of debate included 'pornography', 'rape', 'child sexual abuse', 'incest', 'sexual harassment', and other categories that may or may not overlap with each other. Many of these debates have been at a fairly general level. My approach here is different to much previous work in two ways – first in its attention to specificities rather than broad connections; and second in approaching these questions somewhat less directly, in terms of men's constructions and constructions of men through 'violence' rather than what might be meant by 'sexual violence'.

The Absence and Presence of 'Sex'

Four major forms of connections between sexuality and violence in the context of heterosexuality and heterosexual violence are identified: the taken-for-grantedness of heterosexuality; the separation of sexuality and violence; the implicit articulation of the man's heterosexuality through the woman's heterosexuality, particularly through seeing 'sexual infidelity' as a justification of violence; and the more explicit articulation of the man's own heterosexuality.

Taken-for-Granted Heterosexuality

The men who were interviewed, with three exceptions, operated within a strictly taken-for-granted heterosexuality. All but three of the men talked of violence to women with whom they were married, had been married, were living with or had lived with or had a sexual relationship with. The three exceptions were two men who spoke of violence to mothers, and one man who spoke of violent sexual fantasies about women. One other man spoke of both violence to his sexual 'partner' and violence to a woman friend of his partner.

The vast majority of the men were, in the interview situation at least, located firmly in relation to the women as assumed sexual partner. Thus this was generally not just violence to known women, it was violence to women with whom there was or had been a sexual relationship. The women concerned were thus referred to by their first name, as well as 'wives', 'girlfriends', or 'partner', 'ex-wife' or 'ex-partner', or 'her', and so on. There were three exceptions to this: one man who spoke briefly of an affair with a male neighbour; another man who unprompted described himself as 'heterosexual'; and a third who considered his own violence in more analytical terms acknowledging the possibility of other sexual orientations. As the third of these men put it:

> I've got a sexual bent for the involvement of the domestic and emotional side of things with women, I think it's as banal as that. If I was gay I think I would be the same, the male would take over the more interior life of domestic violence.

The Correspondence Structures of Sexuality and Violence Men's heterosexual violence generally comprises a structural correspondence between the structure of sexual desire and the structure of violence. In almost all the interviews there was an exact correspondence between the structuring of the sexual relationship and the structuring of the violent relationship. This was in one of two ways: (a) current heterosexual relationship/men's violence to women; or (b) previous heterosexual relationship/subsequent men's violence to known women. Although there is a structural correspondence in one of these two ways in most instances, this should not obscure the real variations in which that connection works, how heterosexuality more generally is constructed, as well as the specific form of sexual practices.

Private Closure The private closure of heterosexual violence was often referred to men. The private closure around men's violences instances men's heterosexuality and heterosexual relations:

> They [friends] just don't get involved. I've been in my friend's house when he's been violent towards his girlfriend. I just do not get involved. If my friend got involved, I'd be violent with him.

The private closure of the relationship is often supported by friends or families, or is perceived or reported as such by the man. A man who had stabbed his wife reported afterwards:

> . . . they [his friends] said, 'You've done nothing wrong against us or our families, you're still the same person as you were before.' They said, 'What you've done, you've done something, yes. And any man would have done something more or less similar, maybe not the same thing, or maybe not even anything related, but they would have fought for their children, sort of thing.' They said and when children are involved in any sort of relationship or a man and a woman argue, it's case of domestic and anything can happen.

Separation of Sexuality and Violence

Taken-for-granted heterosexuality is in virtually all cases itself combined with both an absence of talk of sex and sexual sexual violence, and a separation of sexuality and violence. These absences and separations take several forms:

- the silence on sex as part of a taken-for-granted heterosexuality;
- the absence of talk of physical sexual activity;
- the absence of talk of coercive sex and pressurized sex;
- the exclusion of 'sexual violence' from men's definition of 'violence';
- the separation of sex, sexual (sexual) violence from men's definitions and accounts of violence to known women.

In considering violence, sexual violence and sexual sexual violence, Kelly (1987) has convincingly argued that all violence by men to women should for both theoretical and empirical reasons be considered as sexual violence. This is in contrast to the specific labelling of only certain forms of such violence – including rape, sexual assault, child sexual assault, indecent exposure, incest, buggery – as 'sexual violence'. Accordingly, it does seem useful to make further distinctions, for example, 'sexual sexual violence' (Wise and Stanley, 1984) or even overtly sexualized sexual violence, or sexual violence that is sexualized by men.

For almost all the men, violence to women meant 'physical violence' rather than (sexual) 'sexual violence' or sexualized violence or violence associated with sex and sexuality. For men, violence to known women is generally constructed as physical violence that is not seen as specifically sexual. Sexual violence is seen as separate (cf. Kelly, 1988).

In men's accounts, rape appears to be an exception to these general rules. Rape or alleged rape was referred to in a small number of instances where the man had been charged with that offence. Apart from the fact that these are instances of the involvement of the police and the criminal justice system, this may be because rape *is* defined as sexual violence, while other forms of sexual violence are often not. Thus, the talking of alleged or committed rape as sexual violence and indeed as violence may reaffirm a restricted definition of violence. These implications can, of course, apply, *even when rape is denied*:

I took her clothes off and I raped her . . . I can remember ripping her clothes off, but not the raping bit.

I didn't assault. She were alright, she was great with me. We had sex, right. Now she's making out that I forced her to have sex. Well there's nothing to prove that I had, like raped her in a sense. No way. No bruises, nowt torn, nothing. . . . As far as I'm concerned is she knew if she got me on this, I'd be away. And she did. I almost played into a trap in a roundabout way.

They [the police] just said to me, 'We're arresting you on suspicion of rape,' which I couldn't believe. I nearly died when they said that.

In such accounts rape may be constructed as either equivalent to physical violence or occurring alongside other acts of physical violence or as the most serious crime of sexual violence or simply as part of the process of arrest by the police and subsequent charging.

Implicitly Articulating the Man's Heterosexuality Through the Woman's Heterosexuality: 'Sexual Infidelity', Sexual Ownership and Possession

Despite and perhaps because of many men's separation of sex and violence, sexual infidelity by the woman can be seen by some men as justification for their violence. In this view, the woman is not maintaining her self as the man presumes she should. There is a gap and a lack of her being as he presumes she should be. Thus contexts and taken-for-granted assumptions can be made explicit when they are threatened, most obviously through 'affairs', 'adultery', 'separation', 'divorce'. As already discussed (see pp. 127–128), violence is then justified to 'make good' this gap/lack, either as a corrective of the particular instance or as a punishment, even if that is not likely to be 'effective' in changing the situation. The apparent maintenance of a particular kind of heterosexual relationship is one explanation of men's violence, both in men's accounts and in analytical terms.

Sexual infidelity by the woman can also be a clear justification for some men of violence to the other man. Indeed, the violence to the man can be described as both greater in extent and greater in its consequences than that to the woman. Descriptions of violence to men are often more concerned with the outcome, for example, 'I saw him off,' 'I threw him out,' 'I gave him a good going over,' rather than the more formal definition of violence to the woman, 'I hit her,' 'I slapped her.'

The violence to the man is in the context of *excluding* him from a social relation or of punishing him if that is not likely, whereas the violence to the woman is within a given relation and from the man's perspective is usually located in the context of maintaining that relation.

Sexual infidelity of the woman was also one initial motivation for the man being interviewed and talking about his violence. It was as if her breaking of his expectations about her meant that he could then break his silence about his behaviour.

> *Q*: . . . when did that [the violence] begin?
> *A*: Well the violence, it were over a period of years. Let's say, I mean I'd found out she'd been messing about eight years before. She told me herself . . . and it always used to start on a Friday night when she'd been out. . . . She'd come in, carrying on with me, but I wouldn't hit her, so I'd break stuff. . . . I'd just you know pick a load of pots up, just through madness.

Another account of multiple assaults was preceded by the man's descriptions of his anger at the woman's 'messing around':

Things weren't working very well . . . when I went to work there were people telling me she'd been messing around with a man in the warehouse at work . . . and that were playing in my mind.

He then described how, after a mixture of drink and drugs, he hit the woman, attacked a man and his dog, indecently assaulted a second woman friend, and attacked his 'girlfriend':

I'd never been in violence before that's except for when I got married and she started provoking these fights with fellas, flirting and things like that, dancing with people and that lot, used to get me going.

. . . I was moving house and one mate was supposed to be helping me. . . . He was taking her down to this other flat with some of her stuff. And they'd be gone all afternoon, so I decided to find out what was holding them up. They weren't there when I got there, so I went round to her mother's and she hadn't seen them. She'd just come from her sister's, so when he eventually arrived back at the flat I said, 'Where've you been?' So she said they'd been at her sister's. I just went mad, went berserk. Then started beating up. I had her on the floor and was going to kick her head in and she had her hand up so I broke her arm with kicking her arm. . . . I just wanted to hit her. I wanted to hurt the two of them.

Another man attacked both the woman and her lover:

I spent four and a half years in jail cos I caught me wife in bed with me best mate. So I brayed her and I brayed 'im. . . . I says to the judge, 'What would you do then . . . what would you do if you got home today and your wife's in bed with another judge? What would you do? How would you react? You wouldn't just say, "What you're doing?" You'd be straight in there with fists.' I know I would anyway and most of my mates would. Even coppers told me I did right. They said you did right by braying him. You 'ad to bray him. I went to town on him, really brayed him up, pushed 'im through bedroom window and put 'im in hospital for about three months.

In this case, not only is the woman's heterosexuality invoked, but also an appeal is made to the (violent) heterosexuality of another man, the judge.

Perceived sexual infidelity figured in another man's account in a more complex way:

Q: When you say she used to wind you up, what sort of things used to wind you up?

A: It's like er . . . the place where she used to work . . . they'd have like workmen in and they used to laugh, but say one of them would go too far, she wouldn't stop it. You know, like a woman could, she'd say, 'That's enough', she wouldn't. And I used to . . . when it came to draw the line, she'd go over the line. . . . I must admit, I get jealous easy, very easy.

He goes on to argue that because of this

> . . . I was in a state of anger, because of Rosalind, you see. That's the only one way I can explain it.

After a particular incident at the woman's workplace, in which a man there 'kicked her on her behind', they had a 'blazing row. I mean a real blazing row.' The man walked out in the middle of the night and returned in the morning, when he raped and killed a friend of the woman. The man understood this as transferred anger following his anger and jealousy at the woman he lived with.

In all these and many other similar examples the man implicitly articulates his heterosexuality through the woman's heterosexuality.

Articulating the Man's Heterosexuality More Explicitly: 'The Intensity of Feelings'

The explicit articulation of heterosexuality was, as already noted, relatively unusual. However, a few men were able to articulate their heterosexuality and to speak about the intimate connections between their sexuality and their violence.

The connections between sexuality and violence within heterosexuality are also constructed by some men in terms of the emotional intensity of the relationship.

> Alright, violence to me is sometimes, not always, an extension of passion, yes. It's an extension of what's generally known as feelings. . . . What I'm saying is violence really is an extreme form of emotionality, backed up perhaps by a certain type of personality that might consider itself passionate or a certain type of personality that might consider itself insecure. Passion is central to my definition of it [violence], rather than the old 'I'm going to rob a bank.'

This man described the link between sexuality and violence as intense. Indeed, as he put it if there is 'intensity of feeling . . . intensity of action and reaction will be greater'. In other words, the more intense the emotional relationship in a sexual relationship, the more intensive the action, including the violence in that relationship. This man continued by comparing punching a woman to an orgasm.

Another man spelt out the power dimension in slightly less explicit terms. He spoke of there being 'a kind of edge to it', 'it was a kind of thrill where I could have took her life away'. Interestingly, this man in the same response twice 'thanked God', once because, he knew that 'I were near the edge where I didn't go over the edge' and once because though she was near to death, she did not die. He concluded, 'I threw her over the wall . . . as if to say, as calm as you like, one off, that's it, finished. And I got quite a thrill from it.'

A third man, who had murdered, reported:

> I'm a great, I feel passion, I feel love, hate, maybe stronger than others . . . there's a lot of passion, a lot of grief, a lot of sadness, a lot of violence.

What some of the men are saying is that it is the close emotional relationship between them and the woman that helps them to explain why they have been violent. These 'emotions' seem to be a *sine qua non* of the relationship. That is how the relationship *is* and how it works from the man's point of view; and yet it is also these 'emotions' that provide the basis of the violence that may follow.

For example, one man's account included the following, rather allusive explanation:

> Domestic violence, why I'll never know. There's got to be something there. There's got to be a link somewhere along the line where there's something that triggered this off. I think in any relationship, a lot of emotions, and when emotions get frayed I'm afraid anything can happen, anything is possible in that relationship. . . . you know yourself, or you'll likely come across this, or you'll know, any people who set up house or anything like that, the emotion, even setting up a home, you've got to have emotions to start off with. And if anything starts to go wrong, you know, over little things, you can have a big argument over nothing, sort of thing, and it gets blown out of all proportion. One thing leads to another. Alright, the majority of cases do not lead to violence, there's always a trigger with that violence with me, though. And that is a person lifts a hand. I can argue all day, all night, it doesn't bother me. I will sit and laugh with an argument, but if somebody goes to lift a hand, that's when I just snap.

Love   A few men spoke of 'love'. A man who killed his wife spoke of her as follows:

> *A*: . . . there was a hell of a lot of strong feeling between Nina and myself.
> *Q*: What kind of strong feeling do you mean?
> *A*: Like that we loved each other, it was as simple as that.

Later in the interview, he elaborated on this:

> . . . we were the calmest people ever when it comes to discussing anything. Like I say, in the home, never had no arguments, apart from this Sunday and like once before, when I've slapped her sort of thing. And on the Sunday when I happened to kill her. But apart from that, we were that much matched for each other, it was just unbelievable . . . this should never have been because me and her were two happy people.

Another man explained his violence as follows:

> *Q*: . . . why do you think you've been violent to her basically?
> *A*: I don't know. I'll tell you when I find out myself. I just don't honestly know. I can't . . . I just can't work that one out. I really can't. Maybe, and I mean this

> is just a thought, but maybe it's because I loved her so much, and I didn't
> want to lose her, you know. To me that was a way of keeping her, you know,
> by keeping her in check. It could be something like that.

A third man connected his love for the woman with his desire to stop her
drinking as that might kill her. This connection for him justified his violence
designed to stop her drinking and her killing herself, the object of his love.

> I don't want to see her die [through her drinking]. When there's something called
> love between you know. There's lots of violence but I don't want to see her die,
> no way. I just want her to stop what she's doing, drink.

Slightly more pointedly, a man who reported many assaults did make a
tentative connection between his wish to stop his violence and his love for
the woman:

> If I want to be violent I could be violent on home leave [from prison], I'm not
> bothered now. I've probably realised in my mind deep down somewhere, in my
> body somewhere, I love her somewhere. So I thought to myself, 'Well, why have I
> been doing this, all this time?' But there's no answer.

Sexual Attraction, Appearance and Humiliation As with the separation and
general exclusion of 'sex', similarly the attraction of and appearance of
women was rarely spoken of. However, one man did articulate his heterosexuality by talking at length of the woman's attractiveness or lack of
attractiveness to him, how he feared her attraction to other men, and how
he would humiliate her and tell her 'she used to look like shit'. This
particular facet was important to him and his violences, and ultimately
verbal heterosexual humiliation was the link between the two domains.
  Whatever time she came home, he would ask where she had been:

> I'd come home, it didn't matter what time it was. 'Where've you been? Who've
> you been with?' . . . But it wasn't me that should have been like this two years
> ago, it was her you see. Because all the girls I used to go round with on the dance
> floor, chat up, or play around with were like she is now. . . . She was the girl at
> home in the dress and sensible shoes and things. But now she's into big boots and
> the big trainers and the track suit bottom stuff and loose tops. I used to compare
> her with other girls. . . . She was more attractive before. . . . Her life style is more
> attractive to me, but as a person, you know, to actually look at, she was more
> attractive before.

Homosexuality The taken-for-grantedness of heterosexuality also operates
through the separation from 'the feminine' and from gayness/homosexu-
ality. Occasionally this is explicitly articulated. One of the few extended
discussions of homosexuality concerned the risks that one man perceived
from prison:

The very first jail sentence I were 18 year old and I were frightened to death. I were scared of the poofs . . . they offer you money for sex and stuff like that. But if you're straight, you just look at them straight, they leave you alone. . . . They're alright that way.

Later in the interview he describes a drinking spree when his girlfriend had said:

'Stop drinking. Why don't you drink shandies and lemonade and coke and you'll be alright.' And I says, 'I'm no fucking drinking that, I'll be a poof.' Cos I used to go out and drink coke every night for six months. And my mates used to take the piss out of me. 'Go on you fucking poof.' I says, 'I'm not a poof for drinking pop.'

This man remained insistent in telling of his heterosexuality through the interview. When a woman probation officer came into the room during the interview, he remarked:

Wouldn't mind her. She'd just suit me down to the ground, she would. She's a [her home town]-er, and she doesn't like violence. Cos she knows about violence to Olive and she says, 'Why do you do it?' – so I told her – 'Doesn't your husband ever belt you?'

Apart from objectifying the probation officer, the man may well be checking out the possible limits of his domination of her. In terms of recent discussions of masculine psychodynamics, it is difficult to know whether this man is solidly and unproblematically heterosexual, or whether his heterosexuality is actually rather fragile.

Rejection   After, before or in between direct violence to the woman, some men may threaten violence to themselves. This in itself may be a further form of violence to the woman. The threat of violence to the self may be couched in terms of his demand to retain or recover the sexually coupled relationship.

I mean I tried to top . . . kill myself with an overdoses like . . . I've never, ever attempted owt like that before. I'd never do it again. That's how low I were. I'd almost threatened her, you either take me back or I'll kill myself. More or less in a nutshell what I said to her.

Thus this linking of violence to the self and possible rejection affirms heterosexuality.

Finding New Love   Finally, a rare example of the man's articulation of his heterosexuality was through his reference to finding new love:

Q: Were the police ever involved in the violence between you and your first wife?
A: No. No, because she could stand her corner you see. She could stand her corner. She were a nice lass. I went from her after [separated]. There's no ill feeling between us. It's just I went for Daphne [second woman]. That were it. It were love and that's all I can say. I mean I wasn't blind stinking drunk to fall in love with her [Daphne]. No, no way.

This confirms both his more recent and his previous relationships as bona fide 'loving' heterosexual relationships, and him as a loving heterosexual man, in his own terms.

What Kind of Heterosexual Subtext?

This chapter has outlined some of the *particular*, different and sometimes contradictory ways in which violence is connected with heterosexuality. In the first form of connection (taken-for-grantedness), heterosexuality provides the given backcloth within which violence is done and spoken of, neatly paralleling the structure of that backcloth. This involved the maintenance of private closure and the distancing from homosexuality and the feminine. This taken-for-grantedness both provides the backcloth to the subsequent connections, and is a separable and distinct set of connections in its own right.

The general taken-for-grantedness of heterosexuality is given specific form in the silences around sex and (sexual) sexual violence and the separation of physical, sexual and other violences. Thus, in these senses, these separations reproduce the taken-for-grantedness of heterosexuality exactly. The resort to violence following actual or suspected 'sexual infidelity' by the woman could be seen as both reproducing the taken-for-grantedness of heterosexuality and articulating heterosexuality through the woman's heterosexuality. In contrast, the relatively rare articulation of the man's heterosexuality raises some different issues. This is partly simply in terms of making connections *explicit* rather than implicit; it is also sometimes in terms of a rather less closed, less static and more emotionalized set of constructions of sexuality and violence. These different constructions can also be interrelated with each other. While different men may tend to use one or the other, they are all available for men to draw on or refer to, as often as they wish. Thus questions of their own interrelations and their interrelations with constructions of sexuality and violence previously identified are equally important.

Let us now consider how to make sense of this material. First, these accounts presented can be partly understood in terms of competing structured discourses of sexuality. The dominant discourse in these accounts could be compared with the 'have/hold' discourse of heterosexual relations (Hollway, 1984). In this discourse 'sex' is not problematic, it is a taken-for-granted instance of the defined, closed relation; coercive sex and pressurized sex are not defined as 'violence', in keeping with the traditions of marriage, and, until very recently, the non-recognition of marital rape in law. Similarly, 'sexual infidelity' by the woman is placed as a justification for violence to 'maintain' the relationship, to re-include the woman, and re-exclude the 'other man'. In contrast, the 'male sexual drive' discourse (Hollway, 1984) is much less fully developed. It is apparent in the 'special case' of rape, and, on some rare occasions, in the articulation of hetero-sexuality. This provides an excuse, rather than a justification, for violence.

More generally, the relative absence of references to 'sex' in men's accounts of 'violence' evidences many men's ability to compartmentalize and segment different areas of their lives and experiences. This is not simply a matter of a 'division of labour' in men's lives and experience, it is more significant than this in the very formation of the categories of 'sex' and 'violence'. As already noted, a major way in which men reproduce violence is by separating violence off from the rest of their lives and experience.

On the other hand, this separation of sexuality and violence is contra-dicted in a number of ways. First, in a small number of the interviews men *did* talk of sex, the sexualizing of violence and/or the 'positive' sexualized pleasure of violence. Second, longer term research intervention might reveal different ways of talking about sexuality and violence. Third, there are specific questions of men's eroticization of dominance, whether in direct physical relationships or in the production or use of cultural materials.

These complex interplays of the absence and presence of 'sex' in violence are found in and around the *social relation* and the *enactment* of hetero-sexuality. So one of the ways in which sex may be *absent* or apparently absent is because heterosexuality is taken-for-granted by the man. It does not need to be said. Sex is presumed to merely continue as a kind of 'background music' to their particular business of violence. On the other hand, sex remains *present* throughout all of this because heterosexuality is a social relation and social form of sexuality that is usually founded on difference and the eroticization of difference. This applies especially in dominant forms of heterosexuality, such as compulsory heterosexuality (Rich, 1980) and hierarchic heterosexuality (Hearn, 1987). This is also taken-for-granted, so that it also does not need to be said; it is known.

Above all, heterosexuality is a set of structured social relations. These are articulated in a variety of ways. The dominant, though not the only, forms of heterosexuality are closely connected to and reproduced by dominant forms of men (and 'masculinities'). These dominant forms of masculinities have been labelled 'hegemonic' (Carrigan et al., 1985; Brittan, 1989) and hegemonic heterosexual (Frank, 1987). The associated forms of sexuality have been characterized as defined through power (Coveney et al., 1984).

Heterosexuality is *both* the dominant form of sexuality and sexual relations as social relations *and* a particular form of sexual relation and social relation that is usually founded on the eroticization of difference. This *combination* means that *difference* in this context cannot be strictly separated off from *dominance*. This dominance is partly a question of the use of dominance in dominant forms of heterosexuality. Thus (a) hetero-sexuality is dominant; (b) dominant forms of heterosexuality are dominant; and (c) dominant forms of heterosexuality use dominance. Accordingly, difference is eroticized in heterosexuality, as is dominance.

The separation of sexuality and violence that pervades much of these accounts can also be contrasted with the eroticization of dominance in pornography. How can this be explained? One easy explanation is that the accounts are simply showing the *surface* and that there is a 'deeper' structure characterized by the eroticization of violence. Another possible interpretation is that the separation of sexuality and violence is in men's perception but not in women's perception. A third possibility is that the eroticization of dominance and violence operates as a currency *between men* as it may, in men's perceptions, between men and women.

Whereas Dworkin (1982), MacKinnon (1983) and Stoltenberg (1990) speak of the eroticization of dominance, including violence, this material suggests the violencization of eroticism (an eroticism that may itself be partly founded on the eroticization of dominance). This might suggest a reciprocal relationship between the eroticization of dominance and the violencization of eroticism. Furthermore, it is quite possible that what might be defined as the violencization of sexuality in a man's account might be defined as the eroticization of dominance in a woman's account. Accord-ingly, while the interrelation of sexuality (itself violencized) and violence (itself sexualized) is important, there are dangers in reproducing gender differences in accounts in theorizing those experiences.

However, overly deterministic structural accounts need to be treated with caution. Recent contributions to the study of power, and especially feminist poststructuralist perspectives, have emphasized the importance of recog-nizing the embodiment of power in sexual/violent relationships. An extremely useful contribution to these debates on power has been provided by Holland et al. (1994) in their analysis of the embodiment of female sexuality. They concur with Foucault (1979) on the identification of the physical body as a social site where the 'micro physics' of power operate but argue, unlike him, that this conception can be applied specifically to male domination (Holland et al., 1994: 26).[2] This gendering of power in turn 'links the disciplining of bodily activity to institutionalized heterosexuality, the "beauty system", and women's consent and resistance to male hegemony'.[3] These power relations, though not individually held, involve dominance at the level of everyday habits. While male hegemony may be technically precarious, it remains strong since resistance by either women or men is a difficult struggle. Furthermore, 'while men may benefit from male domination in sexual encounters, *they* are also constrained by the social construction of heterosexuality'[4] (Holland et al., 1994: 27; emphasis in original).

Thus in this view, men are not simply free agents, dominating outside of dominant social definitions. The interplay of heterosexuality and violence is, for men, paradoxical. Heterosexual men may keep their sexuality implicit, taken-for-granted. It is made known in a variety of oblique ways. Heterosexual men may relate to each other via women and their sexuality towards women. Indeed seeing women as homosocial currency *between* men is one way of explaining men's relative silence on sexuality in their talk of violence to women. On the other hand, the articulation of heterosexuality may become more clearly explicit when the male sexual narrative (Dyer, 1985; Hearn and Parkin, 1987, 1995) is disrupted, disappointed or unsuccessful.[5] In such situations, heterosexuality may be more fully spelt out, but even then usually by reference to the woman's sexuality and only rarely to 'his own'. In the light of this, it is probably more accurate to understand sexuality and violence as linked in an intimate nexus – the sexuality/ violence nexus – within particular forms of heterosexuality, than to see one as 'causing' the other.

Part III

RESPONDING TO VIOLENCE?

9

In and Around Agencies

After violence a number of things may happen. The woman may or may not take action. Other people – family, friends, neighbours, children – may or may not respond. Such responses may challenge and oppose that violence or may do little, if anything, to stop further violence. Violence may or may not be noticed, named and made public. Thus one major response is silence and not noticing: non-response is a response. Another response is contact with an agency, statutory or voluntary. This chapter reviews these agency contacts by summarizing their basic pattern; considering the particular issues raised in the main types of agency; and concluding with analysis of the relationship of internal organizational dynamics and men's violence to known women.

In discussing agency responses to men's violence to known women, there is an important shift in the status of the material under discussion. It is no longer the accounts of men, with all their limitations, that are relied upon, but connections, triangulations, can be made between men's accounts and agency accounts. In that sense a fuller picture may be available. However, it is important to add that, first, most agency accounts rely on men's own accounts to them; second, some agency accounts rely also on women's accounts and/or the accounts of other agencies; and, third, many agency accounts are also accounts by men in agencies. Thus the status of agency accounts is itself variable. Having said that, there were very few occasions when there was an irreconcilable discrepancy between the men's accounts and agency accounts; rather, agency accounts often provided more detail of the background to the violence, the nature of the violence, and other circumstances in the man's, and sometimes the woman's, life.

One of the key issues in considering the pattern of agency contact is how such contacts begin. Men's initial contact with agencies can occur in several ways: through the man's own initial actions, as, say, with a visit to his GP about problems about drink; or through someone else, often, though not necessarily, the woman concerned. In almost all cases, men reported that the agency contact was initiated by someone outside the agency – another agency or professional, the woman concerned, himself, a neighbour, family member, friends or occasionally a passer-by (with violence in the street).

In theory there are many opportunities for agency staff to initiate contact; in practice this is very rare. Police do not usually just drop into houses on hearing the sound of violent argument. Whereas children experiencing child abuse may be subject to surveillance by teachers, doctors, nurses, and so on, this does not apply in the same way to adults. One of the few professional groups with relatively routine access to women, particularly women with young children, in their own homes is health visitors. In some localities they play an important part in developing awareness of the problem of men's violence, and this is a job that could be expanded. However, even such intervention would not apply to many women without young children. Furthermore, it would still have to engage with issues of embarrassment, shame, even guilt, that accompany dominant constructions of violence in the private realm. To put this more directly, intervention still rests largely on the woman being willing to convert a private conversation with a professional worker to a more public action outside the confines of the home. The private has to become public. Indeed many men continue to have no or negligible contact with agencies.

Even so there is a large amount of agency contact that does take place with men who have been violent to known women. Unfortunately this is usually not directly focused on stopping the violence. The problem may be mentioned in passing; other problems may be attended to instead; or the violence may be dealt with periodically but not necessarily in a way that is likely to reduce or eliminate it. Thus while a large amount of agency time and resources is devoted to the problem both with women and with men, much of this is not directed at countering men's violence.

The Basic Pattern of Men's Contacts with Agencies

Information on agencies has been gathered in six main ways: (a) in gaining the general co-operation of agencies; (b) in gaining research access to men; (c) in the interviews and accounts by individual men; (d) in follow-up interviews and other contacts with agency personnel, following permission from men; (e) in agency policies; and (f) in the routine practice of agencies.

A hundred and thirty follow-up contacts were completed, of which 69 were interviews with agency staff. Organizations that have been involved include the police, the Crown Prosecution Service, the Probation Service, Social Services, HM Prison Service, housing agencies, men's programmes, solicitors, doctors, psychiatrists, and other welfare agencies. The total number of agencies contacted by the 60 men interviewed was 256. Five men reported no agency contacts. On average men in contact with agencies each contacted between four and five agency types. On average men were in contact with far fewer agencies than women, with women in contact with, on average, over eleven agency types (Hanmer, 1995).

Partly because of the way men were recruited for interview, the largest number of agency contacts were with the police and men's programmes. Two thirds of the men had had police involvement in relation to violence to known women, and just under half had contact with therapists, counsellors or men's programmes. Nearly two-thirds had had contact with solicitors, and nearly half with general practitioners. A third had been in contact with Probation and a quarter with various mental health agencies. A sixth or less had had contact with social workers, housing, Social Security, hospital or prison. While men's contact with Social Services is low, there is a considerable contact with GPs, mostly psychologically or medically related rather than focused on violence itself.

The pattern and frequency of men's contact with agencies is rather arbitrary in that only a small proportion go through these agency processes. Agencies vary in their cost per individual and men tend to be in expensive agency systems and interventions. Some men are involved with several criminal justice agencies many times. This uses valuable resources. Men in counselling may consume considerable resources because of their labour-intensive nature. Absence of contact, minimal or irregular contact, and low-quality contact with some men can have dire consequences for women and children.

The Criminal Justice System

The criminal justice system is a large, complex set of organizations. It includes the police, the Crown Prosecution Service, the Probation Service, prisons, solicitors in private practice, the Bar, the judiciary, the magistracy and clerks of the court. This system is involved in a wide range of tasks, including crime prevention, law enforcement, provision of safeguards against injustice, punishment of offenders, and custody of offenders.

Men who have been violent to known women may be located at all points in this system. They may be involved briefly or over a lifetime; they may be involved in relation to one or many acts of violence; they may also be involved in other offences or alleged offences. Where men are located in the system results from several factors: what the man has done or not done; what others, particularly agency staff, have done subsequently; and the man's 'state of mind'. If the man has not murdered, it is likely that he will not be involved with any agency. The more visible the damage is, and possibly life-threatening (the 'more serious' in the terms of the criminal justice system agencies), the greater the likelihood of the man becoming involved in the criminal justice system.

An important general issue, particularly regarding resource use, is that men who had been involved with the criminal justice system had far more contacts with agencies than men who had not, including men who had extensive contacts with 'counselling' agencies (Table 9.1).

While contact with the criminal justice system might be relatively unusual for men who have been violent to known women, once involved, contacts with a whole series of agencies may follow. Thus, moving beyond arrest/caution to charging is a fundamental shift, not only for the man (and, in a different way, the woman), but also for the operation of the state, in terms of time, effort, energy, resources and inter-agency liaison. This may be thought of as a series of stages of agency involvement:

- police arrest/caution;
- police charging/magistrates' court/solicitor/Probation;
- Crown Prosecution Service/magistrates' or higher court/solicitor/Probation;
- Probation;
- prisons and related services (e.g. educational, psychological, psychiatric).

Clearly becoming involved with the criminal justice system, especially beyond arrest, will mean the involvement of more agencies. On the other hand, there is a considerable filtering of cases at every point in the system, so that, for example, of the 16 men from the police referrals, only three were convicted (Table 9.2).

Police involvement was reported by 40 out of 60 men. In five cases, the man said that he himself phoned or asked the police for help; in 36, someone else phoned the police without asking the man. Thirty-six of the men were interviewed by police, leading to arrest for 34 men. For five men the police never showed up. Twenty-seven men had been charged or summonsed to court, and 20 reported they had been convicted for violence to women (one additional man disclosed this elsewhere in the interview). More detailed police responses reported by the men, especially points 4, 8 and 10 in Table 9.3, are major causes for concern.

Several officers described the creation of Police Special Units on domestic violence and child protection (with responsibility also for rape) and the establishment of the force policy to 'act on whatever we come across'. If an offence had been committed, officers indicated that they are aware that they should take the necessary action which they are told to take. On the other hand, officers also indicated an awareness of variations in responses. This might be in terms of whether the assault is 'minor', as defined by them. One officer said that an assault involving 'more than black eyes' would lead to charging. Another officer said there was little to do if the man was calm; if he was, injuries and/or a complaint would be needed before proceeding. Alternatively, proceeding to arrest and charging may occur *without* complaint if, for example, the victim would be in danger of subsequent assault. Some officers were ambivalent to, or even hostile towards, these force

TABLE 9.1 Numbers of agency permissions and agency follow-up contacts by source of referral

Source	No. of men giving permissions	Housing	Social Services	Probation	Police	CPS	Solicitors	Doctors	Men's programmes	Other	Total	Average no. of permissions
Police	14*	–	1 (1)	3* (3)*	13 (28)	4 (4)	8* (3)*	5 (3)	–	4 (4)	38* (46)*	2.7
Men's programmes	11	1 (1)	–	–	3 (6)	1 (1)	2 (2)	2 (2)	10 (10)	1 (1)	20 (23)	1.8
Prison	4	–	1 (1)	6 (6)	5 (5)	5 (5)	3 (2)	1 (1)	–	–	21 (20)	5.25
Probation	7*	–	–	7* (8)*	4 (5)	4 (4)	7* (7)*	1 (1)	–	–	23* (25)*	3.7
Other welfare agencies	4	1 (1)	2 (2)	2 (3)	1 (2)	2 (3)	2 (1)	1 (1)	–	3 (3)	14 (16)	3.5
No agency	2	1 (1)	–	–	–	–	–	–	–	1 (1)	2 (2)	1.0
Total	41*	3 (3)	4 (4)	17* (19)*	26 (46)	16 (17)	21* (14)*	10 (8)	10 (10)	9 (9)	116* (130)*	2.8

* One man referred from both police and Probation.

Figures not in brackets equal number of agency permissions. Figures in brackets equal number of agency follow-up contacts.

TABLE 9.2 *Outcomes in criminal justice system by source of referral*

Source	Total	No involvement with police	Involvement with police	Interviewed by police	Arrested	Charged/ summonsed	Convicted	Probation	Imprisoned
Police	16*	0*	16*	16*	14*	9*	3*	2*	0
Men's programmes									
Project A	11	7	4	3	2	2	2	0	0
Project B	6	2	4	2	3	1	1	0	0
Project C	2	1	1	1	1	1	1	1	0
Total	19	10	9	6	6	4	4	1	0
Prison†									
Prison A	4	0	4	4	4	4	4	4	4
Prison B	3	2	1	1	1	1	1	1	1
Total	7	2	5	5	5	5	5	5	5
Probation	7*	0	7*	7*	7*	7*	7*	7*	3
Other welfare agencies	4	1	3	3	3	3	3	2	0
No agency	8	6	2	2	1	1	0	0	0
Total	60*	19	41*	38	35*	28*	21*	16*	8

* One man referred from both police and Probation.
† Note two men in prison for offences not involving violence to known women.

TABLE 9.3 *Responses of police*

	Yes	No	Don't know
1 Arrested the man	34	6	–
2 Never showed up	5	34	1
3 Told the woman about her legal rights	21	10	9
4 Told the woman to work things out with the man	10	23	7
5 Told her he had broken the law and could be arrested	28	8	4
6 Told him to walk around for a while to cool off	4	35	1
7 Told her about other places to get help, such as refuge	8	24	8
8 Told her they could not do anything	10	25	5
9 Offered to protect her if she tried to leave him	14	21	5
10 Asked her what she had done to make him hit her	14	14	10

policies. One officer saw the force as 'more caring' both through training and practice, but at the same time suggested that 'women manipulate police to expel men after arguments'. He saw the attempt to remove the man as 'slightly unfair', even though he acknowledged that it would probably solve the immediate problem.

While the current policy contrasted with previous policy, which was described as 'up to women to complain', officers often voiced their wish for more discretion, and the use of their judgement to arrest, depending on whether they themselves considered the violence was likely to recommence. Whereas the previous policy encouraged attitudes that meant that there were few arrests for offences against women, the current policy was described as 'compassionate', involving 'listening to both sides' and 'dealing positively with offences disclosed'.

A frequent complaint from officers was that this did not just limit discretion, but its neglect by officers constituted a disciplinary offence for them. Responses to this ranged from, 'I do what I'm told to do' to mis-describing the situation, thus providing a reason not to proceed. As one officer put it: 'she might want him talking to as a warning and they [i.e. certain police officers] will then write off the whole incident, to say that the woman wasn't injured. Now we're only talking about cases where it's very slight injuries, but officers are doing that and risking their careers in the interests of what they think is best in the situation.'

A few officers voiced their concerns around the complexity of 'domestic' situations and the difficulty of devising policy for 'every eventuality'. A few officers also recognized the importance of what was happening with other agencies and of inter-agency links and liaison. Some officers considered that their intervention might not help the situation, for example, by inappropriate arrest.

One officer complained specifically how the Crown Prosecution Service (CPS) often got in touch with them on 'domestics' to ask if the woman wanted to proceed with the case, and that the CPS were checking this to facilitate dropping the case. The officer expressed his frustration at this, in terms of wasting police time rather than the protection of women. A more typical complaint was when women were said to 'change their mind' about wanting the case to proceed, because the man and woman had 'made up'. Some officers saw this as undermining the case whilst others saw this as not necessarily relevant to the prosecution of the case.

Most of the interviews with officers were about one particular 'incident' or occasionally 'series of incidents'. While reference may and should be made to the Domestic Violence Index information system, which catalogues previous personnel and addresses, this is likely to give very limited information on the computerized Viewdata. Individual police officers' understandings of men's violence to women come very largely from their construction as *separate* occasions of violence. What was largely missing in police accounts was a sense of continuity. While Viewdata information may be of some use, it is usually sparse. The continuity of violence by some men is not a prime concern, nor is acting to stop violence beyond the immediate 'incident'. A further important issue is the extent to which *different* kinds of violence are seen as relevant to police intervention and to the police officer. One officer said 'any violence' was relevant; others considered it was physical violence or assault; others included verbal violence and abuse.

For many police, most incidents of what is called 'domestic violence' are defined as relatively isolated or 'one-off' or relatively irresolvable, so that intervention is unlikely to produce change in behaviour. The term 'one-off' is sometimes used to describe relatively isolated incidents, and may carry an ambiguity in terms of it being 'one-off' violence or a 'one-off' call-out. Indeed, according to some officers' reports, arresting is of little use, and may even make the situation worse. Thus men's violence to women is usually understood as either 'inevitable' or discontinuous. It is a very segmented picture that emerges. Even so, only one officer noted that there is no overall co-ordination of agencies in relation to the problem of violence. In most cases, there was little liaison with agencies outside the criminal justice system. The police are centrally concerned with the apprehension of offenders; most are not involved in specific work preventing violence to women, either at policy or individual levels. Eighty-five per cent of even the Special Units' time is devoted to child protection work, rather than violence to women.

A number of areas of concern have become apparent in the work of the police:

- greater attention to the interconnections between men's violence to women and child protection work;
- higher profile to policy and publicity that opposes men's violence to women;
- greater awareness of the continuity of many men's violence to women, and the interconnections between different kinds of violence; need for greater understanding of how some men use excuse and justify violence;
- strict enforcement of force policy;

- greater liaison with other agencies;
- inclusion of all offences, including murder, on the Domestic Violence Index.

The involvement of the Crown Prosecution Service (CPS) follows action of the police and sometimes the courts. A key feature of the CPS's processing of cases is that men's violence to women is defined in terms of alleged offences, which are themselves dealt with in terms of 'legal truths'. Violence is considered as 'incidents' and cases, rather than through continuity over time. CPS involvement begins following police involvement, whether the defendant is charged or summonsed to court. In the latter case, there is both prosecution work and advice work. CPS involvement is then always historical and, in a sense, detached, at a distance from the man and woman concerned.

The processing of cases by the CPS depends on the implementation of *The Code for Crown Prosecutors*. In each agency concerned, violence is defined in a characteristic way by the managers, workers and other staff. These definitions reproduce the agency's function and structure, as well as particular professional and occupational ideologies. This is clearest in the CPS, where there are explicit guidelines on whether or not to proceed to prosecution, in terms of (a) the evidential sufficiency criterion and (b) the public interest criterion. These provide a rational-legal framework for organizational responses to violence. At the time of the research, *The Code for Crown Prosecutors* included the following criteria for determining prosecution: 'likely penalty', 'staleness' (length of time since alleged offence was committed), 'youth', 'old age and infirmity', 'mental disorders', 'sexual offences', 'change in the complainant's attitude' and 'peripheral dependants'. However, all these involve judgement and discretion. 'Presence of slight or minor injuries', 'weak evidence', 'plausible explanation by defendant', 'how realistic is the prospect of conviction?', 'great provocation', 'age', 'previous convictions', 'seriousness' and 'complainant's wishes' were all suggested by CPS staff interviewed.

The revised *Code for Crown Prosecutors*, published in June 1994, is not intended to make substantive changes to the original Code. The new Code is, however, written in clearer language which is more accessible to a non-specialist readership. Accordingly, the section of the Code on 'The Public Interest Test' (rather than 'criterion') is structured through the following sub-sections: 'some common public interest factors in favour of prosecution', 'some common public interest factors against prosecution', 'the relationship between the victim and the public interest', 'youth offenders' and 'police cautions'. Several factors in favour of prosecution are of particular relevance to men's violence to known women. These include: 'the defendant was in a position of authority or trust'; 'the victim of the offence was vulnerable, has been put in considerable fear, or suffered personal attack, damage or disturbance'; 'the offence was motivated by any form of discrimination against the victim's ethnic or national origin, sex, religious beliefs, political views or sexual preference'; and 'there are grounds for believing that the offence is likely to be continued or repeated, for example, by a history of recurring contact'.

There are a wide range of reasons why a case might be terminated. One case began with an alleged assault in December, and was eventually terminated the following May, with the woman complainant dropping the case, and the police unable to trace the complainant, even though it was said that she was still living with the defendant (the man). Even though punching, kicking and bruising to arms and legs, along with shouting and swearing, had been alleged, there was insufficient evidence to proceed.

Another way in which cases are filtered is through the reduction of the charge. Another man was initially charged with Section 47 (assault occasioning actual bodily harm) following stabbing, when he was 'taking the knife off her' (in his statement). Though other injuries were received, no hospital treatment was given. The initial charge was withdrawn; the woman did not want prosecution to proceed. Instead, breach of the peace was admitted by the man. The CPS requested binding over (the taking of recognizances to be of good behaviour to keep the peace). Magistrates declined this, deciding future breach was unlikely; no sanctions were imposed.

CPS files are normally kept only for three years, in accordance with national practice and instruction. The file of a man who was imprisoned for five years, following stabbing his wife, was not requested when he murdered another woman in a different region some years later, after release. This raises two questions: the policy of destruction of files and the monitoring of files between CPS branches.

A number of areas of concern have become apparent in the work of the CPS:

1   The reasons for not proceeding to prosecution with a case are clearly varied. The reasons given by individual CPS solicitors elaborate on the formal reasons for not proceeding, recorded in the *Code for Crown Prosecutors*. This means that even though the CPS is working within a given legal framework, there is room for discretion in particular cases, especially in respect to the public interest criterion. Not proceeding may involve dropping the case or prosecuting a lesser charge. This is especially important in cases where the parties are known to each other. The questions that arise include: How can different CPS solicitors develop a greater knowledge and awareness of the need to prosecute? How can greater consistency be guaranteed between CPS solicitors and between offices in this regard? This may involve a combination of the development of specialist expertise in cases of men's violence to known women and across the board training for all CPS solicitors.

2   CPS work is defined in terms of the prosecution of particular cases. While a great deal of information is collected together on each case, this may not include the full context, such as the continuity of violence over

time. This raises several questions: Can the mass of information collected be put to any further use? Can the context of violence be more fully included? Can the woman's perspective be more fully acknowledged beyond just being a witness to the alleged offence, for example, could there be options for her in changing the situation? The interconnections between men's violence to known women and child protection work are rarely considered in CPS work. The interconnections are important in terms of understanding the full damage of men's violence, and then the need to prosecute cases with maximum urgency; they are also important in terms of the operation of the two separate systems of prosecution. How can these connections be recognized more fully?

3 The liaison of CPS with other agencies is extensive, but primarily for the compilation of evidence to inform prosecution or not. It is not liaison designed to assist the women or alleviate the situation. The question that arises is: Can liaison with agencies be extended in such ways? This includes liaison between the agencies of criminal justice and civil law.

4 The work of the CPS would be eased by being able to obtain statements and other evidential information more quickly. This often relies on police who have their own work demands and priorities. Is it possible to have specific police concerned with CPS-identified follow-up work? Would this assist the process? Speed in obtaining evidence is especially important in cases involving people known to each other.

5 The non-availability and destruction of files is crucial. In a few cases there were problems of obtaining files. The destruction of files is a particular concern when men are released from prison and then re-offend.

The Probation Service[1] and probation officers become involved with men who have been violent to known women within the full range of the Service's activities. These include pre-sentence reports to court, community supervision, the management and staffing of hostels, the work of the probation teams in prisons, supervision of men on life sentence, through-care, the management and staffing of sex offenders programmes, family court welfare work, and liaison with other agencies. Despite this, the amount of ongoing direct work on the problem of men's violence to known women was found to be disappointingly low. Indeed, in one case, the man was referred for the research interview because such work was not being done, and it was thought by the officer that the interview might be helpful to him in addressing his problem. Another officer said they were pleased to have the chance to talk through the case since they had not had the opportunity to do so within the Probation Service as the man was not a lifer.

Sometimes the involvement of Probation is relatively short term. In one case the involvement spanned just three weeks, from appearance in the magistrates' court on charge of Section 47 assault. Because of the bail condition, he entered a bail hostel, until a conditional discharge, when he returned home. A rather different example was of a man on a probation order in relation to several offences that did not include violence to known women. This led to joint work with him and his wife to establish a mutual agenda. In the course of this work, the man's violence to her came to light. However, no energy or commitment to address this was reported by the officer. The man had, however, recognized that he himself might be 'ducking the issue'.

There are also examples of more intensive attempts to deal with the problem. One man was placed on a probation order, following conviction for deception. The problems of alcohol and of violence to his partner were recognized by the officer. This was followed by assault on his partner. The officer's work was aimed at reducing the man's offending, protecting the partner and providing a home for the child. The understanding of the man's violence was complex: drink, insecurity, violence in his childhood, wanting power and control. The officer considered these factors and the man learnt something about his responsibility for violence, but he still did not see himself as a violent person, and therefore would not do any work to reduce it. In fact, during the period of the probation order, he managed to get two Section 47 charges of assault on the woman dropped or dismissed.

Several key issues on the probation response to men's violence to known women emerged from this study:

1 Some cases showed officers' lack of involvement in confronting the problem of the man's violence to known women. Some officers were concerned to get the man to recognize the problem but were unsuccessful or largely so. Rarely did intervention beyond this actually work on the problem. When this was done it was sometimes done so in ways that diverted attention from the man's responsibility. Thus the difficulties found in probation work are of three main kinds:
   (a) avoidance of the problem by the officer;
   (b) avoidance of the problem by the man;
   (c) lack of avoidance, but lack of success, through intransigence of the problem, and the use of inappropriate approaches.
2 There is a need to counter the avoidance of the problem by probation officers. This is being addressed by the 'Domestic Violence Policy and Codes of Practice'. Such policies need careful follow-up by individual officers and teams.
3 There is a need for understanding the complexity of men's violence to known women, rather than explaining it away by 'drink' or 'the relationship'.
4 There is a need for more attention to links between men's violence to known women and child protection work. It was unclear how this latter system interrelated with officers' work on men's violence to known women.

5 There is a need to ensure that developing focused work on men's violence to known women is done in a way that maintains and develops support for women and women's projects.[2]

Social Services

This research found a low level of men's contact with Social Services Departments. Only eight of the men reported contact with Social Services Departments or voluntary social work agencies. In theory, there are many ways in which men who have been violent to known women may come in contact with Social Services Departments. Indeed, this is possible in all the activities and functions of Social Services, including child protection and preventative work with children; community care; mental health and psychiatric work; medical social work; work with people with disabilities, impairments and learning difficulties; and work with elderly people. In practice, Social Services Departments in recent years have become increasingly focused on child protection, work with people with disabilities and mental health problems, and work with elderly people.

The specialization on child protection in Social Services Departments reflects broader movements in the prioritization of certain potential welfare recipients over others. This may reproduce distinctions between 'dangerous'/ 'non-dangerous', 'deserving'/'undeserving' people or families, with the latter in each case not receiving assistance. Such priorities and categorizations may both exclude categories of people from assistance, and neglect the fact that many people in the 'dangerous' or 'undeserving' categories may also be experiencing, or have experienced, violence. These distinctions may also obscure the fact that child abuse is also usually violence to women, and violence to women is also child abuse, when children are present in the home or the relationship (Stark and Flitcraft, 1988; Mullender, 1997). Thus, although child abuse is usually distinguished from violence to women, child protection intervention can often be intervention against violence to women, and intervention against violence to women can often be child protection intervention (see Bowker et al., 1988; Mullender and Morley, 1994).

The limited involvement with Social Services might be considered to be partly the result of the way that the sample was recruited. However, even men who reported a long history of violence to women did not usually report contact with Social Services Departments in relation to their violence. In addition, many other professionals and workers do work that has some similarities with the tasks of social workers and social services. These include Relate counsellors, GPs, psychiatrists, psychotherapists, nurses, group counsellors and therapists, where they are focusing on violence itself, addiction, or some other issue, as well as probation officers. Local authority social services are surrounded by a mass of other agencies that may provide *aspects* of social work to men who have been violent to known women. In this context, Social Services are something of an empty centre to this ring of agencies, other than where specific allegations of child abuse are investigated.

Furthermore, while the *issue* of men's violence to known women can be relevant in all aspects of the work of Social Services, the specific involvement of men in this work is much more problematic. When Social Services Departments offer support and services to 'women fleeing violence' or women who have experienced violence from known men, the primary intention is to do work with the women, not the men. This leaves open the place of direct work with the men who have been violent. While the absence of men from work with women may be welcomed, the absence of men's contact with Social Services is problematic. This is especially so if it simply means men persisting with violence or moving on to be violent to another woman. Thus, in terms of the work of Social Services Departments, men may be both they who need to be resisted in order to change the situation of women and children, and they who need to be assisted to stop the violence and prevent future violence to that woman or other women. These two, and in many ways contradictory, tasks may of course become entangled with all manner of other considerations and potential difficulties and demands, for example, addictions, mental health, disability, the man's own abuse as a boy.

Of the five men who gave permission for follow-up interviews with Social Services, one yielded no records on either the client index or the Child Protection Register, despite the man's own admission of involvement, and his conviction and imprisonment for murder. Of the others, three contacts were in relation to children, and the other was a contact of a more general nature. Three of the men had contacts with Social Services Departments, one had contact with a voluntary social services agency and one had contacts with both.

In the last case, the man was referred to the research from a voluntary social work agency. He was also involved with local Social Services because his 'mentally handicapped' stepson was in care with another Social Services Department, and living at home at trial. This work was focused on reviews of this placement, together with some concern for child protection regarding other children in the man's family. Social Services knew of the man's assault on his wife, his arrest, her hospitalization and then his release to look after the children, as his wife was in hospital. This was at the suggestion of Social Services, as they did not feel that the children were in danger, even though the voluntary social work agency supervising most of the family were not happy with this. The man was convicted for assault with a nine-month suspended sentence. In the research he reported violence to the woman on more than 15 occasions. According to him, the question of his violence was not addressed by the local authority social worker.

The voluntary sector social work agency continued to supervise the rest of the family, while Social Services maintained statutory supervision of the stepson. The violence to the woman was not a focus of Social Services work, and indeed it was affirmed that violence from a man to a woman is never one of Social Services' responsibilities. The social worker concerned did, however, contact a voluntary men's programme, which the man attended for one session and found to be 'a waste of time'.

The voluntary social work agency made a variety of interventions with the family, including:

- working alongside the family member and helping them decide what they wanted to do;
- supporting the wife in taking legal action, advising and counselling her;
- working with the man on how to control his violence;
- letting the man know that the social worker would support the woman if he was violent to her, i.e. help her to find a place to stay if she wanted to leave;
- looking at the circumstances in which violence had occurred with both of the partners, so they could both try to change the situation to prevent these circumstances arising again.

The man became more willing to discuss the issue of his violence when he was facing legal proceedings. The overall outcome was reported by the voluntary sector social worker as an improvement in the man's and woman's relationship, and, as far as the agency knew, the stopping of the physical violence, though some problems remained, and a great improvement in the care of the children.

In general, a number of conclusions can be drawn from these reports on Social Services work:

- the need to relate child protection work and work on men's violence to known women;
- the need to consider men's violence to known women in other sectors of Social Services work;
- the need to consider men's violence to known women as a priority in its own right;
- the need for focused work with men who have been violent to known women while maintaining and developing support for women. This needs to include recording of men's violence to known women, and the development of inter-agency work.

Health Agencies

The health care system is an extremely important part of the pattern of men's contact with agencies. For present purposes, health care agencies include general practitioners, casualty and other hospital services, community health and psychiatric services, and addiction agencies. The general system of health care agencies is concerned with a number of functions and tasks. These include: the prevention of illness and disease; the promotion of health and welfare, both physical and mental; the treatment of illness, disease and injury. The issue of violence is relevant to all of these. There are also a large number of secondary functions and tasks, most of which are relevant to the problem of men's violence to known women. These include pastoral and counselling work, addiction and substance abuse work, psychiatric services, day care, psychotherapy, casualty services, health education, family planning, sexual problems work, health visiting and community nursing.

An important general issue is to consider the relationship of the problem of men's violence to known women with health services and health care agencies. There is a clear, yet often unacknowledged, connection in that violence is bad for your health. Violence causes physical and mental damage, injury, illness, and a host of other negative effects, both immediate and longer term. Specifying the effects for women who have experienced violence from known men has become complicated not least because of the controversies around the 'battered woman syndrome' (Walker, 1979; also see Dobash and Dobash, 1992). This controversy is partly around the danger of reducing women's experience of violence to a syndrome, and in doing so characterizing the woman as a victim, and as unable to speak for herself. Even so the obvious connection of men's violence to women and health services is in terms of women's need for medical and related assistance following violence. There is also, however, the need for preventative and supportive assistance to women from health services. This leaves open the question of men's relationship to health services. Health may affect the ability to be violent; indeed the ability to be physically violent may be seen as an indication of health (Hearn, 1992a).

On the other hand, violence can be seen as to indicate a lack of health, and a need for assistance. In the man's case this lack of health and well-being may be linked to other personal/medical problems, such as drink, drugs, depression, the man's own abuse as a boy, and so on. Men may themselves approach medical and health care agencies for these 'other' problems and then mention violence in relative passing. Another form of referral is for men to become involved with the health service because of a mental health condition or a particular physiological problem following an overdose or long-term addiction. A third referral route is to the psychiatric services following the man's involvement with the criminal justice system. This is especially important in cases of murder and other violent crimes involving major damage. It may also become significant when the violence is not only to the woman but also to animals or himself. It is also important in the case of sexual offences. The point remains that violence to known women is not usually defined as constituting a psychiatric problem. Taken together there are thus a large number of possible reasons for men's involvement with health care agencies in relation to violence.

There is a relatively high level of contacts with health agencies. Of the 55 men who reported contacts with agencies, 26 had had contact with their GP in relation to their violence, 7 had had medical/hospital contact, and 13 had

had mental health contact, including as day patients and outpatients. In addition, 27 had had contact with therapists, counsellors or men's programmes (20 for the last), and one had received assistance from an addiction unit.

Six GP contacts revealed the following range of responses. In one case, the GP reported that he had no knowledge of the man's violence even though he himself considered he had discussed it with the GP. This may be due to a lack of documenting of this aspect of the consultation. A second man saw his GP for 'addiction-related' reasons. He was then seen fortnightly over 18 months during the course of which regular drugs were prescribed with a view to decreasing his use. The violence was never seen by the GP as a significant problem. Another man was also seen weekly for alcohol problems, as well as for general ill-health, insomnia and chronic gastroenteritis. While the man also complained about his wife's drinking, he did acknowledge his own irritability and violence as a problem. The GP saw bringing up the problem of violence as the doctor's responsibility. Moving beyond that was more difficult. Another GP reported concern with the woman and children, especially the possible neglect of the children, rather than with the man. While it was acknowledged that an attempt might be made to get expert help for the woman if she could not control the man's violent behaviour, if the woman's behaviour was 'provocative' then this would not be attempted. Generally, this GP considered there was not much point approaching the man unless he wanted to change. A further GP contact involved violence by the man to the woman and the children, along with problems of alcohol abuse and depression. While the violence to the woman was clearly known about, it was not a focus of the contact. Other GP contacts involved the man's mother intervening with the GP because of her son's violence to himself and property at home, and his overdosing; a psychiatric assessment on another man included no specific mention at all of his violence to the woman; and contact with an addiction unit. In all cases the violence to the woman was not a focus of the intervention.

The only possible successful intervention or involvement was a GP referral of a man to mental health services for his violence. This led to his referral by a psychologist to assessment for group psychotherapy. This intervention was, unusually, focused on his 'violent outbursts' and attempting to constrain his 'violent impulses'. Relationship difficulties and early experiences were focused upon. The intervention was seen as successful but limited. The clinical psychologist considered that a longer term psychotherapeutic group intervention would be appropriate. In the event the man became a committed member of a men's programme.

It is evident that it is rare for medical/health care agencies to intervene directly against men's violence. It may be noted within the confidential clinical relationship, this and other problems of addiction, depression, self-harm, and child abuse may be pursued. But violence to known women is not usually a focus of GPs' involvement; indeed it may not even be uppermost when psychiatric referrals are made for this reason. There is need for:

- more focused recognition of the problem of men's violence to known women;
- more focused work around the problem of men's violence to known women.

To reduce and eliminate violence prevents damage to women's health. It may also assist the health of the men concerned.

Men's Programmes

These programmes, usually organized primarily through group meetings, have received a good deal of attention in recent years. Unlike most agencies, their focus is specifically on the problem of men's violence to known women. Most in the UK have been organized to date on voluntary rather than court-mandated bases. There are, however, signs of a shift towards more court-mandated programmes organized by or contracted out by the Probation Service. Men often come to voluntary men's programmes in order to retrieve relationships with particular women; they are sometimes referred by GPs or other professionals. Such groups may involve structured group seminars, often of a fixed weekly programme, for example, of 14, 16, 20 weeks. There are also sometimes individual sessions. Some programmes also involve work with partners and women's (partner) groups.

The programme leaders understood the violence of the men in a diverse series of ways – men's upbringing, rejection by parents, father's violence to mothers, the man's desire to control and dominate, overcontrol of his emotions, difficulty in dealing with women's assertion, the company with which the man mixed, as well as psychiatric and addiction problems. The key issues here are that:

- the man's violence was the focus;
- the men were seen more as individuals, with different individual histories and 'characters';
- a mixture of psychological and social reasons for the man's violence was often recognized;
- there was a resistance to explaining violence away as a function of addiction;
- there was sometimes an understanding of issues of power, control and domination.

There is increasing interest in, and use of, methods of intervention focusing on men's power over and control of women, rather than simply men's anger control. Furthermore, as there are relatively few such groups, they may attract a relatively diverse group of men in terms of the nature of their problem, whilst tending to mainly attract men who can operate in groups and have the resources to get there. Overall these group-based interventions against men's violence can be understood as ways of enhancing men's health and welfare, of sometimes reducing or even stopping violence, and of sometimes, though not always, assisting women's health and welfare. The part these programmes can play in men moving away from violence is discussed in the next chapter (pp. 193–198).

Reflecting on Organizations and Violence[3]

Men's violence interconnects in various ways with the organizational context, structure and process of agencies. The initial violence by men usually takes place outside the formal agencies that respond to violence; it is generally extra-organizational; and it is often associated with intense emotions, even when the violence is calculated and planned. Organizational responses to such violence transfer the violence into an organizational frame of reference, including rules, hierarchies and organization–client relations.

Agency responses need to be located within the context of men's general domination of women. The various agencies involved operate within their own networks of interorganizational relations, with their own separations and connections. There are in effect arrays of organizations that deal with violence, even though they are rarely considered together in policy or analytical terms. These arrays are diffuse, with many different organizations dealing with violence in different ways and with different definitions, explanations and methods of record-keeping. The complexity of these arrays is increased by the dominant construction of men's violence to women as a private matter, albeit through public discourses. Such constructions are being challenged and are changing, not least through police policy and inter-agency work.

State organizations, professions and other organizations, and their respective interventions around men's violence to women, are themselves gendered. Usually this involves men's domination of managements, men's numerical domination of the criminal justice agencies, as well as the women's greater presence in social work, therapeutic, counselling and medical organizations, especially at the lower and sometimes the middle hierarchical levels. Definitions and explanations of violence by agencies and agency staff are themselves often dominated by men. They may be set within larger systems managed and defined by men, even though there may be room for feminist work by women within those confines. Possible exceptions include some small voluntary organizations and GP practices, though even such small-scale organizations are themselves located within broader spheres of organizational power dominated by men. The organization(s) of violence thus represent a web of men's managements of violence, structured through an impressive, overlapping collection of professional cultures dominated by men (cf. Hearn, 1990: 67). In the case of 'domestic violence' there is the added complication that this has itself become a possible specialization for women within organizational hierarchies which remain dominated by men.

Organizational responses to violence involve interaction *between* individuals and agencies and *between* agencies. These organizations have different relationships to violence, including organizations with legitimated use of violence (police, prisons); organizations created to respond to violence (Probation, CPS, courts, solicitors, men's programmes); and other organizations that are involved in responding but have not been created for that purpose (Social Services, housing, doctors). Different agencies involve both different orientations to violence, in terms of its goals, tasks, definitions and presence/absence of policies on violence, and professional and occupational ideologies. Professional background assumptions include the extent to which anger, stress, aggression and violence are understood to exist or correlate with each other. Formal hierarchical redefinitions are also, in some cases, reinforced by statutory responsibilities and the power of law. This may lead to further conflict, even violence, between those with different access to power, whether within organizations or between the staff and clients.

Violence may be a central part of the organization's work, with that task (though not necessarily the violence) seen as non-problematic. In organizations created to respond to violence, 'violence' becomes both an element in achieving goals, and a part of routine work performance. Violence may be transformed into a file, a case. In other organizations, for example, housing agencies, Social Services and general counselling, the relation to men's violence is less clear. Some housing agencies are engaged in attempting to house men who have been violent; others take a different view, and specifically attempt to bar such men from tenancies.

While police and prisons define and relate to violence in quasi-legal terms, this is supplemented by their legitimated use of violence and their own hierarchical structure. Such definitions may be overlain by professional ideologies that are either tolerant, even accepting of violence, or are unambiguously opposed to violence. Dankwort (1988) also points to how organizational and technobureaucratic forces tend to subordinate more radical practice and dilute ideological positions inconsistent with the prevailing ideological climate. According to this 'logic', management interests go before innovation, and women-centred work, practice and policies become incorporated within dominant professional and managerial ideologies.

Bringing an 'instance' of extra-organizational violence into an organization brings further work relations to that violence. A widespread organizational process is bringing violence into a *collectivity*, and *reference* to that violence being conducted through *talking*. While policy development on men who have been violent to women is not a concern of most agencies, where it does occur, talk is the main medium of agency intervention. Men talking about violence to agency personnel give a descriptive account of the process of events, a subjective justification of them, and are part of the organizational process. *Talking* about violence may occur within the context of such a *collectivity*. Talking may support, condone, reproduce, note, counteract, punish the violence. The collectivity may be involved differentially in that process, with its own dynamics, which may include violent dynamics, whether between workers/staff/members/residents/inmates/managers, and so on. Particular extra-organizational violences may be talked about, and these intersect with (potential) violences in organizations.

While initial police contact usually involves talking about violence, this soon switches to writing about violence and the accumulation of 'evidence' through statements and written reports. Legal process, and the work of the CPS, invests very heavily in the written file, and the establishment of evidential sufficiency and public interest criteria, even though court process valorizes the spoken word. Probation was found to be surprisingly lacking in direct work on men's violence to known women. This may be changing with the adoption of explicit guidelines on work on domestic violence. Prisons convert the organizational availability of violence into concrete form, so that the very structure and form of the organization is custodial. Men on long sentences, such as lifers, not surprisingly often structure their accounts as before and after the relevant crime. This takes place in the context of the availability of organizational violence and violence between prisoners. Most importantly, criminal justice organizations are dominated by men in staffing, management and policies. Accordingly, men's definitions, explanations and ways of writing and talking about violence are dominant in these organizational contexts.

Organizational processes also operated in men's programmes. In these relatively non-hierarchical and non-formal organizations, the main medium was talk in groups and some written notes. Some groups also had individual or couples sessions. The groups were sometimes guided by written documents, such as the MOVE (Men Overcoming Violence) booklet *Be Safe!* (Waring and Wilson, 1990). Some of the current programmes are guided by the Power and Control model set out in the Duluth Program (Pence and Paymar, 1990). Within these programmes, without a clear feminist or pro-feminist direction, it is always likely that the definitions and explanations of violence may be those that derive from the group process and men's experiences there. Violence to women can then always be redefined as something else, as a problem of 'upbringing', of anger management or of group processes (see Gondolf and Russell, 1986). Such programmes may also role-play violence and use dynamics within the group to educate men about violence to women. They sometimes adopt masculinized language from films, sport and violence, such as 'time-outs', 'Peckinpah stills', 'triggers'.

Organizational responses to men's violence characteristically involve negotiation within a zone of uncertainty: about what constitutes violence, why and how violence occurred, what to do about violence. This is not to say that each agency is unified, far from it; rather disunity, tensions and even conflict in definitions can characterisize agencies. This was clearest in the Probation Service where there is considerable variation in the extent to which men's violence to known women is treated as a priority. In addition, Probation straddles the traditions of law and the traditions of social work, so that different officers may develop a different relation to their work, depending on their team location, speciality and personal style. One way in which these tensions between legal and social work traditions are mediated is through explaining violence by drink. This both confirms the man's culpability (in legal discourse) and creates a space for him being different at other times (in social work discourse).

Differentiations of violence and clientdom interrelate with other distinctions around whether organizational personnel are concerned with only men known or potential clients who are now known; with only men who are sought or those who are not sought too; and whether violence is seen as separate from or an integral part of the man's/client's masculinity. In men's programmes, which define violence as the prime problem, it is also seen as part of the 'whole person'. Yet at the same time, such groups are founded on the assumption that it is possible for men to change. They thus embody a tension between a broader view of violence/masculinity, and a commitment to changing that connection.

Responding to violence is likely to involve engaging with the pain and damage from violence, past or present. The place of the violated is under-valued and undervoiced in most organizational contexts. There may even be a sense in which organizational process in the form of talking and writing is (usually) antithetic to the recognition of the full experience of pain from violence. On the other hand, organizing around pain and damage can produce very powerful organizational processes, not least in the movement from violation to anger to action. Such organizational dynamics and con-tradictions may be specially important in organizations of survivors of abuse. Organizations responding to violence, past or present, may develop ambiguous social processes between destructive violating experiences and 'de-violenced' structures and modes of being.

Then there is the place of violence within everyday managerial and work cultures. Violence becomes 'reduced' to the material task and the culture of the organization – it can be processed, reconstructed, ignored, joked about, like any other cultural organizational currency. In one sense, 'violence' is like any other work object, to be worked on and made 'social'.

An example of this is how the work process may relate to the reproduc-tion of masculinities and men's power. Several times in this research I have been told 'horror stories' by men workers; these have either been about particular horrific cases of men's violence to women or men's threats on men professionals. These stories may have several meanings; they may simultaneously convey a sense of both voyeurism and bravado. They may confirm a certain kind of masculinity ('I can take it') while at the same time admitting an emotional response to violence. Past events are objectified and externalized, and simultaneously the worker is saying something for his benefit, dealing with the feelings that persist. This kind of talk can of course easily slip into a verbally or even physically violent work culture, as when

clients are characterized as 'full of shit'. In the context of the men professional workers, such as the probation workers, solicitors and social
workers encountered in this research, there is often a profound ambiguity
between a routine 'straight' masculinity (set within a conventional homosexual subtext) and a less obviously heterosexual, more ambiguous sexuality
that is saying 'I'm not like that.'

A further set of organizational processes derive from *the availability of
organizational violence* to respond to men's violence to women. This applies
within the criminal justice system in different ways to all the relevant state
agencies: police, CPS, courts, Probation, prisons. In particular, police and
prison staff are available to assist the work of the other elements of the
criminal justice system, if need be. An important issue then becomes how
that use of violence is controlled within and outside the hierarchy. Police
officers may thus operate in ways that both maintain rules and hierarchy
and seek to maximize discretion. Among officers interviewed, one of their
common complaints was the lack of discretion in the context of an arrest
policy toward men who have been violent to known women. Some of the
individual men interviewed spoke of police condoning their violence ('I
would've done the same myself'); others saw arrest as less dramatic, even
routine ('They just took me in'); others still complained of violence from the
police ('. . . gave me a good going over').

While there are major divergences between different parts of the system,
the availability of organizational violence is a continuing theme. These very
conditions of making violence available make further violence possible.
Violence is *talked about, written about* and then reconstituted, albeit
unevenly, as *organizational violence*. We thus come full circle from doing to
talking to writing to doing violence again. The exact way in which these
combinations of talking violence, writing violence and (potentially) doing
organizational violence may operate varies considerably in different parts of
the criminal justice system.

In the face of all this, the resort to procedures and proceduralism is
perhaps not surprising. Men's violence to women outside the organizations
in question becomes 'reduced' to an element of the organizational structure,
function, operation and process. This involves interrelations between men's
violence to women, men's explanations of that violence, organizational/
professional–client relations within worker culture, formal organizational
goals and talks, and violence in the organization more generally. Through
these kinds of interconnections we are concerned not only with the links
between client relations and team/work cultures, but with the links between
client relations and patriarchism/anti-patriarchalism in organizations.

Of particular interest is the way in which the accounts given by individual
men and the accounts of staff in agencies that deal with them often mirror
each other. Both individual men and agency men may both avoid the topic
of violence and reproduce it by treating it as a separable activity (Jukes,
1993): this separation of 'violence' from men's power and control in general
is part of the problem. For example, men in contact with Probation may see

their violence to women as secondary to other crime and may talk at length of their violence to men. In contrast, men in men's programmes may accept that violence to women is the central problem and may develop relatively sophisticated explanations thereof; workers in these programmes similarly see violence as central and develop complex understandings of it that relate both general questions of power and control and the individualities of individual men.

Working on and responding to violence involves not just dealing directly with violence but also constructing accounts and explanations of violence. While the place of violence within the structure and function of organizations is very significant in providing the broad contours of organizational responses, it does not fully determine the complexities of violence within the organizational process, and how these are lived and experienced by organizational members.

Concluding Comments

This chapter has analysed organizational dynamics in agency responses to men's violence to known women. In general, such organizational structures and processes are a means of managing, masking and obscuring the pervasiveness of violence. In organizations that respond to violence, particular attention needs to be directed to the reconstruction of violence as work and work routine, and the unanticipated consequences of such ways of working, such as the mirroring of accounts of violence by those who have been violent 'in the first place'.

There is also a need to reflect on the more general relationship of violence, talk, writing and organization. Talking about violence and writing about violence are produced, enacted, reproduced and received materially. Talk and writing are both discursive and material. This theme is explored by MacKinnon (1994) in *Only Words* in relation to pornography – 'to say it is to do it, and to do it is to say it'. Accordingly, she argues, 'Unwelcome sex talk is an unwelcome sex act.' Similarly, unwelcome or threatening talk or writing about violence is an (unwelcome or threatening) violent act. If a man is violent or speaks about his violence in a threatening or unwelcome way, that too may constitute violence. This might concern the minimizing of his violence, the exclusion of violent acts from the definition of violence, and the use of justifications and excuses to explain away violence in order to avoid blame or responsibility respectively.

Minimizing violence, excluding sexual violence and child abuse from violence against women, and providing excuses and justifications for violence may be reproduced in talking and writing. This may be done by men who have been violent, by workers working with these men, and by managers in policy documents and documentation. These definitions and explanations assist in the reproduction of violence in the community, as in the production of agency policies and practices that reinforce violence, whether by implicit or explicit means. Such diminution and reinforcement of men's violences to women may go on alongside the production of greater violence or potential violence by men to men. Such agencies, which are generally dominated by men and generally use men's dominant definitions and explanations of violence, structure the lives of women and men, and in turn the reproduction of violence.

10

Moving Away From Violence?

How do men move away from the use of violence? How do men act against violence? While we can ask what happens after men have been violent, in another sense, once men have been violent there is not an easy division between the past, the present and the future. Past violence continues to form the present, and to affect how the future is understood. In some scenarios, once violent, men never stop, not least in terms of the persistence of threat and potential threat of violence. Furthermore, the mere *presence* of men can be violent and experienced as violating in some situations.

The social processes that occur after violence are characteristically contradictory. For example, the support that men may receive from other men after is likely to be highly ambiguous in its effects – both supportive of change and reproductive of further violence (Hearn, 1996c, 1998c). In this chapter, I focus specifically on how men may move away from violence, and the possible place of agency interventions in that process.

There are a number of different ways of understanding and conceptualizing men's changes. To a large extent these different approaches are based in different theoretical assumptions and as such parallel the different explanations of men's violence (see Chapter 2). They range from psychological to social psychological to sociological to sociopolitical models. Similarly, different models of intervention with men who have been violent to women suggest different models of how men change more generally. For example, Dankwort (1992–3) distinguishes psychodynamic, systemic, social learning (cognitive-behavioural) and pro-feminist power analysis models. This is similar to Adams's (1988) distinction between the following treatment models for men who batter: the insight model (ego psychology and related approaches), the ventilation model ('anger' expression), the interaction model (systems theory), cognitive-behavioural and psychoeducational models (learning theory) and pro-feminist models (power analysis). Edleson and Tolman (1992) have produced a wide-ranging review of interventions for men who batter, using the framework of a 'comprehensive ecological approach'. This is in effect an application of systems theory not just to interaction between the couple, but across the range of social systems from the individual man (microsystem) to the society (macrosystem). Interventions examined include individual treatment, couple treatment, group intervention and 'social system' intervention (that is, prevention and early intervention in educational, religious, medical and employment settings, criminal justice and community interventions). What is equally interesting is that these kinds of classification in relation to intervention and treatment imply different areas of change in men's lives more generally. Thus it is possible to make tentative connections between (a) explanations and theories of men's violence; (b) models of treatment and intervention with men (whether between men's programmes [Dankwort, Adams] or more comprehensively [Edleson and Tolman]); and (c) broader arenas and models of men's change.

These contrasts in approach can thus be made both between different arenas of change, and within interventions in terms of different models of intervention. Or to put it slightly differently, differences in explanation are reproduced both within different interventions and between different arenas, regardless of intervention. The major arenas of change are now examined as follows: the man himself; his relationship with the woman; wider social support and relationships with and responses from family, friends, neighbours and communities; the policy, practice and impact of agencies; and men's programmes.

In each arena there may or may not be attempts to intervene to reduce or stop men's violence to women, just as there may be actions, more or less conscious, which assist in maintaining or even increasing their violence. Furthermore, shifts in one arena are likely to be intermingled with changes in other arenas.

The Individual Man[1]

A first set of questions concerns the individual man who has been violent. What is his relationship to that violence? Is he aware of being violent? What is his orientation to or motivation towards moving away from violence? Is there any possibility of him conceiving of the possibility of not being violent? Is he interested at all in this aspect of his life and others' lives?

A recent evaluation study by Dobash, Dobash, Cavanagh and Lewis (1996a) has identified eight key issues in assessing men's change away from violence to women, as follows: recognition by the man that change is possible; the man's motivation to change; why change?; what change?; internal and external mechanisms for change; shifts in the discourse (of irresponsibility/responsibility); the medium of change; and specific events. They particularly stress the importance of men moving away from (a reliance on) external constraints and control to internal, personally held controls that reflect changes in ways of thinking and the practice of new ways of relating to others. As such, 'from seeing violence as "caused" by external forces, primarily the actions of their partners, they begin to "own" their violence and to recognize they are responsible for their acts and for any transformation that may occur' (Dobash et al., 1996b: 4). This approach has the great advantage of linking change in men with their relationship to agency intervention and indeed surveillance. As such, it is based in social analysis whilst recognizing the importance of individual change.

The emphasis on the shifts from external controls to internal controls has some parallels with the results of the current research. However, here a more complex and more contradictory pattern of factors is discernible. First, this present research found that the extent of violence reported by the man correlated with both increased depression and reduced self-esteem. This is broadly in line with previous research that has stressed the non-assertiveness of men who batter compared with men who are 'non-batterers' (for example, Hotaling and Sugarman, 1986; Maiuro et al., 1986) and the relative depression of batterers (Maiuro et al., 1988). Men may achieve through violence one kind of power but they do not achieve happiness. However, this research found no correlation between the extent of the violence reported and men's sense of 'self-mastery', of ability to control their own future life. One might have expected that a move to greater internal controls might have been indicated by a greater sense of self-mastery. Furthermore, this sense of self-mastery was also not affected by the institutional location of men between, say, prison and the community. Men's sense of control of their own future appears to derive from other sources; it may also conflate men's sense of control of self (including stopping violence) and men's sense of control of others (including women). Furthermore, the existence of personal resources for men – both material and psychological – can serve to either increase or decrease the man's violence. Personal resources are available for changing the man himself or for resisting change (see Hearn, 1996c).

This research also measured the social psychological 'coping strategies' of the men interviewed, and specifically whether the men used active or passive (avoidant) strategies, and whether those strategies were primarily behavioural or cognitive. Interestingly, this showed that the extent of violence reported by the man did not appear to relate to particular kinds of strategies but rather that greater violence was associated with the increasing use of all three main types of strategies, that is, active-behavioural (for example, seeing a relevant agency); active-cognitive (for example, trying to understand or redefine the situation); avoidance (for example, smoking, drinking or eating more). It is as if as men do more violence, they also learn more ways of surviving with that (possibly) uncomfortable fact. The menu of coping strategies increases along with the menus of violence and ways of talking about violence. In this way, doing more violence may be accompanied by doing more forms of 'coping' and producing more variety in accounts of those violences. More generally, this research casts doubt on the applicability of the concepts of 'coping' and 'coping strategies' to men who have been violent to women. This is not least because 'coping' is a profoundly contradictory notion – it can refer to managing a situation so that a tolerable life can be lived by the self or others, or it can mean tolerating the intolerable, in this case violence.

Thus the concept of coping is a complex one when applied to men doing violence. For men to 'cope with' their violence might mean that men are attempting to find ways of changing the situation. This might involve stopping the violence and leaving the woman. Coping might also refer to men's attempts to minimize any effects upon them even if the violence is continued. This could involve avoiding legal intervention and ignoring or distancing from the effects of the violence. For men, 'coping' can simultaneously increase and reduce the likelihood of further violence. It can also be simultaneously cognitive and behavioural.

A few men may not 'cope' to the extent of choosing to destroy themselves through suicide, self-mutilation or addiction. For men to kill themselves is clearly violence against themselves; it can also be experienced by others or interpreted in some cases as a development or extension of their violence against women, and indeed sometimes children.

The Man's Relationship with the Woman

A second arena or aspect of change is the nature of the man's relationship with the woman – this includes the length of the relationship; the power relations in and around it; the occurrence of key changes or crises; its beginning and possible end. While these kinds of conditions provide the setting of the man's violence, what is of most relevance is the way in which most of the men interviewed were able to abstract the violence from these broader questions of the relationship between themselves and the women. Thus violence, the events leading up to the violence, and even the attempt to reduce or stop violence might be described in some detail, but it was rare to find accounts of the way in which their relationship was at the level of everyday life – housework, childcare, intimacy, sexuality, family responsibilities, and so on. The key issue here is men's ability to look at the whole of their relationship to the woman concerned, and change all forms of control and controlling behaviour (Pence and Paymar, 1990).

The men who appeared to be the most committed to stopping their violence were thus concerned with the broad picture of their relationship, not only their violence in isolation. Interestingly, even here there was a possible problem, in the sense that men's reflection on the whole of the relationship with a woman was still focused on that particular relationship rather than their more general relations with women, and indeed men and children. For example, one man who attempted to change his behaviour argued that 'I never got the chance to put it into practice' – as the woman had left him. Similarly, even men who appeared keen to stop their violence did not reflect on their (hetero)sexuality or the relationship of their sexuality and their violence. Thus the man's relationship with the woman, even when examined closely by the man, was generally itself abstracted from wider social and societal issues, including those of family, friendship, community, agency and social structures.

A significant way of men stopping violence, if only temporarily, is for the man or woman to leave. This can occur in a number of ways. First, the man may leave the immediate place where he has 'been violent' to the woman. Men frequently end an account of such violence by adding, 'I just left,' 'I went out,' 'I fucked off,' 'I went to go for a drink.' Second, there is the act of leaving the relationship either temporarily or permanently. This may be initiated and then carried out by the man himself or by the woman. Third, the man may leave the situation through being arrested, placed in custody and possibly imprisoned. This can be for days, weeks, months, years or a life sentence.

Having said that, there are two important caveats that must be added in any analysis of the processes of leaving. First, the period around separation and particularly after leaving may be an especially dangerous one for women, as some men remain insistent on seeking violent contact with the woman. Second, leaving and separation may only be a step to moving to another relationship with another woman, where the man may be as violent or more violent.

Social Support from Family and Friends

Another aspect of men's possible change that was examined in this study was the extent of men's social support networks. Again this notion is contradictory. Social support can help the reproduction of men's violence or it can oppose men's violence. Social support might refer to men's informal networks of friends and relatives, or it might refer to formal agency support that a man might receive, for example, from a counsellor.

At first sight, it might be expected that the more social support a man has the less likely he is to be violent in the first place; this, however, may not be the case in many instances.[2] Indeed this formulation does nothing to account for the violence of those men who enjoy violence, find it satisfying, or see it as a development of passions, even cathartic intimacy. Additionally, some research has shown association between men's 'male peer support and woman abuse' (DeKeseredy, 1990).

Then there is the question of the form of social support in relation to violence. Social support in this respect might be to bolster and support the man's violence and/or its continuation. This may be particularly important in terms of social support from other men (DeKeseredy, 1990). Social support may also be sought and obtained by some men for changing their violent behaviour or for stopping their violence, for example, in men's programmes against violence to women.

In most cases men indicated that family members do not take a lead in directly confronting the man over his violence. A man who had been violent 'loads' of times reported: '. . . our family minds our own business. If he clouts his wife, he clouts his wife. If I clout mine, I clout mine.' Sometimes initiatives are taken indirectly with the man by way of supporting the woman concerned. A 50-year-old man with a long history of assaults said, 'Why don't they [her family/parents] just keep out of it? My mother never interferes with us, my sister doesn't. . . . They never interfere. I resent that [their interfering] with [from] her family, I told her that.' Men from the woman's family rather than the man's own family may attempt to intervene. For example, a man who was imprisoned for multiple assaults on the woman described rather dolefully how: 'They [her brothers] could come up at any time because like I were having a lot of trouble with her brothers. I never got on with her brothers and that. It were just any time. Places where I went.' This was understood by the man as a significant incon- venience in his relationship with the woman and his social life more generally, but not a significant factor in stopping his violence.

It is also important to draw attention to the importance of the character of men's friendships and other social contacts with each other. These may be small or extensive in size but are rarely close in emotional content and built around a critique of men's violence to women (DeKeseredy, 1990; Hearn, 1998c). Often violence to women is associated with patterns of friendship between men in which men explicitly or implicitly either condone such violence or take the position that it is the individual man's business in which friends should not interfere. A number of studies have shown 'that men who have abusive friends are more likely to abuse their own wives or girlfriends. . . . Some researchers have also found a strong relationship between the frequency of abusers' contacts with their friends and female victimization' (Dekeseredy, 1990: 130). Indeed, in some cases for men to 'interfere' is to risk violence between the men concerned.

In this research, the pattern of men's contacts with men was rather similar to that with relatives. However, with men friends direct intervention against the man's violence was even more unusual. Men reported that their men friends either did not intervene at all or gave active support to the violence:

> You don't get involved. I don't get involved, so I don't expect the [friends] to get involved with mine [woman].

Some men have a positive expectation that their men friends will be violent. Accordingly, absence of violence is viewed with suspicion:

> . . . I know men who couldn't be violent even when it's probably better for them and the woman. I think because they're not fully developed people. I'm a bit wary of men who are never violent.

With such attitudes from men and men's friends, it can be very difficult for men to find the kind of social support from friends that would assist in moving away from violence.

This study thus found a complex mixture of contradictory systems of 'social support' for men. In contrast to some earlier findings, greater violence reported by men was moderately correlated with greater social isolation, and yet also the existence of empathic responses from friends. In general it was the qualitative character of informal social support that appeared more significant than the quantitative size of social networks or frequency of social contacts.

Social support can of course help men to change. However, this depends on the nature of that support. If a man who has been violent to a known woman has a close 'supportive' social network that condones or encourages such violence, then that closeness is itself likely to assist him in maintaining that violence. If, on the other hand, the man has a close social network that opposes violence to women, then that 'support' is likely to assist him in moving away from violence. Thus for these reasons the evaluation of the significance of social support in men moving away from violence has to entail quite specific measures of the nature of that 'support' and/or close reference to the accounts of those involved.

These processes are necessarily dialectical, even contradictory. Thus, for example, a man with major personal resources (money, job, education) may use those resources to continue violence or against his own violence. Similarly, social support from family or friends can condone violence or even be violent in a further way itself, or it can intervene against violence. These processes also transcend the individual and the social; they also operate simultaneously for the woman concerned. Accordingly, increasing men's resources, support and coping have to be considered very cautiously, especially if that is likely to mean a diminution of women's resources, support and coping.[3]

Contact with Agencies

A further area of men's change is through contact with agencies. There has been considerable debate about what kind of contact with agencies might be most appropriate. The most usual response has been that little should be done. Indeed this has been the official state response until relatively recently. Since it has been recognized that this is a problem for the state, there have been a number of possible avenues of intervention. These include 'having a word', cautions, injunctions, fines, occasionally imprisonment.

The evaluative study of men's programmes and other criminal justice interventions by Dobash et al. (1996a) has examined the different ways in which men can change, and how this is interrelated with different kinds of intervention (principally men's programmes or other criminal justice system interventions). They suggest that some men cannot or will not change despite intervention; others engage in limited, short-term change whilst under a watchful eye or when faced with the threat of future sanctions; and some change their behaviour and attitudes, and become responsible for their own behaviour.

Agencies can play a significant part in assisting men to move away from violence to women. They can involve the man in talk, in doing and saying different things to usual, in removing him from the home, and occasionally in placing him forcibly elsewhere, so that he cannot continue his violence to women for that time at least. Thus custody has the effect of moving him away from violence to known women, if only temporarily. However, most agency contacts are not directed at moving men away from violence. Finding an agency worker who focuses *primarily* on the violence is extremely unusual. The problem is more usually either defined in other terms or subordinated to another problem, for example, alcoholism, depression, marital relations, even offending with a specific reference to his violence.

Men were sometimes particularly appreciative of the assistance they had received from individual professionals, specifically solicitors, doctors and probation officers. Generally, this appreciation was based on how they had given the man individual time and attention. In the case of solicitors, this usually meant their success in getting the charge dropped or the man acquitted. Solicitors generally saw these cases of 'domestic violence' as relatively routine tasks to be dealt with and dispensed with. Doctors and GPs rarely intervened directly against men's violence: they generally defined the problem in terms other than the violence to known women. Indeed there were a number of examples where the man considered discussion of his violence had been part of the consultation but it had not been known of or noted by the doctor. In the space of a few minutes of a typical consultation there is room for considerable misunderstanding between patients and doctors over the significance of or even the presence of violence as a problem. It is perhaps for this reason that men can often see doctors as valuable support even though and perhaps because they generally do little to directly confront the violence.

For men who become involved in the criminal justice system, there are different considerations. At each stage in the criminal justice system, and indeed in related parts of the welfare system, men may be filtered out from further agency contact. This can be for a variety of reasons, for example, lack of evidence, decision not to proceed on the basis of 'public interest', the woman's decision not to pursue the case. It can also sometimes be the result of the initiative of the worker, because of other priorities and demands, or even through intimidation from the man. In this sense, the gender of workers and the implication of this for different kinds of work are especially important.

In the light of this an important way of assessing men's violence and abuse may be their conduct with agency staff. Some men, for example, may attempt to take control of the situation, including the agency worker, in a particularly overbearing way. Thus the ease or difficulty of actually contacting the man may be a way of categorizing men. On the other hand, agencies can also act as significant social support for men – providing them with time, attention, resources, understanding of their violence, and even justifications and excuses.

Many men structured their account around their contacts with the criminal justice system, and especially their arrest, though not necessarily charging or prosecution, and their imprisonment. However, some men did not understand the difference between being cautioned, bound over and receiving a suspended sentence, and some considered with all of these they had not been 'convicted'. Interestingly, Dobash et al.'s (1996a) study of the men's programmes and criminal justice system interventions found that all intervention had some impact. Seventy-five per cent of men sanctioned through the criminal justice system other than through the men's programmes (fines, community service, probation order, custody) committed one violent act, and 37 per cent committed five or more violent acts during the following year; 10 per cent were prosecuted for violence against their partners during the following year from the initial criminal justice intervention.

The involvement of agencies in response to men's violence also has complex implications for friends and family of the man concerned. The involvement of agencies, and especially the police, may be the point at which family and friends respond to the man's violence. In such instances, it is state organizations that produce the display of the family rather than vice versa. This sequence of events also shows it is mistaken to see the private and the informal as somehow more flexible or responsive; on the contrary, organizational responses can also construct the context of private, informal and domestic responses. There are of course a number of different ways of explaining such apparent lack of responses from family and friends: the difficulty of 'knowing', the power of other men, the constraints on women's action, the intransigence of particular situations, the resistance to intervention by the police and other social agencies. Even so, it is significant to note that family and friendship networks are often embedded in the public domain and organizational networks.

The Case of Men's Programmes

This research does not provide the material for the evaluation of the effectiveness of such focused group intervention. Individual men and group leaders/facilitators reported the range of responses from 'waste of time' to 'completely successful'. However, it is important to consider that these interventions are, first, focused, and, second, directed to talking about 'effectiveness' and 'degrees of success' in reducing or eliminating violence. Such interventions cannot be evaluated in general as there is a wide variation in the methods and approaches used.

In particular, firm assessments of effectiveness need to be treated with caution. Some men enter such groups to rescue failing or failed relationships with a woman. Rescuing the relationship appears to be the main aim for such men; stopping or reducing their violence appears to be the means to that end. Certainly for a substantial proportion there appears to be a reduction or stopping of physical violence whilst they are in the group. However, as some of the group leaders reported, 'what I find with men in the group is that the physical violence stops probably within the first week. They over-compensate then by increasing the verbal, emotional and psychological [violence], because they've nowhere to off-load the tension you see. That takes a long time.' Another group leader considered that for one man the violence did not stop but would have got far worse but for his involvement in the group. For a few men, such groups can be dangerous as they can, through their group participation, learn or increase their knowledge of the particular ways, physically or non-physically, that are experienced as most harmful or hurtful to the particular woman. This points to the crucial importance of the process of assessment in the selection of group-based members.

Since the late 1970s and early 1980s there has been increasing interest in attempts to move men away from violence through treatment and/or education. The clearest example of this has been the development of men's programmes specifically designed for men who have been violent to known women. There are several roots to these ideas. They include faith in personal change, whether of liberal individualism, the counselling society or indeed psychoanalysis; the ineffectiveness of custodial and other criminal justice interventions; costliness and low cost-effectiveness of such interventions; the search for causes of and allocating responsibility for men's violence; and the continuing interaction of feminist and pro-feminist politics.

Men's programmes were developed in the late 1970s and early 1980s in the United States as a parallel development to women's refuges and shelters. Indeed some of these programmes were developed in collaboration with women's projects. These 'shelter adjunct programmes' might be for the partners or ex-partners of women in the shelters, or for other men in the district. This tradition has not developed in the UK, partly because the women's refuge movement has operated largely within the context of a policy of minimizing contact with men, and certainly not allowing men into refuges. The idea of men's programmes has been taken up for other reasons – as part of pro-feminist politics, as a self-help movement (comparable to Alcoholics Anonymous), as an element in mental health provision. More recently, men's programmes have been developed in Canada, parts of the United States, Scotland and Wales in conjunction with the courts and the criminal justice system sometimes to be used for court-mandated treatment (see Hamberger and Hastings, 1993). Men's programmes are now found in North America, Australia and in many European countries. A major growth of programmes has occurred in Canada and especially Ontario. In addition to the various locations and traditions that have been influential in the expansion of men's programmes, there are other variations in terms of the specific theoretical approach that underpins the intervention.

There is an extensive literature, especially from the United States, on the different theoretical, political and practical approaches to men's programmes (for example, Gondolf, 1985, 1987; Caesar and Hamberger, 1989; Pence, 1989; Edleson and Tolman, 1992; Dankwort, 1992–3; Pence and Paymar, 1990, 1995). These can range from psychoanalytic to structural and pro-feminist approaches. A fundamental question is to what extent men are directed to look at their responsibility and intentionality, and the effects of their violence on women and children. There are also variations which to some extent interrelate with location, tradition and theoretical approach, in sources of funding, relationship to the state, style of working, and gender politics. This last issue can concern whether the programme is run only by men or by women and men, or occasionally only by women. It also concerns the use of single or co-leadership of groups and programmes. Inevitably, there are many other variations between projects, such as around formality/informality; structure and structurelessness; existence or lack of evaluation; record-keeping; and the impact of particular individuals. Above all, programmes can be mandatory or voluntary. Accordingly, it is very difficult to argue that such programmes are either all good or all bad – it depends on the form they take.

Dobash et al. (1996a) found that court-mandated men's programmes (based on cognitive-behavioural and power analysis) were much more successful in reducing violence and associated controlling and coercive behaviours than other criminal justice interventions. During a one-year period following a court sanction, 33 per cent of men participating in one of the men's programmes committed another violent act against their woman partner, compared with 75 per cent of men sanctioned in other ways. The equivalent figures for five or more violent incidents during the following up period were 7 per cent and 37 per cent respectively. Dobash et al. conclude that men's programmes are effective ways of providing the group context for building on initial motivations to change; in particular, the programmes assign the shift from external to internal controls of men. Overall, the possible strength of men's programmes is that they can act as a focus of action against men's violence, not just for individual group members, but also educationally and politically (Gondolf and Russell, 1986; Horley, 1990; Dankwort, 1992–3; Lees and Lloyd, 1994).

In this research, collaboration was developed with three men's pro-grammes of widely varying kinds. Project A was run as a voluntary effort by a woman and had a strong collaborative and self-help ethos to it. It was serious and open in tone. Project B was co-run by a woman and a man, had some small financial assistance, and operated much more on a model of worker and client. Accordingly, this project appeared to have a less cohesive and more individualized ethos. Project C was part of a forum of state and community organization, and hence was the only one of the three with official organizational backing. It still relied on voluntary effort. It was also the project with the clearest feminist/pro-feminist stance, and the strongest professional support and leadership.

These kinds of projects are typically small in scale. They are often main-tained and expanded by one person or a small group of workers and leaders. Sometimes these are women, sometimes men. The men may be involved because of a generalized political commitment against men's violence and/or their own movement away from violence in the model of 'new careers'. For some politically motivated men, such projects have sometimes seemed to be one of the few concrete things that can be done in public that put pro-feminism into practice. Sometimes present in these projects is the element of charismatic leadership, with all its advantages and disadvantages.

This small-scale and charismatic forum may be complicated by a number of factors: the fact that there is great pressure for survival of the project; the fact that as projects are far and few between a variety of men may attend; and the fact of whether or not a formal pre-defined programme should be rigidly adhered to. Thus in many projects there may be a tension between different elements and forces just as one might expect in any organization. However, it is necessary to emphasize the particular tension between the charismatic, even evangelical, aspects of programmes, for both leaders and group members, and the more routinized aspects of the organization. In the last few years there has been a movement towards the more routinized, reflecting the development or adoption of specific training-type programmes, the transferability of programme content and methods between staff, the search for evaluation and the movement to a more educative (rather than, say, expressive) model of personal change. For all these and other reasons it is extremely difficult to make generalizations about the effectiveness of men's programmes.

This leads us on to the evaluation of the idea of 'treatment' of men who have been violent. What this assumes is that it is possible to 'treat' this problem and that this problem is carried by the bearer of the problem *between* violent acts. In this sense, the problem of violence is both *separate from* other parts of the person and at the same time is *borne* by the person. While this paradox applies to almost all problem-focused interventions, there is a special difficulty with this approach in relation to violence. In particular there is a problem if violence is treated (in both senses) as if it is a separate part of the person. This is itself part of the form of violence and part of the way in which violence is perpetrated – as being a thing that can be talked about separately.

As 'violence' is but a shorthand for actions and experience that can happen for such a wide variety of reasons, it is more accurate to say that it is the person or the social relations of the person that need treatment and changing, not just the violence. To focus on the violence *in isolation* or as if it is a separate phenomenon is very likely to be self-defeating.

The dynamics of men's programmes are complex. In the interviews with men, a major theme was the daunting nature of joining the group. This was generally quickly overcome and the main response to being in the group was often an interesting, and, in some ways, paradoxical, relation between men's sense of similarity with other men in the group and men's sense of difference from other men (Hearn, 1998c). Many men appear to be 'comforted' by their feeling of similarity with other men, especially in the initial stages of the programme. This can be used either to move away from violence or to continue the violence. Subsequent feelings of difference from other men can also be a means of deciding to stop violence (because other men are not doing that) or to carry on with it (because of denial that one is like other men). These feelings of similarity and difference themselves feed into more general ways of being men – of maintaining bonding with other men, and of asserting independent autonomy from other men respectively.

Although men's assessments of the programmes inevitably varied, only a few were negative – one found the programme 'a waste of time'; most were positive, and a few argued that the programme had completely changed their life. The only men in this research who had become unequivocally committed against violence were members or 'graduates' of the men's programmes.

A few men spoke extremely positively about the whole experience of their men's programme. One man with a history of 15 years of violence, who attended a programme for 18 months, concluded as follows:

. . . I finally got to the point where I am today, where there is no violence whatsoever. There is a certain amount of unwanted verbal abuse, but that is entirely down to me. It is entirely through slovenly attitude, letting myself slip into irrational thinking rather than thinking, 'Well it's your own insecurity. . . .'

I recognize that the violence was all about power, about wanting. I had to have my own way, and by any means I would get my own way. And usually the quickest means was violence. At the same time I always used to think that I never got my own [way] but in effect I did. I always got my own way. . . .

. . . I realise now that in the past 18 months that my life has done a complete turnaround. I no longer, well I say no longer, 'I want to have power' there are times when I allow myself to regress when I shouldn't do. But I'm not willing now to let things ride as I did before. . . .

And I'm generally taking life less seriously than ever I have done before because the attitude I have now is that life is to be enjoyed, and as long as you don't hurt anybody else, which is ironic in what behaviour I've displayed in the past 15 years, it doesn't matter what you do. I'm actually now getting to a stage where I'm not in overt but covert ways trying to philosophize with the people I work with, and trying to guide people through things I've learnt through the group [men's programme]. . . . Taking responsibility for my own actions rather than laying the blame with anybody else.

I couldn't praise the group enough, I really couldn't.

The question of social support is especially important in formulating practical responses and opposition to men's violence to known women, for example, the organization of men's programmes and other focused interventions against men's violence. In such interventions there is typically a tension between support of men, both between the facilitators and each other (Lees and Lloyd, 1994: 38–39). Within this tension, there are certainly ways in which peer support between men can be positive in changing men away from violence.

As with social support more generally (see pp. 189–191), social support from facilitators/leaders or group members can itself be contradictory. It may support change away from violence; it may also provide more general support to the man, whilst sometimes also supporting the woman. For these reasons, 'social support' is not a unified concept. At the very least it may mean distinctions being made between support in relation to the (a) man's violence; (b) the stopping of men's violence; (c) men's welfare other than the violence. These distinctions, though analytically important, are not, however, watertight in the case of individual men's lives. Social support may involve being very unsupportive in certain respects, especially in the immediate, short term or in relation to particular aspects of men's lives.

There are a number of problems that men's programmes have to face. First, do they direct attention and resources away from women's projects? Ideally it could be argued that resources for both are vital; in practice, both may be competing for the scarce funds available. Linked to this is the question of whether they should be in the voluntary or community sector or be part of state intervention, most obviously within the Probation Service. Second, do they provide opportunities for men to gain further power? This can be by 'saving' marriages that are oppressive or by men learning other forms of violence, such as emotional violence, or by men learning the *precise* action that is most distressing to the women. Thus for certain men, men's programmes could be more dangerous. The violence could be exacerbated by 'the cure'. More generally still, such projects usually operate within a heterosexual norm and thus contribute to the maintenance and development of heterosexual power, usually in the taken-for-granted form and ideology. Third, do such programmes mystify men's power by obscuring the extent to which men's violence is embedded in the structures of patriarchal society?

Reconceptualizing Men's Change

There are many ways of conceptualizing men's change, and lack of change, in relation to violence. I have noted the range of theoretical assumptions that may inform the analysis of change, and how they are mirrored in both the emphasis on different areas of change, and the form of possible interventions within men's programmes and across the range of interventions. Similar debates and tensions seem to recur in terms of theory, interventions and arenas of change.

A central challenge in understanding men's change away from violence is how to focus on the individual man's responsibility without losing sight of broader social and political structures. The focus on the individual man is a complex matter. While it may be tempting to conceptualize men's change away from violence as an individual 'journey' that begins with the man's realization of the possibility of change, and the affirmation of his motivation to change, and ends some time later with the 'saved' non-violent man, this does not capture the contradictions and complexities of the change process.

The use of violence by men is the resort to a cowardly and simple solution to what may be relatively complex problems. On the other hand, for men to consciously stop being violent may involve, in terms of the man's definition of the situation, some degree of courage. This is so on several counts: it involves admitting the violence in the first place – it involves overcoming denial; it involves doing things differently, unlearning earlier ways of behaving; it may also involve a major reorganization of how the man sees himself and how he lives his life; it also involves the man *admitting he was wrong*. When I refer to being wrong, I am not simply meaning the moral case against the use of violence at particular times and particular places. What I am thinking of is a much broader sense of a man coming to realise that he might be wrong in his view of the world. Being wrong is very hard for most men to imagine. It is rare. It can be quite threatening to most men's sense of themselves, of what is usually called 'identity'.

A major qualification is worth adding to this idea of men consciously stopping violence. This is that this state of mind is a temporary definition of the situation. For a man to define himself and his life in that way, as some of the men in the men's programmes did, does not mean that is the case for all time. That kind of self-definition, and indeed that focused effort, work and intervention, is something that may happen at certain times of men's lives. It does not *make* men non-violent. Men can always be violent. Indeed in a different sense, almost all people can always have the potential for violence; exceptions might be those who are unconscious, dying or severely disabled.

So the point here is that moving away from violence is a meaningful process not an outcome. It is quite possible for a man to 'successfully' redefine himself as not violent and then subsequently to be violent. So the task seems to be to continually oppose violence, not just to redefine oneself as having stopped violence. The latter is merely reactive to past violence, albeit that which is now recognized; the former is continued and active. It also acknowledges the potential and threat of violence that is there. Thus moving away from violence or the decision to stop being violent always has to be understood as a provisional state of mind and being, not as the 'successful' outcome of personal change.

Men changing against violence are not simply on a '*career*' that goes through various set stages. The contexts, interventions and processes of change are themselves constructed through men's social power and characterized by complexity and contradictions. For men to change against violence involves change that has to take place within and throughout patriarchies. While it is important to maintain responsibility for violence with the individual man, understanding his possible change away from violence involves much more than the charting of a motivated career. Instead there is a need to consider men's change in terms of a very broad combination of the social forces that sustain and act against that violence. There are in effect individual motivational and social structural *parameters* of the processes of moving (or not moving) away from violence to women. Men's possible change from violence needs to be understood in the context of the dominant patriarchal system of social relations; it is within this spectrum that the man has been violent and he may or may not move away from that violence.

While violence to women is generally not a problem for the man, it can become or lead to problems for men in a variety of ways. Most obviously, it can lead to a deteriorating relationship with the woman. It may lead to an unsatisfying and unpleasant relationship for the man; it may mean the woman's attempted removal of sexual services or her refusal to cook food or her decision to go out more to avoid him or some other way of changing the relationship. Second, it can lead to the end of the relationship. This may of course be what the man wants. Indeed one way of thinking of men's violence is a means of worsening, destroying or ending relationships without overtly saying so, not at least to the woman concerned. Third, it may lead to the death of the woman. The man may kill the woman, that is, kill her through his own direct physically violent actions. He may also hasten her death in other ways through drink or drugs or physical illness. Fourth, men's violence may contribute to the ill-health of the woman, which may increase her dependence on him, through, for example, disability, lack of employment. Fifth, violence can lead to responses from others, family and friends, including moral censure, physical punishment and ostracism. A problem specifically arises when an individual man gains a reputation for violence to women. As one man put it: 'I were getting a name for myself.' Accordingly, 'all her family . . . people in street who she knew and all that . . . wanted me off the estate'. This is a form of social control, initiated probably by the woman and by women and men in the community. It is also a threat to patriarchal relations. It draws attention to men's violence to women. Sixth, violence can lead to the intervention of social agencies, most obviously the police. This can include interview, arresting, cautioning, charging, and then, in due course, prosecution, trial, conviction, custodial or other sentencing, imprisonment. Each of these may be unwanted by men, even though at each stage there may be organizational mechanisms which operate in the favour of men's rather than women's interests or in ways which *do not mean* that violence becomes a problem for men. To put this differently, the response of agencies to men's violence, including those in the criminal justice system, are themselves constructed in the context of men's domination of women.

Bearing in mind there is a high degree of tolerance of certain amounts of men's violence to women, why does the state act against men's violence? The answer seems to lie in a mixture of reasons that are themselves somewhat contradictory. The state may take on a response initiated by neighbours and others in the community. This may well pose a threat to 'law and order' in a locality, especially if individuals attempt to punish the man directly through physical violence. Community responses may of course become more formalized through the action of tenants' and residents' groups, community organizations and women's organizations. Such actions may contain or respond more fully to violence; they may also create further demands on the state; in some localities they may even pose a threat to the rule of the state. This is clear in parts of inner cities and in paramilitary-controlled districts, but also applies on a much smaller scale in Women's Aid refuges that exclude men, including men as agents of the state.

Patriarchal control includes state control and so the action of individual men (fathers, husbands, heterosexual partners, sons, and so on) are secondary and subordinate to that control. This is comparable to capitalist control overriding the interests of individual capitalists, though not the class interests of capitalists.

Those, relatively few, men who are held in custody because of their violence or alleged violence lose their freedom to go where they wish, if only temporarily, even if they eventually are not charged or are charged and found 'not guilty'. It is as if patriarchies continue through rather restrained local conflicts between factions of men, including those who have the high technology and organizational/operational capability of the state; and those who are dispersed in households and families. These two factions come together on rather uneven terms. In one sense, this may involve a civil conflict between men, in which women are the means or currency of dominance but not the end. In another, men's violence to women cuts across social divisions of men, by class, race and age, and one group of powerful men continue to be protected by another group of powerful men. Men at the centre of the state and the criminal justice system, with their own family, living and sexual relationships, interact with the power dynamics of individual women and men in families and other living and sexual relationships.

Part IV

REVIEWING THE PROBLEM

11

Key Issues for Theory, Politics, Policy and Practice

Men's violence to known women is an urgent political problem – the kind of problem that is often obscured and ignored in dominant constructions of 'politics'. This chapter reviews and debates a range of key questions around men's violence to known women. In each case the attempt is made to both discuss the issue concerned and develop some provisional conclusions. It is more important to move debate on than to argue prematurely for some false solution.

Violence and the Recognition of Violence

The doing of violence affects the construction – the very recognition – of violence, of what counts as violence. The more that violence occurs, the greater the number of violent occasions or the greater the intensity of violence, the more that violence is likely to be taken-for-granted. Thus the greater the violence, the less awareness of violence there is likely to be. This might apply to individuals, agencies and whole societies. And of course the greater the awareness of violence, the more that violence is likely to be identified.

As men do more violence, they are able to diminish previous violences, in terms of both their impact and their recognition as violence. Doing more violence may both diminish consciousness of violence and lead to increasing ways of accounting for violence. As men do more violence, their threshold of what counts as violence is raised. With more violence, it becomes more taken-for-granted as part of their ordinary life rather than as something exceptional. Furthermore, as violence is subject to social disapproval, raising the threshold of what counts as violence is one way to discount at least some violence from consideration and possible dispute. Apart from those men who live by violence and who take their violence completely for granted, for most men there is a degree of ambivalence, embarrassment and even shame in doing and disclosing violence. They may see violence to known women, 'their' woman, as partly legitimate and partly illegitimate. This ambiguity can pervade the doing of violence, the accounting for violence, and the reduction and stopping of violence.

An important aspect of this issue of the moving threshold of violence is to what extent it is conscious, unconscious or less than fully conscious. The doing of violence may desensitize and objectify not only the receiver of violence, but also in a different sense the doer of violence. For violence to be continued the doer may become less than fully conscious of himself and his bodily force, which may become naturalized and increasingly, with greater and more repeated violence, taken-for-granted.

Consciousness of violence can of course change with the man's telling of *his story* about his violence. This may happen with police intervention and arrest, prosecution and court appearance, conviction and sentence. It may also occur in a quite different way with the presentation of an ultimatum in the relationship with the woman, for example, with her leaving or threatening to leave, or his request or demand that she leaves. It may also occur with the movement of the man towards his own personal confrontation with his own violence, for example, in a counselling, therapeutic or educational context. Greater consciousness of violence can also occur through being interviewed about violence, when men may sometimes reflect on their actions for the first time. Either way, consciousness of violence may be centred on the re-telling of the man's story, usually around a specific event or series of events. In such a scenario specific violences, or more accurately men's accounts of specific violences, become critical incidents within the telling of the man's story and the development of his consciousness of his violence.

There is, however, a paradox to be noted: namely that re-telling the man's story may lead to his distancing from the violence. The talk can be a defence. Furthermore, in some contexts re-telling may involve the man taking on others' professional accounts and recounting them 'in his own words'. Such professionalizations of men's accounts and re-telling of violence are important in many agency contexts. These processes of re-telling the critical incident are even more important when the violence concerned is defined as 'serious' or 'very serious', and where and when the man's life is transformed through the violence. This most obviously applies with a man's arrest, prosecution and conviction for murder, and sentence to life imprisonment. Thus the very specific series of events and experiences of men and women, before, during and after violence, construct the recognition of those violences.

Men's Violence and Social Theory

Focusing on men's violence, and specifically men's violence to known women, raises many questions for social theory. Indeed it is more than interesting how much social theory has been developed *without* attending to the pervasiveness of men's violence. There are many aspects of social theory that can usefully be rethought through remembering the presence of violence. The notion of *historical and cultural constructions*, the concepts of *meaning* and of *individual action*, the relationship of *organization and social structure*, the place of *experience* in the creation of knowledge, the conceptualization of *power*, and the *deconstruction of the 'self'* are all examples of key issues in social theory that can be re-viewed through a focus on men's violence, especially that to known women.

For example, in most social theory violence is not understood as a *characteristic* or *pervasive* form of interpersonal or structural relations. Interpersonal relations are easily assumed to involve 'rational individuals', each with a 'unified self' who conducts their (or his!) affairs in a reasonable, liberal, tolerant and mutually adjusting manner. This model continues to inform much study of families, groups, organizations and indeed individuals' relation to social structures. In this scheme, violence is portrayed as a relatively isolated and isolatable exception to 'normal life'. Violence is rarely understood as integral, embedded or immanent in social relations, and social relations are rarely characterized by or as violence, actual or potential. Accordingly, when a man is violent to a woman 'he loves' or 'is married to' or 'has a sexual relationship with', the violence is usually constructed, by men, as aberrant. Even in discussions of gender and power, violence may not be understood as fundamental. In order to develop social theory that deals with this satisfactorily, it is necessary to begin with the recognition of the place of violence in relation to social relationships and not as an afterthought.

There are close parallels to be drawn between men's accounts of their own violence and the way that men have generally developed social theory. Violence is constructed as occurring in 'incidents'; it is constructed as 'incidental', it is incidentalized. Violence is constructed as occurring as exceptions to supposedly 'non-violent, ordinary normal life'. The dominant constructions of social theory by men, and of 'men' within social theory, in turn construct violence and men's violences as central or peripheral, explicit or implicit (Hearn, 1996d).

The general distribution of violence also has profound implications and effects on the differential experiences of women and men that in turn contribute to, or even often lay the basis for, the construction of what is called *knowledge*. Violence, and the experience of violence, is clearly of great significance for both the understanding of knowledge, or what we call knowledge, and the nature of being, including whether we exist at all. The extent and acquisition of knowledge, about both violence and other areas of life, is itself affected by violence. These constructions provide the criteria for judging the reliability of further, other knowledges, whether about violence or not. The experience of being, of being alive, is similarly affected by decisions on what counts as validity and valid knowledge, whether about violence or not.

In considering these differential experiences of women and men in relation to violence, and the processes of other possible knowledge formations, a distinction needs to be drawn between, first, the direct experience of a particular (kind of) event or particular (kind of) effects, and, second, the experience of being a part of a particular social category, in this case women or men. In the first case, I would not want to argue that people have to have direct experience of a certain kind of event or effect for that kind of event or effect to be understood or for knowledge to be formed in relation to such events or effects. To argue for this would mean that only those who directly experience a certain kind of event or effect could understand such events or effects, or possibly even speak knowledgeably on them. However, such a view does not solve the problem of how events and effects are grouped together in certain categories so that *certain kinds* of events and effects can be talked of at all. It also does not resolve disputes of what might be meant by 'speaking knowledgeably' on a particular topic.

In the second case, I would argue that certain kinds of knowledge are only available to people within certain categories. For example, men do not know what it means to be a woman experiencing violence from a man or a known man. Indeed, even if the same knowledge appears to be generatable by both women and men, the meaning of that knowledge is likely to be different because of women's and men's different power locations. Furthermore, being part of the social category of 'women' or the social category of 'men' necessarily places people in a different relationship to not only dominant social arrangements but also dominant forms of knowledge. Thus even without saying anything, and even more so having said something, women and men are differently located in relation to knowledge. Similarly, dominant forms of knowledges, to which women and men relate differently, are themselves the product of different historical silencing, violation and killing of women and men. This is of course not to say that only women are silenced, violated and killed; that is clearly not the case. What is the case is that it is men who do the vast majority of the silencing, amongst other things, in the gendered structuring of knowledge and theory.

The placing of gendered silencing, violation and killing *centrally* within the regimes of constitution of objectivity and subjectivities opens up many major questions. Some of these have recently been discussed in a brilliant essay by Dean MacCannell and Juliet Flower MacCannell (1993) on 'Violence, Power and Pleasure'. They detail the complexities of the effects of violence on experience and knowledge, particularly from the perspective of women who have suffered violence from men. These effects are damaging, multiple, subjectively felt, recurrent, intense, and often at odds with dominant 'truths' of law, order and authority. They may involve a fraying of order and a fragmentation of the women's experience. The effects are particularly complex in the realm of (sexual) pleasure, so that the woman's relationship to her own pleasure may become mediated by violence, and she may become isolated from intimate relationships except those linked to her violation. Such complexities of experience and knowledge, objectivity and subjectivities, have to be ever present as part of the analysis of men's 'objectivity' and 'subjectivities'. They also exemplify the kind of differential experiences of women and men, and the differential processes of knowledge formation that may follow from them. It is not appropriate to attempt to isolate men's knowledge from such complex effects. Considering the reconstitution of men's objectivity and subjectivities involves attention to the transformation of men and men's knowledge, and the relation of those changes to women and women's knowledge. Within this, there is a danger of returning to the recentring of men.

For these and other reasons, being a member of the category 'men' places men in a different relation to knowledge to being a member of the category 'women'. And it is for these and other reasons that it is possible to relate men's subjectivity as subjects to what is socially constructed as objectivity, whatever differences between men are made apparent. To say this implies a particular and *structured* relation between the *individual* man and the *category* of 'men' that is not open to simple definition through acts of will.

The differential expression *of women and men* in relation to violence, and indeed more generally, should not obscure the very real differences that persist *between women and between men*. Differenced forms of experience are available to different men, and in turn differenced forms of theorizing can be produced by men in different social locations, according to age, economics, class, racialization and other social divisions, including violence. In particular, men in relatively disadvantaged categories, for example, gay men, black men, older men, may be likely to theorize 'men' in relation to those categories. This question of differenced, situated knowledge is particularly important in relation to violence. For example, if a man is talking about his own violence to a woman, this talk has to be analysed with a view to the power relations between them, and particularly the way in which such talk can be part of the rationalization, justification and reproduction of violence. In contrast, men talking about violence to women may also refer to their violence, for example, as boys. This may be used to excuse their violence to women. Sometimes professionalized discourses are used by men to explain and excuse their adult violence. Of these the idea that the abused may become the abuser is especially powerful. Thus men's accounts of earlier abuse and violation may, on the one hand, be part of a contemporary rationalization of excuses for, and even act as reproductions of, violence to women whilst, on the other hand, being recollections of times of relative powerfulness rarely recounted. As such, for individual men talking about violence and men's relation to violence is usefully informed by notions of situated knowledges.

A task for men, or at least pro-feminist men, is to move towards overcoming the separation of subject and object, not just the reconstitution of some new subjects or new objects. An initial movement to 'objectified subjectivity' is but one stage in the further move to transcending subject and object. I remain much more doubtful, indeed more doubtful than ever, about the *general* possibility and potential of men gathering knowledge of direct emancipatory value *simply* on the basis of a resort to subjectivity. I also remain (rather less) doubtful of the possibility of the creation of such knowledge through an act of will. On the other hand, subjectivism of men may well generate information on the nature of men's power and oppression of others, women and men – and this, however oppressive it might be, may *in turn* be of emancipatory value for others, women or men, or even those men themselves or other similar men in the longer term. Indeed this might be the case, for example, in researching men who have been violent to women about that violence. This is very different to men speaking on, say, their abuse as boys. Though major difficulties remain as to the extent to which men are able to understand that which constitutes the category 'men' of which they/we/I am a part, either generally or specifically, for men to critically theorize men necessitates an engagement with these reconstitutions of objectivity and subjectivities.[1]

The Explanation of Men's Violences: Structure and Process

Virtually all people, both men and women, have the potential to be violent to others. So how is the preponderance of men's violence to be explained? In many attempts to do so, it has become usual to relate men's practice of violence to other social divisions, principally divisions of economic class, but also age, locality, region, religion, and so on. In particular men's violence to men is often related to age, economic class and locality; while men's violence to women is often related to gender and sexuality. This all makes clear sense. The continual temptation to try to explain men's violence *by reference to 'something else'* may seem obvious and sensible enough but it does not quite capture the *autonomy* of violence and systems of violence. In particular it is important to note that the practice of violence is itself a form of social division and social inequality. It is a social distribution of *who does what to whom*. Violence is not simply a subset of some other social division. Violence *distinguishes* people, both individually and structurally. Violence is a form of profound bodily discrimination.

These structural conditions of violence do not just exist in analysis: they recur in the lives of individuals within structures. For example, capitalist relations of employment and unemployment might affect the gendered expectation and experiences of men and women, so that when men formerly defined as 'breadwinners' become unemployed and identified as redundant they may reassert their selves through violence. A related process may occur for young men who have no prospects of employment at all. Now such connections are only possibilities; they are not causal relations. Most important, such changes in capitalist employment relations *do not cause men's violence*; it is the *gendered* nature of those relations that *makes possible* such connections, *structurally and individually* in structures and in consciousness.

In *The Wretched of the Earth*, Franz Fanon (1967) argues that violence from the colonizers towards the colonized follows from the former's incredulity at the latter's incomprehension of their ideology of supremacy. Faced with this incomprehension, the colonizer asserts his way through violence. Violence is an attempt to enforce that which is already not the case. Thus violence is associated with change and uncertainty. The implications of this view of violence for an analysis of men's violence to known women are dramatic. This would suggest that one way of 'making sense' of men's violence to known women is an attempt to enforce an ideology that is already beyond incredulity – such as the ideology of love and romance in marriage.

In this sense, when men are violent to known women, that might suggest that those women have most likely already decided upon the inaccuracy of the ideology of male supremacy. This is clearly not to be taken to mean that the women are in any way to blame; rather that they have seen through the ideology, and *then* the men respond by attempting what are likely to be unsuccessful material re-exertions of that ideology. Violence thus might come from men to these women who least agree with men. Of course the reasons for a lack of agreement by women with men's ideologies could be several. Incredulity, that is, women's incredulity of men's ideologies of supremacy, may be obvious, intuitive, reasoned, the result of prolonged study. Perhaps this may be why different women in very different social situations may experience violence. These may include when women occupy very different worlds from men, for example, strict divisions of labour, strict separation of private and public worlds; when women's consciousness is raised, for example, through feminism; and when women do not understand or are not interested in men's ideologies for other reasons.

Another source of disjunction may be where women or indeed men are changing the pattern of their activities, such as a returning to education, which brings its own sets of different experiences and expectations. Just as high levels of harassment have been reported when women enter new occupational arenas, a similar process may operate in relation to women who are wives, partners and girlfriends. In practice several processes may operate at once.

This leaves the question of variation in men's propensity to violence. If there is complete male supremacy there may be no need to use violence at all. If, on the other hand, there is a need to assert or reassert male supremacy, then violence may be used. If violence can be got away with, it may be used without hesitation or with very little hesitation. Men's violence to women can be a form of *raw power*, the way that authority is enforced by coercion, or it may be a *response* to challenges of that authority. It can of course also be both. In the first case, violence may reinforce or maintain domination; in the second, the countering of resistance may mean that further violence is not necessary. Violence from subordinates who resist domination is analytically distinct, even if this may sometimes be difficult to isolate specifically. Alternatively, if a man becomes aware of the impli-cations of his actions or if his use of violence or potential violence threatens his own livelihood, violence may be self-monitored and less likely.

Men's violence to women is not just a given structure; it is a structure, a process, a set of practical actions and an outcome of men's societal domination – of what may be called as a shorthand 'patriarchy'. Such violence is a structure of patriarchal relations in itself; a patriarchal process; and an outcome of other forms of patriarchal domination. For example, other patriarchal structures, such as hierarchic heterosexuality, fatherhood, and the state (Hearn, 1987, 1992b) may all be *maintained* and sometimes intensified by men's violence. The means is men's violence and potential violence to women, children and each other. As Dworkin (1985)[2] has argued, subordination is a social-political dynamic consisting of four parts: hierarchy, objectification, submission and violence. In her view, violence is the element of subordination that may follow from the previous three – 'whenever you see a social situation in which violence is widespread' and normalized, 'you know you already have the other three existing elements solidly in place'. The social subordination by men of women and children thus consists of hierarchies in which men predominate over women and children; men's objectification of women, children (and possibly each other); women's, children's (and indeed some men's) submission to men; and men's violence to women and children.

A closely related political and theoretical issue is the question of whether men's violence is simply a means to an end of maintaining patriarchal institutions and men's power, or whether it is an end in itself. In other words, do men live simply to do violence to women (and children and other men)? If this question is answered 'yes', it could suggest that it is violence that is the central dialectic of patriarchy rather than simply a means of control of reproductive and other patriarchal relations.

While there are individual women who are violent, they are generally so in reaction to or in aberration from the category of women/woman. In contrast, for men the experience of violence is much more *routine*. The experience of violence is essentially part of that which is constitutive of the category of men. The notion of essentialism has been colonized by various forms of biological determinism; indeed essentialism has been redefined as biological determinism; in contrast, essentialism is here used to refer to the essentialism of men that is socially constructed. Thus the experience of violence is socially routine and routinized for men, such that the *reference* to violence (men's violence) is that which forms and informs *the category of men* of which men, individual men, are a part. The category of 'men' is a social one and not a natural or biologically determined one. Thus in one sense the reason that men are violent to women, known women or women who are not known is because they are men, or more precisely because they are constructed as 'men'. This is not as tautological as it might sound. For example, the reason that children may be violent to other children is not because they are children when these children who are being violent are boys, that is, male children. Thus a mere description of a person does not necessarily explain the activity or behaviour of that person. Men are violent to known women because it is the case that they are men. Being men is the case that explains why they are violent to known women.

All these kinds of 'explanation' should not, however, be taken to exclude or demean other types of explanation. Indeed different explanations can simultaneously exist. These may co-exist; they may complement each other; they may also contradict each other. As Goldner and her colleagues put it 'To say violence, domination, subordination and victimization are psychological does not mean they are not also moral, material or legal' (Goldner et al., 1990: 345). Simultaneous and differing explanations need to be acknowledged and embraced.

This may also be important in considering different kinds of explanation for different kinds of violence. While different forms of violence have been understood as located along a continuum of prevalence and experience (Kelly, 1988), they may also be characterized as *clusters* or *sediments* of actions where different *rules* of interrelation of structure and agency operate. For example, murder might be contrasted with verbal abuse. The latter might be built into the very structuring of social relations; the former might be the action of particular individuals acting contrary to general social norms. These sediments overlay each other and to a large extent reinforce each other. Routine abuses operate at a very taken-for-granted and wide-spread level; assaults are more localized; murders more exceptional.

The Explanation of Men's Violences: Agency, Rationality, Choice and Responsibility

While men are often constructed as 'naturally violent' (see Elshtain, 1981; Sydie, 1987), it may be more appropriate to move full circle and see men's violence as a social choice, a clear intention to do harm, for which men are individually responsible. Some men use clear and deliberate intentions in their accounts:

> So, basically, I grabbed hold of her and thumped her one. But it's like the thing was, I thumped her hard enough to hurt her, but not hard enough to knock her down, because I didn't want to hurt the baby. I knew what I was doing.

Men may use exactly the amount of violence that is necessary to achieve their ends. In this sense, violence may be 'rational', not something that is 'out of control'. Men talk about violence to women as being relatively easy, and more restrained than violence to men. Violence may also be used so that the woman is not visibly damaged more than is deemed necessary by the man. One man described how he had damaged the face of the woman, and so inconveniently for him he decided that he had to stay in the whole of the next week:

> . . . these two massive black eyes and a broken nose, I couldn't believe it. I had two weeks off work. Anybody come to the door, I had to go to the door, I wouldn't let anybody in. Cos I felt ashamed of what I'd done. She wouldn't even go cash us child benefit. I had to go. I had to lock her in the house, take the keys with me. Lock her in the house in case somebody came.

From the man's point of view he had gone 'too far', and this brought him into possible contact and difficulty with agencies and others outside the home.

Violence can be used to achieve certain ends, to enforce controls, and sometimes to end the relationship, either temporarily or permanently. However, developing an adequate theory of agency, choice and responsibility in relation to men's violence remains a problem area. Violence can certainly be understood as an approach to action *chosen* by some men, as knowledgeable social actors in doing violence. Thus, a pervasive way of understanding men's violence to women is in terms of a series of particular actions performed by individual people, for which they are *individually* responsible. This is certainly the dominant construction within legal discourse; indeed it is possible for collectivities or organizations to be 'individuals' in a legal sense. From rather different perspectives, the notion of individual responsibility is also invoked in right-wing conservative and social democratic ideologies. In the first case, this fits neatly with a model of the isolated non-gendered economic individual; in the second case, the notion of the 'responsible individual' is located within social market forces. Even so this more societal perspective still retains the notion of the 'responsible individual' as the agent of violence and crime in the last instance. This seems to be related directly to the need to maintain the institutions of the law, the state, welfare services, trade unions and indeed capitalist organizations, which are in turn capable of reform and progressive improvements.

A rather different set of considerations is brought to bear in the feminist constructions of responsibility. This includes the various meanings of 'the personal and the political', and the various attempts to change men's behaviour by explaining men's responsibility, collective and individual, for their oppressive and violent behaviour. Thus the clarification, statement and use of 'responsibility' by men has its own politics and political tensions and problems. On the one hand, it has been clearly pointed out in feminist theory and practice that men are responsible for men's violence. This is clear. This position has been developed in a direct reaction to advocates of women-blaming who use in their analysis of men's violence such concepts as (women's) 'learned helplessness': the responsibility for men's violence is clearly men's.

On the other hand, the notions of responsibility and choice need to be treated with care; they can feed into a simple liberal individualism that is itself subject to critique. In particular the idea of individual choice is open to critique through the deconstruction of the autonomous, unified rational individual, as well as for opening the way to a neglect of structural location. Despite the importance and complexity of individual responsibility, it is important to understand men's violence as much more than a collection of individual actions. Without a more societal/structural discourse, under-standing men's violence to women or indeed men can seem the equivalent of women's violence to men or indeed women. In fact without a more struc-tural perspective violence is reduced to the particular behaviours without attention either to their meaning to those concerned or to the social forces that construct gendered people in the first place. The prevalence of liberal individualism and in a different sense the liberal individual is one of the major obstacles to the formulation of a more societally based understanding of men's violence, and this is itself necessary if men's violence is to be changed, reduced and abolished.

Explanations of Violence and Talking About Violence

Men's talk about violence is not merely descriptive; it creates social reality for men and women. Similarly, agency policy and practice generally emphasize the importance of talk. Indeed men's accounts and agency accounts may themselves have close correspondence. Violence, talk about violence, and responses to violence by both individuals and agencies are all simultaneously material and discursive (Hearn, 1996b).

Explanations of violence are kinds of talking about violence, usually talking in written form. Accounts of violence by men are also forms of talking. They provide information on men's motives in doing violence but they cannot be assumed to give any kind of complete explanation. More-over, explanations of men's violence, especially by professionals, can be re-used by men as excuses and rationalizations of violence within their accounts of violence. Thus there is a not so hidden danger in the develop-ment of explanations of men's violence. In such ways, explanations can be transmuted to excuses and rationalizations, and they in turn can be transmuted to denials.

One of the ways in which violence is perpetuated is by its isolation as something separate from the rest of men's lives. This can be done by the man himself; it can also be done by those who have professional and other contact with the man, for example, psychiatrists. Those professionals and other workers who have met with men who have been violent to known women can have a particularly important effect on reinforcing the assump-tion of the separation and isolation of violence from other aspects of the man. Consequently, explanations of violence, professional or otherwise, can be *used* to explain choice and responsibility, or to deny it.

Thus the construction of analytical or social scientific explanation has to proceed with caution and not simply so that men's accounts are reproduced 'with capital letters'. To be slightly more precise, when a man *invokes* a particular cause or explanation of his violence, such as his own ill treatment as a child, he may be providing valuable information on the explanation of his violence, but he may also be presenting a diversionary rationalization. Either way we have here an example of an 'explanation-in-use', *regardless of its accuracy or truth*. This kind of explanation should be distinguished from explanations and causes in which the man is determined by forces such that he is not held responsible. This may apply with, for example, types of mental illness. It also needs to be distinguished from 'macro explanations' that operate at the level of the collective *regardless* of what men themselves say. Furthermore, in this study an interweaving between 'explanations-in-use' and 'macro explanations' has been attempted. This combination, what might be called 'composite explanations', points to the intertextuality of accounts and social scientific explanations, such that each draws on and invokes the other.

What is the relationship to be drawn between the social construction of men and masculinities and the ways in which men talk about their violence? Men and masculinities are formed by the full range of social and political forces in society. In this context, the most important issue is the social construction of men's relations and reference to violence as a relevant element in the doing of masculinities. So when men talk about their violence they are continuing being men and doing masculinities as well as giving specific accounts of those violences. The doing of men's talk is just one more aspect of the social construction of men and masculinities. It is not a separate activity that needs to be read off and interpreted from *prior* social constructions of the way men have been 'brought up' or the way masculinities have been 'formed'. Men's talk about violence is not an effect of the past, it is men doing masculinities themselves *in the present*.

Power

One of the most important general issues raised in this book is the conceptualization of power. The power and control model has become increasingly influential as a way of understanding men's violence to known women (Pence and Paymar, 1990). This research can be seen as a sympathetic extension of the power and control model. Men's violence to women is clearly a form of power: it arises from and is underwritten by men's domination of women as a social group and it persists as a form of power in individual situations. However, the operation of power is complex.

Violence can be conceptualized as a form of power in many ways. The key question is: How is a theory of power to be constructed that adequately and fully deals with the complexity of men's violence to women? This has to recognize:

- societal realities of men's structural power over women;
- the power relations embedded in family ideology and family forms, heterosexuality and marriage;
- the specification of interpersonal relations;
- intrapersonal/intrapsychic relations of those involved.

Men's dominance is a characterizing feature of each of these relations. In explaining men's violences, there is a particular danger of seeing it as part of a *one-way system* of men's power that removes women's agency and resistance, and that may also remove men's agency and responsibility, as well as some men's resistance to that system. In addition, there are further complications, as follows:

1 Men's dominance is not complete.
2 Women resist and may indeed dominate in certain situations, regardless or even because of men's structural dominance.
3 Men who are dominant through direct violence to women may maintain that dominance, and in doing so may destroy the woman, the relationship, others (for example, children present) and/or themselves. The destruction of the self of men through themselves is a further illustration of men's dominance.
4 Other men control the processes of dominance, control, punishment and destruction of men.

Violence occurs within dialectical social processes. Men's control of women in heterosexual relationships may be achieved through violence; it may also be undermined and ended, especially where the woman resists, and indeed leaves. Men may use violence to exert direct or indirect control over women in heterosexual relationships. This can be with respect to (the woman's) sexual fidelity/infidelity, assumed or known; control of housework, childcare and mothering; the woman's appearance, drinking, autonomy, movement, friends and activity; 'provocation' by the woman; retaliation of the woman. The use of violence may be effective or ineffective in exerting this control; it may indeed produce the opposite effect (still in the terms of the man's definitions). It may, for example, mean that the woman resents and resists his attempted control of her autonomy to a greater extent and indeed may leave him. These processes are most easily understood as dialectical – in several senses. They involve participation in the contradictions of controlling and being controlled, dominance and deference, power and resistance, that themselves develop differentially over time. The interrelations of power, control, intimacy and sexuality are especially complex and contradictory. To reduce intimacy and sexuality to a simple by-product of men's power and control of women may also be to dismiss women's experience.

In addition, men's power through violence to women is complicated in some cases by the processing of men through the criminal justice system. Despite recent policy changes in arrest and prosecution, this remains rare, with custodial sentences rarer still. For some such men, their lives are clearly 'in a mess' – through drink, drugs, psychological difficulties, work and money problems.

These considerations demand a multifaceted conceptualization of men's power in relation to violence. It needs to examine how it is that men who may attempt to maintain or increase power through violence may not experience powerfulness, and may in *some* cases go on to psychiatric illness, suicide, murder/attempted murder, imprisonment. This particular form of violence in this particular historical form of patriarchy involves some men being controlled by other men, particularly men in the state. Attention to such a question in no way diminishes women's experience of power, violences and control. Rather this general view of men's power entails consideration of men as husbands/partners, men as state agents, women as wives/partners, and women as state agents, and the interrelations of the various groupings.

Futhermore, men who have been violent to known women exert power in specific and connected ways. They embody men's power more generally and they have also personally embodied their violence. Men may be powerful through size, strength, control of the body, use of muscles, control of money and sources, the specificity of violent acts and actions, the use of objects, as well as through the control of words, speech, emotional relations and emotional distance. Yet the men interviewed rarely saw these acts of power in that way. They often reported experience of relative powerlessness – which might be understood as 'less power' relative to their expectation of 'more power' or to their taken-for-granted 'all-powerfulness'. These are all acts of men's cultural power.

Power also operates in time and space. Men's violence to women involves the use of domination of physical and social space – not only in particular locations (for example, living rooms, bedrooms, kitchens, the streets), but also in terms of the occupation of spaces between people. Violence occupies space; it takes up space, forges gaps and physical *connections*; it also controls the space of the violated person. Most important, the use of space that occurs in and through violence is a basic form of *existence* in itself, and not just a reflection of *some other determinant* of behaviour, such as social role, or *some other measure* of behaviour, such as the use of time.

Such complications of power and the oppression of women provide a framework for the differential understanding and interpretation of men's experiences around being violent to known women. They are simultaneously material and discursive: they articulate a relationship of doing power and talking power, and a way of rethinking what is called power and politics in the first place.

The Category of Men and Types of Men

Researching men's violence to known women involves using and engaging with the social category of 'men'. This category is a basic building block in use – it is that which is set up, worked on, refined, poured over, and redefined. The category is, however, itself problematic: it is a taken-for-granted category of the social world, and accordingly it needs to be treated with sociological caution. The taken-for-grantedness of the category is one of its most important social features.

The deconstruction of the category 'men' does not necessarily dilute power relations, as in men's violences; indeed, it may serve to illustrate the mythologies that surround men, including men as a gender class. In the case of men's violence, a particular challenge is to deconstruct 'men' whilst recognizing both men's power as a gender class and the physical embodiment of men as males when violent or potentially violent. 'Men' may become recognized as such at least partly through their violence, as well as their talking about violence. Violence and talking about violence are resources for not just the construction of masculinities (cf. Messerschmidt, 1993), but also the construction of men.

Interviewing men who have been violent to known women makes it clear that men vary in their relationship to violence, and *in that sense* there are different types of men – that is, different men talk about very different types of violence, explain their violence in very different ways, and have very different orientations to their violence. There are also differences and varieties in terms of: the length of the interview; the amount of detail provided; the extent of self-disclosure and ownership of responsibility of the violence; the construction of violence as 'something inside' the man or 'something between people'.

However, whilst recognizing these and other differences, it is not accurate to distinguish *clear and separate types of men*. Even so, a number of analysts have attempted to construct typologies of men who are violent to known women. For example, distinctions have been drawn between sporadic, chronic, antisocial and sociopathic batterers (Gondolf, 1988, 1993); and between emotionally volatile, family-only and generalized aggressors (Saunders, 1992). To construct a typology of men in terms of men's violence to known women, it is necessary to begin not from the particularities of reported violence of this kind but rather from the totality of men's relations with known women. Such relations include social structural relations and interpersonal social relationships of men to known women. Two major interrelated principles need to be recognized: the universality of men's violence and potential violence; and the differences between men in terms of violence and potential violence.

While all the men were in some way involved with violence to women, and all were involved in relations of power and dominance over women, these unities and commonalities have to be understood alongside differences. There are a number of ways of describing these differences among men in relation to violence to known women. First, there is the question of men's location in relation to agencies, and in particular the criminal justice system. Second, there are differences in terms of the violence. Third, there are differences in the men's relationship to those violences. These three differentiations overlap to some extent. Paradoxically, unities of men's power are maintained through difference, and differences are obscured in the maintenance of unities (Hearn and Collinson, 1993).

The major experience that men have in common is itself power and control in relation to women. This is often, indeed usually, taken-for-granted. Sometimes it is, however, very specifically talked of. On the other hand, there are many differences between men:

- men who are regularly violent to women *and* men over a lifetime;
- men who are regularly violent only to women (or a particular woman) over a lifetime;
- men who are occasionally or less regularly violent to women;
- men who are occasionally violent to women, and may be to men too;
- men who are violent on a one-off occasion;
- men who are violent to children;
- men who are violent to men, because of their involvement with particular women;
- men who are violent mainly to men, but also may be occasionally to women.

Similarly, it is possible to describe characteristic types of activity by men that may be distinct for some individual men but may more usually overlap or occur in combination. In other words, distinctions may be made between ideal-typical forms of violence by men. These characteristic types of men's violence (rather than types of men) include the following:

1 Men use violence that is a part of violence to control or to resolve disputes across their relationships with women or men.
2 Men use violence that is part of violence to control or resolve disputes with women.
3 Men use violence that is in contrast to their usual behaviour in relation to women.

Men's Sexuality and Violence

Another recurring, if often implicit, theme (see Chapter 8) throughout this research has been the relationship of men's violence and men's sexuality. The dominant ideological tendency to construct sexuality and violence as separate entities was reproduced in the accounts of men talking about their violence. This constructed separation in the words of men should not be taken to suggest that there are not intense connections between men's sexual life, men's violent life, and indeed the very notion of men's sexual violence itself. It is of course tempting to evaluate whether it is men's (hetero)sexuality that underlies or 'causes' men's violence or whether it is men's violence that underlies or 'causes' men's (hetero)sexuality. This is, however, to miss the point. Both men's heterosexuality and men's hetero-violence are constructed in relation to each other. They are part and parcel of the same set of social forces, *not* so that one inevitably follows from the other, but rather that they each form the social framework of the other. Men's violence to women is structured *through men's* heterosexuality and vice versa. Thus it is more useful to consider each as part of a broader social system of heterosexual violence. To argue this is not to suggest that all heterosexual forms are associated with violence; it is rather that the dominant forms are founded on inequality, subordination and men's control and oppression of women. While such a form is paramount, other forms, such as where women are dominant, or where equal relations operate, or where quite different social forces and contexts pertain, are also possible.

Violence to Women and 'Child Abuse'

It has become relatively common to see the violation of children, as in child abuse, as a major 'cause' of men's violence to women. This of course fits well with a socialization model of boys, men and men's violence. However, such a cyclical notion of violence should be treated with great caution. Indeed in many senses it is a dangerous framework for understanding men's violence to women in that it usually incorporates gender in a naturalized way. To put this rather simply, it is assumed that violated boys go on to become abusing men, while violated girls go on to become abused women: men become 'natural' violators and women 'natural' victims. What this does not explain is why such gender power dynamics might operate or how men might 'choose' not to be violent as adults or how women avoid being further violated, or indeed why some men not only abuse as adults but go to great lengths to continue that abuse after the end of relationships.

Despite these kinds of theoretical and empirical problems with cyclical or socialization models of men's violence there is of course plenty of evidence that different kinds of men's violence and abuse are strongly interrelated. Thus what we have is something of a disjunction between the various combinations of violence that particular men may produce, and the inadequacy of understanding such combinations as following naturally and inevitably from any previous abuse. One way of making sense of this is to distinguish between the levels of explanation and levels of personal responsibility. At a general level of explanation men who have witnessed violence as boys may be more likely to be violent as adults; however, this in no way takes away from the specific responsibility of specific men in doing violence, or not doing violence.

Another way of considering presence or absence of a link between violence to women and child abuse is in terms of the domestic situation. Men's violence to known women is certainly affected by women's differential responsibility with regard to children. Women with children, and particularly young children, are likely to be more dependent on men and thus vulnerable to men's violence and abuse (Hanmer and Saunders, 1984).

Men's violence to known women may be performed in the presence or hearing of children; it may involve direct violence to both the woman and the children; it affects the well-being of the woman as a mother, and undermines her ability to control situations and define reality for herself. In all of these and other ways men's violence to known women may be child abuse. Indeed, as I have discussed, elsewhere (Hearn, 1988, 1990), the very term, 'child abuse' is problematic and would be better labelled men's violences or sexualities towards young people. Similarly, 'child abuse' can be reconceptualized as men's violence to known women.

Furthermore, it is necessary to recognize that the connections between violence to women and child abuse are affected by the different living situations of the people involved. These include never living together, being separated after living together, living together long term, intermittent living or not living together. Such different domestic situations necessarily construct the exact connections and relationships of men's violence to known women and child abuse.

Finally, all of these connections or lack of connections have implications for the organization of policy and practices. Policy intervention against men's violence to known women and children is generally now conducted within separate systems. A major challenge is to bring these systems closer to each other, without treating women as children or children as women.

Violence and Organizations

The practice of violence by men to known women in the domestic, private and other realms, such as the street, should not divert attention from the implications of such violence for organizations and organizational practice. Most obviously, there is the whole range of organizational responses and non-responses to such violence. This is particularly from the criminal justice system but also other parts of the state sector, the voluntary sector, and increasingly the private sector, as the first two sectors become subject to various forms of privatization and commercialization. Thus men's violence can be literally profitable for some. Organizations of many different kinds are therefore involved in the business of responding to men's violence to known women. This affects their goals, structure, functioning, internal processes and dynamics, work cultures, and individual and collective relations with clients and users (Hearn, 1994c).

These responses to violence are not the only way in which organizations and violence interconnect. Men in organizations, whether workers or managers, bring their own experiences of being or not being violent, just as do women managers and workers. Organizations are thus inhabited and constructed by men and women, with their own differential experiences of violence. These of course have specific implications for organizations, such as when individuals are in personal crisis arising from violence and find difficulty in completing organizational tasks. More generally, individuals are gendered and reproduced as organizational actors and subjects partly through their relationship to gendered violence, both outside and within organizations.

Ambivalence, Ambiguity and Paradox

Throughout all of this engagement with violence, there has been a recurring difficulty – of how to reduce the ambiguities and paradoxes of social life to the printed page. Men talking about violence usually do so with a good deal of ambivalence – a chance to tell their story, as well as a chance to confess, to lay some ghosts. Men may be simultaneously very keen and very reluctant to talk. Ambivalence persists. In describing their violence, men are constantly invoking paradoxical aspects of power – of *feelings* of power-fulness and control and feelings of powerlessness and being out of control. Such contradictory feelings and reports cannot of course be taken at face value. The reproduction of feelings of powerlessness and being out of control can easily be one mode of maintaining power and control. And yet while men are certainly engaged, through the doing of violence, in maintaining and elaborating power and control, in another sense some men are also not fully in control of themselves – whether through drink or drugs, through rage, through the lure and excitement of the violent movement. That sense of not being in control of themselves is, however, still knowable and to an extent predictable. Thus for the vast majority of men, the knowledge, power and control remain about *their own* possible feelings of sometimes being out of control. The most obvious example of this is the knowledge that drinking may be associated with feelings of loss of control. To reduce all this and the numerous variations on such themes to a sentence or a paragraph or a page is difficult, if not impossible.

Similarly, doing research and writing about men's violence to known women is an ambiguous process. For me, it brings both progressive and optimistic feelings, and regressive and pessimistic ones. It simultaneously provides hope and disappointment. Research and writing on violence are not to be taken lightly by men.

Making Links

Analysing men's violences to known women invites the segmentation of the phenomena and the experiences around it. However, it is equally important to acknowledge that each element of analysis – for example, contested definitions of violence, the attribution of responsibility, the explanation of action, the construction of knowledge about violence – is interlinked with the others. Particular definitions, such as very narrow ones, suggest particular versions of responsibility and explanation, such as those that minimize men's culpability and particular forms of knowledge, such as those that are partial and derived from men's experience. Elements of analysis interlink and reinforce each other. Links need to be recognized between different methodological approaches to violence: those that draw on social psychological models, discourses and discursive practices, and materialist analyses of violence and violent acts. Similarly, parallel connections need to be drawn between theory, politics, policy and practice.

Policy Development

Agency policy development clearly remains vitally important in confronting men's violence. In addition to the specific policy arenas already discussed (see Chapters 9 and 10), there are particular agency responses to the problem of men's violence to known women that are relevant across agencies (Hearn, 1995, 1998a). These include:

- educating men on what violence is;
- dealing with the problem as the responsibility of the statutory sector;
- producing clear, general policy statements;
- developing public campaigns;
- changing the conditions that produce and sustain men's violence;
- addressing other oppressions;
- developing appropriate and detailed policy and practice;
- monitoring, maintaining and improving policy and practice;
- working against violence with men in contact in a focused way;
- placing issues of power, control and responsibility as central in focused work with men;
- developing inter-agency work with men;
- making men, men's power and men's violence explicit in agency and inter-agency work;
- addressing the need to change men in agencies;
- dealing with ambiguous issues of men's support for men;
- reaching out to men not in contact with agencies.

Throughout all of these, it is important to attend to and change men's practice in organizations. It is not possible, on the one hand, to work with men against *their* violence and, on the other, to behave in violent and abusive ways as men. Developing ways of managing that are non-oppressive, non-violent and non-abusive is a high priority (Hearn, 1996c: 113; also see Collinson and Hearn, 1996).

Any innovations in work by men and/or with men has to supplement broader public policy, including consistent police and prosecution policy and practice; inter-agency work with women experiencing violence; improved housing provision for women; and state support for Women's Aid and other projects for women. Men's violence to women represents a clear challenge to the development of agency policy and practice by men and in relation to men. There is thus a need for a national commitment against violence. As the Gulbenkian Foundation Commission Report (1995), *Children and Violence*, stressed as its first priority recommendation:

> Individuals, communities and government at all levels should adopt a 'Commitment to non-violence', of similar standing to existing commitments to 'equal opportunities'.

The Report continued:

> The aims of the commitment are to work towards a society in which individuals, communities and government share non-violent values and resolve conflict by non-violent means. Building such a society involves . . . consistent disavowal of all forms of inter-personal violence – in particular by opinion-leaders.

Governmental and other policies and strategies should embody a clear opposition to violence by boys and men, should tell boys and men not to be violent, advocate policies that encourage men to behave in ways that facilitate women's equality, and make it clear that the realization of such changes depends partly on men in politics and policy-making, and their own understanding of their gendered actions. These issues equally apply beyond the nation in international and global contexts. Mullender (1997: 28) summarizes recent initiatives as follows:

> Wife abuse only became a formal international priority in the 1980s during the United Nations' Decade for Women. . . . In 1992, a UN Declaration recognised violence against women and children as a human rights issue, and the UN Platform of Action from the Fourth World Conference on Women, held in Beijing in 1995 . . . built upon this by including violence against women as one of its critical areas of concern.

These initiatives need to be taken on board by men in changing men.

Changing and Improving Men's Personal Practice

Finally, and most importantly, the point of all this is to change and improve men's personal practice. What this means specifically is stopping, or better still not starting, violence and abuse to women. It also means giving attention to this priority in all possible social arenas – in families, at school, amongst friends, in workplaces, in the media, and throughout politics (Hearn, 1998a). It is a problem to be faced by men in our relations with each other, just as much as in our relations with women and children. It is our responsibility not to collude with each other, and so make such violence intolerable and simply out of the question. This entails focusing on action against violence, and yet seeing violence in a broad and open-ended way that does not separate it off from other parts of personal life; it also entails recognizing the many close connections that there are between violence and sexuality in dominant forms of men's practice, and opposing and transforming those connections. It involves changing all those elements of gender inequality that support men's violence. Men's personal practice without violence is not only a better way of living one's life, but also a prerequisite for men to be involved in professional intervention, policy development, and indeed research on men's violences against women. It is time that men came out against men's violence to women; it is time for men to change.

Appendix: Summary of Men in Interview Sample

Source of referral	Age	Relation to woman at time of violence	No. of children	No. of times of violence reported*	Violence described by man in interview	Violence Index	Place in criminal justice system
Police	33	M & LT	1	30×	Mental torture, beat up, 6 counts of assault	9	Charged and cautioned, not convicted
Police	47	M & LT	2	?	Thrown and smacked, attacked woman's man friend	7	Arrested, breach of the peace, bound over for 1 year, £100 fine, not charged for assault
Police	55	M & LT	3	2×	Hit with fist, kicked	7	Charged with ABH × 2, both charges dropped
Police	37	M & LT	5	5×	Beat up	8	Convicted of ABH × 2, £50 compensation, £38 costs, 2 years probation
Police	50	M & LT	3	1×	Pushed, shoved, threatened, smacked	7	Charged with ABH, charge dropped
Police	20	NM & LT	0	'loads'	Beat up, lifted by the throat	9	Arrested, not charged
Police	32	M & LT	2	1×	Assault	7	Charged with ABH, bound over for 12 months for £100
Police	24	M & LT	1	10×	Criminal damage to door, slapped, kicked	8	Arrested, not charged
Police	41	M & LT	4	1×	Pushed, shoved, slapped	7	Charged, not convicted
Police	30	M & LT	4	'loads'	Beat up, threatened with knife	9	Charged with ABH, convicted, £20 fine

Police	25	Son	0	1×	Pushed, shoved, threw things	6	Arrested, not charged
Police	28	M & LT	1	5×	Pushed, shoved, thrown, threatened, poured water over	8	Arrested, not charged
Police	29	M & LT	2	7×	Pushed, shoved, slapped, threw things	8	Arrested, not charged
Police	24	NM & LT	1	?	Pushed, shoved, hit, threw things	7	Arrested, not charged
Police	30	M & LT	1	1×	Pushed, shoved, slapped	7	Convicted of ABH, £50 fine, £50 costs
Probation/ Police	21	NM & LT	1	2×	Slapped, beat up	9	Convicted of ABH and GBH, 2 year probation
Probation	50	M & LT	2	>30×	Beat up	9	Convicted of ABH, bound over (3 years according to the man?)
Probation	35	NM & LT	1	5×	Beat up	8	Convicted of GBH, bound over 1 year, probation
Probation	27	NM & NLT	2	2×	Assault, indecent assault	7	5½ year imprisonment
Probation	27	NM & LT	1	'loads'	Pulled hair, hit with stick, assaults, humiliation	9	Convicted of ABH × 4, imprisonment, 7 months, 2 months, 4 months, 15 months
Probation	37	M & NLT	3	3×	Kidnapping, assault, indecent assault, false imprisonment	8	Imprisonment for ABH, kidnapping; false imprisonment and indecent assault dropped
Probation	32	NM & LT	4	>30×	Beat up, threatened with knife	9	Charged >3×. Some charges dropped, some acquitted, probation
Prison	27	NM & NLT (Neighbour)	0	3×	Assaults, manslaughter, rape	10	Convicted of ABH, GBH, manslaughter, rape, life imprisonment
Prison	42	NM & LT	4	2×	Beat up, assault, use of knife, murder, ripped up clothes	10	Convicted of GBH, 4 years imprisonment; murder, life imprisonment

continued

APPENDIX (*cont.*)

Source of referral	Age	Relation to woman at time of violence	No. of children	No. of times of violence reported*	Violence described by man in interview	Violence Index	Place in criminal justice system
Prison	38	NM & LT	2	2×	Assault, murder	10	Convicted of GBH, 4 years imprisonment; murder, life imprisonment
Prison	40	NM & LT	3	'loads'	Assaults, wounding, use of knife	9	Imprisonment for ABH and wounding
Prison	23	NM & NLT	0	5×	Verbal, throwing, smashing	8	None for violence to women
Prison	34	M & LT	2	?	Denied violence	10	Convicted attempted murder, and murder of wife's lover, life imprisonment
Prison	39	M & LT	3	'loads'	5 assaults, threw things, threatened, verbal	9	None for violence to women
Men's programme	33	M & LT	2	5×	Hit with fist, beat up, pushed, shoved	8	None
Men's programme	38	M & LT	1	20×	Assaults, beat up, threw things	9	Convicted of ABH, fined £75, £15 costs
Men's programme	44	M & NLT	2	>15×	Assaults	9	Convicted of ABH ×2
Men's programme	43	NM & NLT	2	'fairly persistent'	Hit with fist extremely hard, 'loads'	9	None
Men's programme	29	(1) Divorced (2) NM & LT	2	50×	Beat up, punched	9	Police interview, not charged
Men's programme	46	M & NLT	2	7×	Pushed, grabbed, thrown	8	Convicted, fined
Men's programme	31	NM & NLT	2	'lots'	Hit, pushed, slapped	9	None

Men's programme	34	M & LT	2	'lots'	Beat up, pushed, slapped	9	Police interview, not charged
Men's programme	24	NM & LT	0	2×	Pushed, shoved, punched	7	None
Men's programme	23	NM & LT	2	'loads'	Hit, punched, pushed	9	Arrested, not charged
Men's programme	34	NM & LT	0	7×	Punched, hit, pushed	8	None
Men's programme	32	M & LT	0	10×	Assaults, beat up, use of knife	8	Convicted of ABH × 2, 250 hours community service and £30 fine, charges on use of knife dropped
Men's programme	25	NM & LT	0	10×	Pushed, slapped, thrown, threw things	8	None
Men's programme	35	M & LT	3	20×	Slapped, thrown, pushed, shoved	9	None
Men's programme	65	M & LT	4	10×	Slapped, hit, threatened, threw things	8	None
Men's programme	43	NM & LT	3	2×	Slapped, hit with fist, threatened, pushed	7	Police interview, no arrest
Men's programme	29	NM & LT	0	?	Violent fantasies	1	None
Men's programme	32	M & LT	1	>30×	Grabbed neck, pulled hair, kicked	9	None
Men's programme	30	M & LT	2	5×	Beat up	8	Arrested, not charged
Social services	41	M & LT	5	2×	Pushed, shoved, slapped, threw things	7	Convicted of ABH, bound over for 12 months, £150 fine, probation
Welfare agency	43	NM & LT	2	10×	Hit, punched, slapped	8	Convicted drunk and disorderly and affray, 12 months probation
Welfare agency	47	M & LT	4	'lots'	Beat up	9	Convicted of ABH, 9 month suspended sentence for 3 years

continued

APPENDIX (cont.)

Source of referral	Age	Relation to woman at time of violence	No. of children	No. of times of violence reported*	Violence described by man in interview	Violence Index	Place in criminal justice system
Welfare agency	34	M & LT	2	>30×	Everything apart from murder	9	None
No agency	38	M & LT	1	8×	Pushed, shoved	5	None
No agency	32	M & NLT	4	3×	Hit with fist	8	None
No agency	30	M & LT	0	'lots'	Verbal, psychological	3	None
No agency	40	M & LT	1	10×	Hit, slapped, threw things	8	Police interview, not arrested
No agency	19	Son	0	1×	Attacked mother's partner	4	None
No agency	29	NM & NLT	0	1×	Wrestling	2	None
No agency	39	M & LT	2	5×	Verbal, psychological	3	None
No agency	24	M & LT	2	5×	Pushed, grabbed, slapped, thrown, assault	8	Charged, not convicted

* Reported on questionnaire. Note descriptions of violence in interview may not correspond.

M = Married
NM = Not married
LT = Living together
NLT = Not living together
Violence Index from 1 to 10 based on all information on men, including from agencies.
1 = violent fantasies 2= ambiguous wrestling 3 = verbal and psychological violence 4 = physical violence to woman's friend/partner 5 = pushed, shoved 6 = pushed, shoved, threw things 7 = 1 or 2 physical attacks involving more than pushing and showing 8 = 3–15 physical attacks 9 = more than 15 physical attacks 10 = murder, manslaughter, attempted murder
ABH = Actual bodily harm
GBH = Grievous bodily harm

Notes

1 Introduction

1. There is now a growing history of these 'crises' and questionings of men (for example, Kimmel, 1987), including those that have been developed self-consciously by pro-feminist men (Strauss, 1983; Kimmel and Mosmiller, 1992).

2. Citing Smith, 1989; Mirrlees-Black, 1994; Mooney, 1994.

3. This section draws on Hearn, 1996d: 24–27.

4. The Research Study is ESRC No L2606 25 2003: 'Violence, Abuse and the Stress-coping Process Project 2' (Hearn, 1993b).

5. With two exceptions, these were all men who talked directly of their own violence to known women. These two exceptions were one man who talked of violent fantasies, and another who had been convicted of attempted murder but denied the offence.

2 Definitions and Explanations of Men's Violence

1. This section and the references cited draw heavily upon Kemper's (1990) important study of the interrelation of social structure and testosterone.

2. A further link is between testosterone, aggression and norepinephrine, which carries nerve impulses across the synaptic gap within the Sympathetic branch of the Autonomic Nervous System (Kemper, 1990).

3. Citing Straus et al., 1980; Straus and Gelles, 1990.

4. Citing Monahan, 1981.

5. Citing Star, 1978; Coleman et al., 1980; Straus et al., 1980; Rosenbaum and O'Leary, 1981; Fagen et al., 1983; Kalmuss, 1984; Sonkin and Durphy, 1985.

6. Citing Rosenbaum and O'Leary, 1981; Kalmuss, 1984; Hotaling and Sugarman, 1986.

7. Citing, Bard and Zacker, 1974; Coleman and Straus, 1983; Van Hasselt et al., 1985; Kantor and Straus, 1987.

8. The extent to which stress can be separated off from a broader social analysis is discussed in Hanmer et al., 1993. Also see Seymour, 1992, 1998; Williams, 1992, 1998.

9. One way out of this conundrum is to argue that men and women are much more comparable to each other in their violence, as in much of the work that has derived from the use of the Conflicts Tactics Scale (Straus, 1979). This approach has subsequently been thoroughly critiqued (Dobash and Dobash, 1992; Dobash et al., 1992; Nazroo, 1995).

10. For discussions of violence and differentiations within patriarchy/patriarchies, see Walby, 1986, 1990; Hearn, 1987, 1992b. These kind of analyses point to the

danger of reifying patriarchy. This issue is addressed directly by Poon (1995) (drawing principally on the work of Scott [1990], who in turn draws on the work of Giddens [1979, 1981, 1984]). In her review of conceptual issues in defining male domestic violence, Poon (1995) distinguishes between 'male domination as a system and the specific patriarchal structures as rules and resources that reproduce the general pattern of male domination'. Such a framework 'allows conceptual space for differences in social location, such as class, ethnicity' (Poon, 1995: 250). It is through these rules and resources that gendered subjectivities are produced. This kind of approach has much in common with Messerschmidt (1993), who draws more directly on Connell (1987), as well as Giddens. His particular focus is on the intersection of class, gender and race relations, social structures and social action in the framing of gendered crime, including violence.

11. Citing Hanmer and Saunders, 1984, 1987, 1993.

12. The distinction between studies that focus on explanations of men's violence (in general or as a generalized phenomenon) and men's violence to women is itself of interest. The fact that some explanations of men's violence do not attend to its gendered nature is itself a form of gendering. Non-gendering of explanations is itself gendered. Non-gendering is most often accomplished by men. Indeed non-gendering in explanations is one way of those with gender power (usually men) of maintaining or protecting that power, by virtue of diverting attention from their gender power. This process can be individual or collective, conscious or unconscious. For a discussion and application of the gendering of analyses, see Hanmer and Hearn, 1998.

3 Studying and Researching Men's Violence to Known Women

1. For further discussion on these questions, see Morgan, 1981, 1992; Hearn, 1987, 1989, 1994d, 1999; Hearn and Morgan, 1990.

2. For further discussion of the relationship of subjectivity and objectivity in Critical Studies on Men see Hearn, 1993d, 1994d.

3. For a further discussion of relevant issues see Hearn 1993d.

4. A fascinating account of demands for confidentiality in researching rapists is provided by Scully (1990).

5. The idea of emancipatory communication is developed in Critical Theory (for example, Habermas, 1971; Fay, 1975; Held, 1980). What is not developed, in this tradition, however, is a gendering of such communicative forms. There is also a lack of attention to the link between forms of communicative acts and the emancipation of 'others' not directly participating in those acts, but affected by them.

6. Dunn explores the hazardous nature of qualitative research, specifically in doing research on 'the meaning of battering to women who had been victims' (Dunn, 1991: 389).

4 Violence and Talking About Violence

1. A comparison can be made here with the attempt to 'talk the body'. See Jardine, 1987; Jackson 1990.

2. For useful discussions of context and the 'inherent contextuality' of action, see Knorr, 1979, and Cooper and Fox, 1990, who also emphasize the importance of connectedness, complexity and tacitness (also see Hosking and Fineman, 1990).

3. See Hearn and Parkin, 1987, 1995; Smith, 1987, 1989, 1990; Benschop and Doorewaard, 1995, 1998.

4. For other non-gendered discussions of the relation of the material and discursive, see Hunt, 1989; Kaye, 1991; Kalb, 1993; for gendered discussions see Hearn, 1992b, 1993a, 1994c; Hennessy, 1993; Landry and Maclean, 1993.

5 The Contexts of Violence

1. The distinction between strategy and tactics is well developed in military, business and systemic thinking (see, for example, Schützenberger, 1954). There has been considerable recent interest in the use of the concept of strategy in sociological analysis (see Crow, 1991; Edwards and Ribbens, 1991; Morgan, 1991).

2. Citing Scott and Lyman, 1968. For further discussions of the production of accounts of problematic behaviour see Lyman and Scott, 1970; Schönbach, 1980; Antaki, 1981; Semin and Manstead, 1983. Further consideration of alternative accounts is provided in Chapter 7.

3. All placenames have been disguised, just as all personal names are pseudonyms.

6 The Text of Violence: (1) How Men Describe Their Violence

1. Goading is what is done to animals, especially cattle or oxen when they are urged on by the use of a pointed stick. The term is also used when horses are excessively whipped. The figurative use of goading is 'to assail or prick as with a goad; to instigate or impel by mental pain or annoyance'.

2. Harassment is a term that seems to be never used by men when talking about their violence to women they know.

7 The Text of Violence: (2) How Men Account for Their Violence

1. In a particularly interesting study of 'narrative characters' in accounts of violence, in this case violence by New Zealand police against anti-apartheid campaigners during the 1981 Springbok tour, Wetherell and Potter (1989) draw on Atkinson and Drew's (1979) work on the management of accusation in courts and on Semin and Manstead's (1983) synthetic typology of excuses and justifications. Wetherell and Potter discuss accounts of justifications of and excuses for the violence of the police. In particular they focus on excuses. They address the way that excuses may or may not draw on the pressure of a self of the speaker in talking about, giving accounts of, and above all giving excuses for, the violence. Also see Hydén, 1994, for a discussion of narrative in interviewing women about violence to them from men, and Richardson, 1990, for a more general examination of narrative and sociology.

2. The reference to the real self does not imply any question of honesty, merely a reference by the man to authenticities. See Marshall and Wetherell, 1989.

8 The Sexual Subtexts of Talk About Violence

1. This chapter is a development of Hearn, 1994a, 1996a.

2. Citing Jackson, 1982; Coveney et al., 1984; Hite, 1987; Thompson, 1990.

3. Citing MacCannell and MacCannell, 1987; Lesko, 1988; Martin, 1989; Bartky, 1990; Bordo, 1990.

4. Citing Holland et al., 1993.

5. In some complex and contradictory accounts it may be more accurate to think of there being an anti-narrative – a persistent and ongoing disruption of a cohesive story.

9 In and Around Agencies

1. For further details of the responses of Social Services, Probation and men's programmes, see Hearn, 1995, 1998b.

2. There has been considerable recent interest in the development of improved policy and practice in Probation. See Burn et al., 1990; Cordery and Whitehead, 1992; Jenkins, 1994; Pringle, 1995; Mullender, 1997.

3. This section draws on material discussed in Hearn, 1994c.

10 Moving Away From Violence?

1. For further discussion of individual and collective change, see Hearn, 1998a.

2. A more extensive discussion of the ambiguities of men's support for men who have been violent to known women is developed in Hearn, 1998c.

3. This way of conceptualizing resources, support and coping is a critique of the 'stress-coping' paradigm (Titterton, 1989) that has been promoted as a 'new paradigm' in the analysis of personal welfare. It moves the emphasis from individual stress and distress to social power, pressure and oppression. Also see note 2:8.

11 Key Issues for Theory, Politics, Policy and Practice

1. For further discussion on this question, see Hearn, 1994d, 1999.

2. Cited by Hanmer, 1990: 41–42.

Bibliography

Adams, D. (1988). Treatment models with men who batter: a pro-feminist analysis. In M. Bograd and K. Yllö (Eds.), *Feminist Perspectives on Wife Abuse* (pp. 176–199). Newbury Park, CA: Sage.

Annett, M. (1976). *Evolution, Genetics and Social Behaviour*. Milton Keynes: Open University Press.

Antaki, C. (Ed.) (1981). *The Psychology of Ordinary Explanations of Social Behaviour*. London: Academic Press.

Ardrey, R. (1961). *African Genesis*. New York: Atheneum.

Ardrey, R. (1966). *The Territorial Imperative*. New York: Atheneum.

Atkins, S. and Hoggett, B. (1984). *Women and the Law*. Oxford: Blackwell.

Atkinson, J.M. and Drew, P. (1979). *Order in Court: The Organization of Verbal Interaction in Judicial Settings*. London: Macmillan/SSRC.

Austin, J.L. (1961). *Philosophical Papers*. London: Oxford University Press.

Bagarozzi, D. and Giddings, C.W. (1983). Conjugal violence: a critical review of current research and clinical practices. *The American Journal of Family Therapy*, 11, 3–15.

Bandura, A. (1973). *Aggression: A Social Learning Analysis*. Englewood Cliffs, NJ: Prentice-Hall.

Bandura, A. (1977). *Social Learning Theory*. Englewood Cliffs, NJ: Prentice-Hall.

Bard, M. and Zacker, J. (1974). Assaultiveness and alcohol use in family disputes: police perceptions. *Criminology*, 12 (3), 281–292.

Barry, K. (1984). *Female Sexual Slavery*. New York: New York University Press.

Bartky, S.L. (1990). *Femininity and Domination: Studies in the Phenomenology of Oppression*. London: Routledge.

Bell, V. (1993). *Interrogating Incest: Feminism, Foucault and the Law*. London: Routledge.

Bell, V. (1995). Bio-politics and the spectre of incest: sexuality and/in the family. In M. Featherstone, S. Lash and R. Robertson (Eds.), *Global Modernities* (pp. 227–243). London: Sage.

Beneke, T. (1982). *Men on Rape*. New York: St Martin's Press.

Benjamin, J. (1988). *The Bonds of Love: Psychoanalysis, Feminism and the Problem of Domination*. New York: Pantheon; 1990 London: Virago.

Benschop, Y. and Doorewaard, H. (1995). *'Covered' by Equality: the Gender Subtext of Organizations*. Mimeo. Department of Business Studies, Katholieke Universiteit Nijmegen.

Benschop, Y. and Doorewaard, H. (1998). Six of one and half a dozen of the other: the gender subtext of Taylorism and team-based work. *Gender, Work and Organization*, 5 (1): 5–18.

Bergman, B. and Brismar, B. (1992). Family violence is a learned behaviour. *Journal of Public Health*, 106, 45–52.

Bhatti-Sinclair, K. (1994). Asian women and violence from male partners. In C.

Lupton and T. Gillespie (Eds.), *Working With Violence* (pp. 75–95). London: Macmillan.

Binney, V., Harkell, G. and Nixon, J. (1981). *Leaving Violent Men*. London: Women's Aid Federation, England.

Bordo, S. (1990). Material girl: the effacements of postmodern culture. *Michigan Quarterly Review*, Fall, 653–676.

Bowker, L.H. (1983). *Beating Wife-Beating*. Lexington, MA: Lexington Books.

Bowker, L.H., Arbitell, M. and McFerron, J.R. (1988). On the relationship between wife beating and child abuse. In K. Yllö and M. Bograd (Eds.), *Feminist Perspectives on Wife Abuse* (pp. 158–174). Newbury Park, CA: Sage.

Brannen, J. (Ed.) (1992). *Mixing Methods: Qualitative and Quantitative Research*. Aldershot: Avebury.

Bristol Women's Studies Group (1979). *Half the Story: An Introduction to Women's Studies*. London: Virago.

Brittan, A. (1989). *Masculinity and Power*. Oxford: Blackwell.

Brophy, J. and Smart, C. (1982). From disregard to disrepute: the position of women in family law. In E. Whitelegg, M. Arnott, E. Bartels, V. Beechey, L. Birke, S. Himmelweit, D. Leonard, S. Ruchl and M.A. Speakmann (Eds.), *The Changing Experience of Women* (pp. 207–225). Milton Keynes: Open University Press.

Brownmiller, S. (1975). *Against Our Will*. Harmondsworth: Penguin.

Bull, R. and Shaw, I. (1992). Constructing causal accounts in social work. *Sociology*, 26 (4), 635–649.

Burn, D., Boyle, J., Copsey, M., Cordery, J., Dominelli, L., Lambert, J., Smallridge, M., Whitehead, V. and Willis, S. (1990). Offending and masculinity: working with males. *Probation Journal*, 37 (3), 106–111.

Caesar, P.L. and Hamberger, L.K. (Eds.) (1989). *Treating Men Who Batter: Theory, Practice and Programs*. New York: Springer.

Campbell, A. (1993). *Out of Control: Men, Women and Aggression*. London: Pandora.

Carrigan, T., Connell, R.W. and Lee, J. (1985). Toward a new sociology of masculinity. *Theory and Society*, 14 (5), 551–604.

Chodorow, N. (1978). *The Reproduction of Mothering*. Berkeley: University of California Press.

Cobbe, F.P. (1878). 'Wife torture in England'. *The Contemporary Review*, April, 55–87.

Cobbe, F.P. (1894). *Life of Frances Power Cobbe by Herself, Vol. 2*. London: Bentley.

Cockburn, C. (1983). *Brothers*. London: Pluto

Coleman, D. and Straus, M. (1983). Alcohol abuse and family violence. In E. Gottheil (Ed.), *Alcohol, Drug Abuse and Aggression*. Springfield, IL: Charles Thomas.

Coleman, K., Weinman, M.L. and Hsi, B.P. (1980). Factors affecting conjugal violence. *Journal of Psychology*, 105, 197–202.

Collier, R. (1995). *Masculinity, Law and the Family*. London: Routledge.

Collinson, D.L. and Hearn, J. (1994). Naming men as men: implications for work, organizations and management. *Gender, Work and Organization*, 1 (1), 2–22.

Collinson, D.L. and Hearn, J. (Eds.) (1996). *Men as Managers, Managers as Men: Critical Perspectives on Men, Masculinities and Management*. London: Sage.

Connell, R.W. (1987). *Gender and Power*. Cambridge: Polity.

Cooper, R. and Fox, S. (1990). The texture of organizing. *Journal of Management Studies*, 27 (6), 575–582.

Coote, A. and Campbell, B. (1982). *Sweet Freedom: The Struggle for Women's Liberation*. London: Picador.

Cordery, J. and Whitehead, A. (1992). 'Boys don't cry': empathy, warmth, collusion and crime. In P. Senior and D. Woodhill (Eds.), *Gender, Crime and Probation Practice*. Sheffield: Sheffield City Polytechnic PAVIC Publication.

Coveney, L., Jackson, M., Jeffreys, S., Kaye, L. and Mahoney, P. (1984). *The Sexuality Papers: Male Sexuality and the Social Control of Women*. London: Hutchinson.

Craib, I. (1987). Masculinity and male dominance. *Sociological Review*, 34 (3), 721–742.

Crow, G. (1991). The use of the concept of strategy in recent sociological literature. *Sociology*, 23 (1), 1–24.

Dabbs, J.M., Frady, R.L., Carr, T.S. and Besch, N.F. (1987). Saliva testosterone and criminal violence in young adult prison inmates. *Psychosomatic Medicine*, 49, 174–182.

Dankwort, J. (1988). *Batterers' Programs and Issues of Accountability: A Critical Evaluation from Quebec*. Unpublished master's dissertation, Montreal, Quebec.

Dankwort, J. (1992–3). Violence against women: varying perceptions and intervention practices with woman abusers. *Intervention* (Quebec), 92, 34–49.

DeKeseredy, W.S. (1990). Male peer support and woman abuse: the current state of knowledge. *Sociological Focus*, 23, 129–139.

Delphy, C. and Leonard, D. (1992). *Familiar Exploitation: A New Analysis of Marriage in Contemporary Western Societies*. Cambridge: Polity.

Dobash, R.E. and Dobash, R.P. (1979). *Violence Against Wives: A Case Against the Patriarchy*. London: Open Books.

Dobash, R.E. and Dobash, R.P. (1984). The nature and antecedents of violent events. *British Journal of Criminology*, 24 (3), 269–288.

Dobash, R.E. and Dobash, R.P. (1992). *Women, Violence and Social Change*. London and New York: Routledge.

Dobash, R.P., Dobash, R.E., Wilson, M. and Daly, M. (1992). The myth of sexual symmetry in marital violence. *Social Problems*, 39 (1), 71–91.

Dobash, R.P., Dobash, R.E., Cavanagh, K. and Lewis, R. (1996a). *The Evaluation of Programmes for Violent Men*. Edinburgh: Scottish Office.

Dobash, R.P., Dobash, R.E., Cavanagh, K. and Lewis, R. (1996b) *Re-education Programmes for Violent Men – An Evaluation*. Research Findings No. 46. Croydon: Home Office Research and Statistics Directorate.

Dunn, L. (1991). Research Alert! Qualitative research may be hazardous to your health. *Qualitative Health Research*, 1 (3), 388–392.

Dworkin, A. (1982). *Pornography: Men Possessing Women*. London: Women's Press.

Dworkin, A. (1985). A word people don't understand. *MS*, 46, April, cited in Hanmer, 1990.

Dyer, R. (1985). Male sexuality in the media. In A. Metcalf and M. Humphries (Eds.), *The Sexuality of Men*. London: Pluto.

Edleson, J.L. and Tolman, R.M. (1992). *Intervention for Men who Batter: An Ecological Approach*. London: Sage.

Edleson, J.L., Eisikovits, Z. and Guttman, E. (1985). Men who batter women: a critical review of the evidence. *Journal of Family Issues*, 6 (2), 229–247.

Edwards, R. (1990). Connecting method and epistemology: a white woman interviewing black women. *Women's Studies International Forum*, 13 (5), 477–490.

Edwards, R. and Ribbens, J. (1991). Meanderings around 'strategy': a research note on the strategic discourse in the lives of women. *Sociology*, 25 (3), 477–489.

Edwards, S. (1989). *Policing Domestic Violence*. London: Sage.

Ehrenkranz, J., Bliss, E. and Sheard, M.H. (1974). Plasma testosterone: correlation with aggressive behaviour and social dominance in men. *Psychosomatic Medicine*, 36, 469–475.

Eichenbaum, L. and Orbach, S. (1984). *What Do Women Want?* London: Fontana/Collins.

Elias, M. (1981). Serum cortisol, testosterone, and testosterone binding globulin response to competitive fighting in human males. *Aggressive Behaviour*, 7, 215–224.

Elshtain, J.B. (1981). *Public Man, Private Women*. London: Martin Robertson.

Eysenck, H. (1964). *Crime and Personality*. London: Routledge and Kegan Paul.

Fagen, J.A., Stewart, D.K. and Hanson, K.V. (1983). Violent men or violent husbands? In D. Finkelhor, R.J. Gelles, G.T. Hotaling and M.A. Straus (Eds.), *The Dark Side of Families: Current Family Violence Research* (pp. 49–67). Beverly Hills, CA: Sage.

Fanon, F. (1967). *The Wretched of the Earth*. Harmondsworth: Penguin.

Fawcett, B. (1996). Women, mental health and community care: an abusive combination? In B. Fawcett, B. Featherstone, J. Hearn and C. Toft (Eds.), *Violence and Gender Relations: Theories and Interventions* (pp. 81–97). London: Sage.

Fay, B. (1975). *Social Theory and Political Practice*. London: Allen and Unwin.

Foucault, M. (1979). *Discipline and Punish*. New York: Vintage Books.

Foucault, M. (1988). Technologies of the self. In L.H. Martin, H. Gutman and P.H. Hutton (Eds.), *Technologies of the Self* (pp. 19–49). Boston: University of Massachusetts Press; London: Tavistock.

Frank, B. (1987). Hegemonic heterosexual masculinity. *Studies in Political Economy*, 24, 159–170.

Freeman, M.D.A. (1987). *Dealing with Domestic Violence*. Bicester, Oxon: CCH Editions.

Friedman, S. and Sarah, E. (Eds.) (1982). *On the Problem of Men*. London: Women's Press.

Fuller, P. (1995). *Masculinity, Scripting and Child Sexual Abuse*. Unpublished doctoral thesis, University of Essex.

Ganley, A.L. (1989). Integrating feminist and social learning analyses of aggression: creating multiple models for intervention with men who batter. In P.L. Caesar and L.K. Hamberger (Eds.), *Treating Men Who Batter. Theory, Practice and Programs* (pp. 196–235). New York: Springer.

Garfinkel, H. (1967). *Studies in Ethnomethodology*. New York: Prentice-Hall.

Geffner, R., Mantooth, C., Franks, D. and Rao, L. (1989). A psychoeducational, conjoint therapy approach to reducing family violence. In P.L. Caesar and L.K. Hamberger (Eds.), *Treating Men Who Batter: Theory, Practice and Programs* (pp. 103–133). New York: Springer.

Gelles, R.J. (1974). *The Violent Home*. Beverly Hills, CA: Sage.

Gelles, R.J. (1983). An exchange/social control theory. In D. Finkelhor, R.J. Gelles, G.T. Hotaling and M.A. Straus (Eds.), *The Dark Side of Families*. Beverly Hills, CA: Sage.

Gelles, R.J. and Cornell, C.P. (1985). *Intimate Violence in Families*. Beverly Hills, CA: Sage.

Gerth, H. and Mills, C.W. (1953). *Character and Social Structure*. New York: Harcourt, Brace and World Inc.

Giddens, A. (1979). *Central Problems in Social Theory: Action, Structure and Contradiction in Social Analysis*. Berkeley, CA: University of California Press.

Giddens, A. (1981). *A Contemporary Critique of Historical Materialism, Vol. 1*. Berkeley, CA: University of California Press.

Giddens, A. (1984). *The Constitution of Society: Outline of the Theory of Structuration*. Berkeley, CA: University of California Press.

Godenzi, A. (1994). What's the big deal? We are men and they are women. In T. Newburn and E.A. Stanko (Eds.), *Just Boys Doing Business: Men, Masculinities and Crime* (pp. 135–152). London: Routledge.

Goldner, V., Penn, P., Sheinberg, M. and Walker, G. (1990). Love and violence: gender paradoxes in volatile attachments. *Family Process*, 29 (4), 343–364.

Goldstein, J.H. (1989). Beliefs about human aggression. In J. Groebel and R.A. Hinde (Eds.), *Aggression and War: Their Biological and Social Bases* (pp. 10–19). Cambridge and New York: Cambridge University Press.

Gondolf, E.W. (1985). *Men Who Batter: An Integrated Approach for Stopping Wife Abuse*. Holmes Beach, FL: Learning Publications.

Gondolf, E.W. (1987). Seeing through smoke and mirrors: a guide to batterer program evaluations. *Response*, 10 (3), 16–19.

Gondolf, E.W. (1988). Who are those guys? Towards a behavioral typology of men who batter. *Journal of Interpersonal Violence*, 3, 275–289.

Gondolf, E.W. (1993). Male batterers. In R.L. Hampton, T.P. Gullotta, G.R. Adams, E.H. Potter III and R.P. Weissberg (Eds.), *Family Violence: Prevention and Treatments* (pp. 230–257). Newbury Park, CA: Sage.

Gondolf, E.W. and Russell, D. (1986). The case against anger control treatment programs for batterers. *Response*, 9 (3), 2–5.

Grosz, E.A. (1987). Feminist theory and the challenge to knowledges. *Women's Studies International Forum*, 10 (5), 475–480.

Groth, N. (1979). *Men Who Rape: The Psychology of the Offender*. New York: Plenum.

Gulbenkian Foundation Commission Report (1995). *Children and Violence*. London: Calouste Gulbenkian Foundation.

Habermas, J. (1971). *Knowledge and Human Interests*. London: Heinemann.

Hamberger, L.K. and Hastings, J.E. (1993). Court-mandated treatments of men who assault their partner: issues, controversies and outcomes. In N.Z. Hilton (Ed.), *Legal Responses to Wife Assault: Current Trends and Evaluation* (pp. 188–229). Newbury Park, CA: Sage.

Hamberger, L.K. and Lohr, J.M. (1989). Proximal causes of spouse abuse: a theoretical analysis for cognitive-behavioral interventions. In P.L. Caesar and L.K. Hamberger (Eds.), *Treating Men Who Batter: Theory, Practice and Programs* (pp. 53–76). New York: Springer.

Hanmer, J. (1990). Men, power and the exploitation of women. In J. Hearn and D. Morgan (Eds.), *Men, Masculinities and Social Theory* (pp. 21–42). London: Unwin Hyman.

Hanmer, J. (1993). *End of Award Report: Violence, Abuse and the Stress-Coping Process. Project 1*. Report to the ESRC. University of Bradford.

Hanmer, J. (1995). *Patterns of Agency Contacts with Women who have Experienced Violence from Known Men*. Research Unit on Violence, Abuse and Gender Relations, University of Bradford, Research Paper No. 12.

Hanmer, J. (1996). Women and violence: commonalties and diversities. In B. Fawcett, B. Featherstone, J. Hearn and C. Toft (Eds.), *Violence and Gender Relations: Theories and Interventions* (pp. 7–21). London: Sage.

Hanmer, J. and Hearn, J. (1993). *Gendered Research and Researching Gender*. Paper presented at the British Sociological Association Annual Conference 'Research Imaginations', University of Essex. Mimeo. University of Bradford.

Hanmer, J. and Hearn, J. (1998). Gender and welfare research. In F. Williams, J. Popay and A. Oakley (Eds.), *Welfare Research*. London: UCL Press.

Hanmer, J. and Saunders, S. (1984). *Well-Founded Fear: A Community Study of Violence to Women*. London: Hutchinson.

Hanmer, J. and Saunders, S. (1987). *Women, Violence and Crime Prevention*. Report of a Research Study Commissioned by West Yorkshire Metropolitan County Council. November.

Hanmer, J. and Saunders, S. (1990). *Women, Violence and Crime Prevention: A Study of Changes in Policy and Practice in West Yorkshire*. Research Unit on

Violence, Abuse and Gender Relations, University of Bradford, Research Paper No. 1.

Hanmer, J. and Saunders, S. (1993). *Women, Violence and Crime Prevention.* Aldershot, Avebury.

Hanmer, J., Radford, J. and Stanko, E.A. (Eds.) (1989). *Women, Policing and Male Violence: International Perspectives.* London: Routledge.

Hanmer, J., Hearn, J. and Bruce, E. (1993). *Gender and the Management of Personal Welfare.* Report for ESRC Management of Personal Welfare Initiative. Mimeo. Research Unit on Violence, Abuse and Gender Relations, University of Bradford.

Haupt, H.A. and Rovere, G.D. (1984). Anabolic steroids: a review of the literature. *American Journal of Sports Medicine*, 12, 469–484.

Hearn, J. (1983). *Birth and Afterbirth: A Materialist Account.* London: Achilles Heel.

Hearn, J. (1987). *The Gender of Oppression: Men, Masculinity and the Critique of Marxism.* Brighton: Wheatsheaf; New York: St Martin's Press.

Hearn, J. (1988). Child abuse: sexualities and violences towards young people. *Sociology*, 22 (4), 531–544.

Hearn, J. (1989). Reviewing men and masculinities – or mostly boys' own papers. *Theory, Culture & Society*, 6, 665–689.

Hearn, J. (1990). 'Child abuse' and men's violence. In Violence Against Children Study Group, *Taking Child Abuse Seriously: Contemporary Issues in Child Protection Theory and Practice* (pp. 63–85). London: Unwin Hyman.

Hearn, J. (1992a). *Health, Bodies and Men's Violence: Making Connections.* Research Unit on Violence, Abuse and Gender Relations, University of Bradford, Research Paper No. 2..

Hearn, J. (1992b). *Men in the Public Eye: The Construction and Deconstruction of Public Men and Public Patriarchies.* London and New York: Routledge.

Hearn, J. (1993a). Emotive subjects: organizational men, organizational masculinities and the (de)construction of emotions. In S. Fineman (Ed.), *Emotions in Organizations* (pp. 142–166). London: Sage.

Hearn, J. (1993b). *End of Award Report: Violence, Abuse and the Stress-Coping Process. Project 2.* Report to the ESRC. University of Bradford.

Hearn, J. (1993c). How men talk about men's violence to known women. In *Masculinity and Crime: Issues of Theory and Practice* (pp. 36–54). London: Brunel University of West London.

Hearn, J. (Ed.) (1993d). *Researching Men and Men's Violence.* Research Unit on Violence, Abuse and Gender Relations, University of Bradford, Research Paper No. 4.

Hearn, J. (1994a). *'It Just Happened': A Research and Policy Report on Men's Violence to Known Women.* Research Unit on Violence, Abuse and Gender Relations, University of Bradford, Research Paper No. 6.

Hearn, J. (1994b). *Men's Heterosexual Violence to Women: The Presence and Absence of Sex in Men's Accounts of Violence to Known Women.* Paper presented at the British Sociological Association Annual Conference 'Sexualities in Context', University of Central Lancashire. Mimeo. University of Bradford.

Hearn, J. (1994c). The organization(s) of violence: men, gender relations, organizations and violences. *Human Relations*, 47 (6), 731–754.

Hearn, J. (1994d). Research in men and masculinities: some sociological issues and possibilities. *The Australian and New Zealand Journal of Sociology*, 30 (1), 47–70.

Hearn, J. (1995). *Patterns of Agency Contacts with Men who have been Violent to Known Women.* Research Unit on Violence, Abuse and Gender Relations, University of Bradford, Research Paper No. 13.

Hearn, J. (1996a). Heteroseksuaalinen väkivalta lähipiirin naisia kohtaan: sukupuolistunut väkivalta miesteu kertomuksissa. *Janus: Sosiaalipolitiikan ja Sosiaalityon Tutkimuksen Aikakauslehti*, 4 (1), 39–55.

Hearn, J. (1996b). *Men and Men's Violence to Known Women: the 'Lure' and 'Lack' of Cultural Studies Approaches.* Paper presented at Crossroads in Cultural Studies International Conference, Tampere University. Mimeo. University of Manchester.

Hearn, J. (1996c). Men's violence to known women – men's accounts and men's policy development. In B. Fawcett, B. Featherstone, J. Hearn and C. Toft (Eds.), *Violence and Gender Relations: Theories and Interventions* (pp. 99–114). London: Sage.

Hearn, J. (1996d). Men's violence to known women: historical, everyday and theoretical constructions. In B. Fawcett, B. Featherstone, J. Hearn and C. Toft (Eds.), *Violence and Gender Relations: Theories and Interventions* (pp. 22–37). London: Sage.

Hearn, J. (1998a). Educating men against violence to women. Unpub. ms. University of Manchester.

Hearn, J. (1998b). Men, social work and men's violence to known women. In A. Christie (Ed.), *Men and Social Work.* London: Macmillan.

Hearn, J. (1998c). Men will be men: the ambiguity of men's support for men who have been violent to known women. In J. Popay, J. Hearn and J. Edwards (Eds.), *Men, Gender Divisions and Welfare* (pp. 147–180). London: Routledge.

Hearn, J. (1999). Theorizing men and men's theorizing: men's discursive practices in theorizing men. *Theory and Society,* 28.

Hearn, J. and Collinson, D.C. (1993). Theorizing unities and differences between men and between masculinities. In H. Brod and M. Kaufman (Eds.), *Theorizing Masculinities* (pp. 97–118). Thousand Oaks, CA: Sage.

Hearn, J. and Morgan, D. (Eds.) (1990). *Men, Masculinities and Social Theory.* London: Unwin Hyman.

Hearn, J. and Parkin, W. (1987). *'Sex' at 'Work': The Power and Paradox of Organization Sexuality.* Brighton: Wheatsheaf; New York: St Martin's Press.

Hearn, J. and Parkin, W. (1989). Child abuse, social theory and everyday state practices. In J. Hudson and B. Galaway (Eds.), *The State as Parent* (pp. 229–236). Dordecht: Kluwer.

Hearn, J. and Parkin, W. (1995). *'Sex' at 'Work': The Power and Paradox of Organisation Sexuality.* Rev. edn. Hemel Hempstead: Prentice-Hall; New York: St. Martin's Press.

Hearn, J., Raws, P. and Barford, R. (1993) Working guidelines: men interviewing men. In J. Hearn (Ed.), *Researching Men and Researching Men's Violence* (pp. 33–53). Research Unit on Violence, Abuse and Gender Relations, University of Bradford, Research Paper No. 4.

Hearn, J., Sheppard, D., Tancred-Sheriff, P. and Burrell, G. (Eds.) (1989). *The Sexuality of Organization.* London: Sage.

Held, D. (1980). *Critical Theory: An Introduction.* London: Heinmann.

Hennessy, P. (1993). *Materialist Feminism and the Politics of Discourse.* New York and London: Routledge.

Hester, M., Kelly, L. and Radford, J. (Eds.) (1996). *Women, Violence and Male Power.* Buckingham: Open University Press.

Hite, S. (1987). *Women and Love.* London: Penguin.

Holland, J., Ramazanoglu, C. and Sharpe, S. (1993). *Wimp or Gladiator? Contradictions in Acquiring Masculine Sexuality.* WRAP/MRAP Paper 9. London: Tufnell Press.

Holland, J., Ramazanoglu, C., Sharpe, S. and Thomson, R. (1994). Power and desire: the embodiment of female sexuality. *Feminist Review,* 46, 21–38.

Hollway, W. (1981). 'I just wanted to kill a woman': Why? The Ripper and male sexuality. *Feminist Review,* 9, 33–40.

Hollway, W. (1984). Gender differences and the production of subjectivity. In J. Henriques, W. Hollway, C. Urwin, C. Venn and V. Walkerdine, *Changing the Subject* (pp. 227–263). London: Methuen.

Horley, S. (1990). Responding to male violence against women. *Probation Journal*, December, 166–170.

Horsfall, J. (1991). *The Presence of the Past: Male Violence in the Family*. North Sydney: Allen and Unwin.

Hosking, D. and Fineman, S. (1990). Organizing processes. *Journal of Management Studies*, 27 (6), 583–604.

Hotaling, G.T. and Sugarman, D.B. (1986). An analysis of risk markers in husband to wife violence: the current state of knowledge. *Violence and Victims*, 1 (2), 101–124.

Hunt, L. (Ed.) (1989). *The New Cultural History*. Berkeley, CA: University of California Press.

Hydén, M. (1994). *Woman Battering as a Marital Act: Interviewing and Analysis in Context*. Stockholm: Institutionen för Socialt Arbete, Stockholms Universitet.

Jackson, D. (1990). *Unmasking Masculinity: A Critical Autobiography*. London: Unwin Hyman.

Jackson, S. (1982). *Childhood and Sexuality*. Oxford: Blackwell.

Jacobs, P.A., Brunton, M., Melville, M.M., Britain, R.P. and McClemont, W.F. (1965). Aggressive behaviour, mental sub-normality and the XYY male. *Nature (London)*, 208, 1351–1352.

James, J.S. (1986). *Stroud's Judicial Dictionary of Words and Phrases, Vol. 1* (5th edn). London: Sweet and Maxwell.

Jardine, A. (1987). Men in feminism: odor di uomo or compagnons de route. In A. Jardine and P. Smith (Eds.), *Men in Feminism* (pp. 54–62). New York: Methuen.

Jenkins, J. (1994). *Men, Masculinity and Offending*. London: Acton Trust/Inner London Probation Service.

Jukes, A. (1993). *When Men Hate Women*. London: Free Association Books.

Kalb, D. (1993). Frameworks of culture and class in historical research. *Theory and Society*, 22, 513–537.

Kalmuss, D.S. (1984). The intergenerational transmission of family aggression. *Journal of Marriage and the Family*, 46 (1), 11–19.

Kanter, R.M. (1977). *Men and Women of the Corporation*. New York: Basic.

Kantor, G.K. and Straus, M. (1987). The 'Drunken Bum' theory of wife beating. *Social Problems*, 34 (3), 213–230.

Kaufman, M. (1987). The construction of masculinity and the triad of men's violence. In M. Kaufman (Ed.), *Beyond Patriarchy: Essays by Men on Pleasure, Power and Change* (pp. 1–29). Toronto: Oxford University Press.

Kaye, H.J. (1991). *The Powers of the Past*. Minneapolis: University of Minnesota Press.

Kelly, L. (1987). The continuum of sexual violence. In J. Hanmer and M. Maynard (Eds.), *Women, Violence and Social Control* (pp. 46–60). London: Macmillan.

Kelly, L. (1988). *Surviving Sexual Abuse*. Cambridge: Polity.

Kemper, T. (1990). *Social Structure and Testosterone: Explorations of the Socio-Bio-Social Chain*. New Brunswick, NJ: Rutgers University Press.

Keverne, E.B. (1979). Sexual and aggressive behaviour in social groups of talapoin monkeys. In *Symposium on Sex, Hormones and Behaviour* (pp. 217–297). Ciba Symposium 62. Amsterdam: Excerpta Medica.

Kimmel, M.S. (1987). The contemporary 'crisis' of masculinity in historical perspective. In H. Brod (Ed.), *The Making of Masculinities: The New Men's Studies* (pp. 121–153). Boston and London: Allen & Unwin.

Kimmel, M.S. (Ed.) (1990). *Men Confront Pornography*. New York: Crown.

Kimmel, M.S. and Mosmiller, T.E. (1992). *Against the Tide: Pro-feminist Men in the United States, 1776–1990*. Boston: Beacon.

Kirkwood, C. (1993). *Leaving Abusive Partners: From the Scars of Survival to the Wisdom for Change*. London: Sage.

Knorr, K. (1979). Contextuality and indexicality of organizational action: towards a transorganizational theory of organizations. *Social Science Information*, 18 (1), 79–101.

Kress, G. and Hodge, R. (1979). *Language as Ideology*. London: Routledge and Kegan Paul.

Kreuz, L. and Rose, R.M. (1972). Assessment of aggressive behavior and plasma testosterone in a young criminal population. *Psychosomatic Medicine*, 34, 470–471.

Landry, D. and Maclean, G. (1993). *Materialist Feminisms*. Cambridge, MA and Oxford: Blackwell.

Lee, R.M. (1993). *Doing Research in Sensitive Topics*. London: Sage.

Lees, J. and Lloyd, T. (1994). *Working with Men Who Batter Their Partners (An Introductory Text)*. London: Working with Men/The B Team.

Lesko, N. (1988). The curriculum of the body: lessons from a Catholic high school. In L.G. Roman and L.K. Christian-Smith with E. Ellsworth (Eds.), *Becoming Feminine* (pp. 123–142). London: Falmer.

Lorenz, K. (1966). *On Aggression*. New York: Harcourt, Brace and World.

Lukács, G. (1971). *History and Class Consciousness*. London: Merlin.

Lyman, S.M. and Scott, M.B. (1970). *Sociology of the Absurd*. New York: Appleton-Century-Crofts.

MacCannell, D. and MacCannell, J.F. (1987). The beauty system. In N. Armstrong and L. Tennenhouse (Eds.), *The Ideology of Conduct* (pp. 206–238). London: Methuen.

MacCannell, D. and MacCannell, J.F. (1993). Violence, power and pleasure: a revisionist reading of Foucault from the victim perspective. In C. Ramazanoglu (Ed.), *Up Against Foucault* (pp. 203–238). London: Routledge.

McGregor, H. and Hopkins, A. (1991). *Working for Change. The Movement Against Domestic Violence*. Sydney: Allen and Unwin.

McKee, L. and O'Brien, M. (1983). Interviewing men: 'taking gender seriously'. In E. Garmarnikow, D. Morgan, J. Purvis and D. Taylorson (Eds.), *The Public and the Private* (pp. 147–161). London: Heinemann.

MacKeganey, N. and Bloor, M. (1991). Spotting the invisible man: the influence of male gender on fieldwork relations. *British Journal of Sociology*, 42 (2), 195–210.

MacKinnon, C.A. (1983). Feminism, Marxism, method and the state: towards feminist jurisprudence. *Signs*, 8 (4), 635–658.

MacKinnon, C.A. (1994). *Only Words*. London: HarperCollins.

McWilliams, M. and McKiernan, J. (1993). *Bringing It Out in the Open: Domestic Violence in Northern Ireland*. Belfast: HMSO.

Maiuro, R.D., Cahn, T.S. and Vitaliano, P.P. (1986). Assertiveness deficits and hostility in domestically violent men. *Violence and Victims*, 1, 279–290.

Maiuro, R.D., Cahn, T.S., Vitaliano, P.P., Wagner, B.C. and Zegree, J.B. (1988). Anger, hostility and depression in domestically violent versus generally assaultive men and non-violent control subjects. *Journal of Consulting and Clinical Psychology*, 56, 17–23.

Malseed, J. (1987). Straw men: a note on Ann Oakley's treatment of textbook prescriptions for interviewing. *Sociology*, 21 (4), 629–631.

Mama, A. (1989). *The Hidden Struggle: Statutory and Voluntary Sector Responses to Violence against Black Women in the Home*. London: The London Race and Housing Research Unit.

Mann, L. (1993). *Domestic Violence within Lesbian Relationships*. Paper presented at the British Sociological Association Annual Conference, University of Central Lancashire. Mimeo: Staffordshire University.

Manning, A. (1989). The genetic bases of aggression. In J. Groebel and R.A. Hinde (Eds.), *Aggression and War: Their Biological and Social Bases* (pp. 48–57). Cambridge: Cambridge University Press.

Marshall, H. and Wetherell, M. (1989). Talking about career and gender identities: a discourse analysis perspective. In S. Skevington and D. Baker (Eds.), *The Social Identity of Women* (pp. 106–129) London: Sage.

Martin, E. (1989). *The Woman in the Body*. Milton Keynes: Open University Press.

Matza, D. (1964). *Delinquency and Drift*. Englewood Cliffs, NJ: Prentice-Hall.

Mazur, A. and Lamb, T.A. (1980). Testosterone, status and mood in human males. *Hormones and Behaviour*, 4, 236–246.

Messerschmidt, J.W. (1986). *Capitalism, Patriarchy and Crime: Toward a Socialist Feminist Criminology*. Totowa, NJ: Rowman and Littlefield.

Messerschmidt, J.W. (1993). *Masculinities and Crime: Critique and Reconceptualization of Theory*. Lanham, MD: Rowman and Littlefield.

Miedzian, M. (1992). *Boys Will Be Boys*. London: Virago.

Mills, C.W. (1940). Situated actions and vocabularies of motive. *American Sociological Review*, 5, 904–913.

Mirrlees-Black, C. (1994). *Estimating the Extent of Domestic Violence: Findings from the 1992 BCS*. Home Office Research Bulletin No. 37. London: Home Office Research and Statistics Department.

Mitchell, R. and Hodson, C. (1983). Coping with domestic violence: social support and psychological health among women. *American Journal of Community Psychology*, 11 (6), 629–654.

Monahan, J. (1981). *Predicting Violent Behaviour: An Assessment of Clinical Techniques*. Beverly Hills, CA: Sage.

Montagu, M.F.A. (Ed.) (1968). *Man and Aggression*. Oxford: Oxford University Press.

Mooney, J. (1994). *The Prevalence and Social Distribution of Domestic Violence: An Analysis of Theory and Method*. Unpublished PhD dissertation, Middlesex University.

Morgan, D.H.J. (1981). Men, masculinity and the process of sociological enquiry. In H. Roberts (Ed.), *Doing Feminist Research* (pp. 83–113). London: Routledge and Kegan Paul.

Morgan, D.H.J. (1991). Strategies and sociologists: a comment on Crow. *Sociology*, 23 (1), 25–30.

Morgan, D.H.J. (1992). *Discovering Men*. London: Routledge.

Mowrer, O.H. and Lamoreaux, R. (1946). Fear as an intervening variable in avoidance conditioning. *Journal of Comparative and Physiological Psychology*, 39, 29–50.

Mullender, A. (1997). *Rethinking Domestic Violence: The Social Work and Probation Response*. London: Routledge.

Mullender, A. and Morley, R. (Eds.) (1994). *Children Living With Domestic Violence: Putting Men's Abuse of Women on the Child Care Agenda*. London: Whiting and Birch.

Nazroo, J. (1995). Uncovering gender differences in the use of marital violence: the effect of methodology. *Sociology*, 29 (3), 475–494.

Newburn, T. and Stanko, E.A. (Eds.) (1994). *Just Boys Doing Business? Men, Masculinities and Crime*. London: Routledge.

Oakley, A. (1981). Interviewing women: a contradiction in terms. In H. Roberts (Ed.), *Doing Feminist Research* (pp. 30–61). London: Routledge and Kegan Paul.

Oakley, A. (1987). Comments on Malseed. *Sociology*, 21 (4), 632.

Pagelow, M.D. (1981). *Women-battering: Victims and Their Experiences*. Newbury Park, CA: Sage.

Pankhurst, C. (1913). *The Hidden Scourge and How to End It*. London: E. Pankhurst.

Pence, E. (1989). Batterer programs: shifting from community collusion to community confrontation. In P.L. Caesar and L.K. Hamberger (Eds.), *Treating Men Who Batter: Theory, Practice and Programs* (pp. 24–50). New York: Springer.

Pence, E. and Paymar, M. (1990). *Power and Control Tactics of Men Who Batter*. Duluth: Minnesota Program Development.

Pence, E. and Paymar, M. (1995). *Education Groups for Men Who Batter*. New York: Springer.

Peterson, R. (1980). Social class, social learning and wife abuse. *Social Services Review*, 54 (3), 390–406.

Platt, J. (1981). On interviewing one's peers. *British Journal of Sociology*, 32 (1), 75–93.

Plummer, K. (Ed.) (1992). *Modern Homosexualities*. London: Routledge.

Poon, N. (1995). Conceptual issues in defining male domestic violence. In T. Haddad (Ed.), *Men and Masculinities: A Critical Anthology* (pp. 245–261). Toronto: Canadian Scholars' Press.

Pringle, K. (1995). *Men, Masculinities and Social Welfare*. London: UCL Press.

Ptacek, J. (1985). *Wifebeaters' Accounts of Their Violence: Loss of Control as Excuse and as Subjective Experience*. Unpublished master's dissertation, University of New Hampshire.

Ptacek, J. (1988). Why do men batter their wives? In K. Yllö and M. Bograd (Eds.), *Feminist Perspectives on Wife Abuse* (pp. 133–157). Newbury Park, CA: Sage.

Rice, M. (1990). Challenging orthodoxies in feminist theory: a black feminist critique. In L. Gelsthorpe and A. Morris (Eds.), *Feminist Perspectives in Criminology* (pp. 57–69). Milton Keynes: Open University Press.

Rich, A. (1980). Contemporary heterosexuality and lesbian existence. *Signs*, 5, 631–660.

Richardson, L. (1990). Narrative and sociology. *Journal of Contemporary Ethnography*, 19 (1), 116–135.

Rosenbaum, A. and Maiuro, R.D. (1989). Eclectic approaches in working with men who batter. In P.L. Caesar and L.K. Hamberger (Eds.), *Treating Men Who Batter: Theory, Practice and Programs* (pp. 165–195). New York: Springer.

Rosenbaum, A. and O'Leary, K.D. (1981). Marital violence: characteristics of abusive couples. *Journal of Consulting and Clinical Psychology*, 49, 63–71.

Rosengren, W. and Lefton, M. (1969). *Hospitals and Patients*. New York: Atherton Press.

Roy, M. (Ed.) (1982). *The Abusive Partner: An Analysis of Domestic Battering*. New York: Van Nostrand Reinhold.

Russell, D. (Ed.) (1993). *Making Violence Sexy*. Buckingham: Open University Press.

Saunders, D.G. (1992). A typology of men who batter: three types derived from cluster analysis. *American Journal of Orthopsychiatry*, 62, 264–275.

Schechter, S. (1982). *Women and Male Violence: The Visions and Struggles of the Battered Woman's Movement*. Boston: South End Press.

Schönbach, P. (1980). A category system for account phrases. *European Journal of Social Psychology*, 10, 195–200.

Schützenberger, M.P. (1954). A tentative classification of goal-seeking behaviours. *Journal of Mental Science*, 100, 97–102.

Scott, D. (1990). *Feminist Explanations of Wife Assault: Coping with Diversity in the Experiences of Battered Women and their Partners*. Paper presented at the Annual Meetings of the Canadian Law and Society Association, Victoria, BC.

Scott, M.B. and Lyman, S.M. (1968). Accounts. *American Sociological Review*, 33, 46–62.

Scully, D. (1990). *Understanding Sexual Violence: A Study of Convicted Rapists*. London: Unwin Hyman.

Segal, L. (1990). *Slow Motion: Changing Men, Changing Masculinities*. London: Virago.

Select Committee on Violence in Marriage (1975). *Report, together with the*

Proceedings of the Committee Vol. 2: Report, Minutes of the Committee and Appendices. London: HMSO.

Semin, G.R. and Manstead, A.S.R. (1983). *The Accountability of Conduct: A Social Psychological Analysis*. London and New York: Academic Press.

Seymour, J. (1992). *Construction of the Meaning of Key Concepts*. Report for the ESRC Management of Personal Welfare Initiative. Mimeo. Social Policy Research Unit, University of York.

Seymour, J. (1998). The construction of the meaning of key variables. In F. Williams, J. Popay and A. Oakley (Eds.), *Welfare Research*. London: UCL Press.

Sheffield, C. (1987). Sexual terrorism: the social control of women. In B.B. Hess and M. Marx Ferree (Eds.), *Analyzing Gender: A Handbook of Social Science Research* (pp. 171–183). Newbury Park, CA: Sage.

Smith, D.E. (1987). *The Everyday World as Problematic: A Feminist Sociology*. Boston: Northeastern University Press.

Smith, D.E. (1989). Sociological theory: methods of writing patriarchy. In R.A. Wallace (Ed.), *Feminism and Sociological Theory* (pp. 34–64). Newbury Park, CA and London: Sage.

Smith, D.E. (1990). *The Conceptual Practices of Power: A Feminist Sociology of Knowledge*. Boston: Northeastern University Press.

Smith, L. (1989). *Domestic Violence: An Overview of the Literature*. Home Office Resarch Study 107. London: HMSO.

Snell, J., Rosenwald, R. and Robey, A. (1964). The wifebeater's wife. *Archives of General Psychiatry*, 11, 109–114.

Sonkin, D. and Durphy, M. (1985). *Learning to Live Without Violence: A Handbook for Men*. San Francisco: Volcano Press.

Staats, A.W. (1975). *Social Behaviorism*. Homewood, IL: Dorsey Press.

Stanko, E.A. (1994). Challenging the problem of men's individual violence. In T. Newburn and E.A. Stanko (Eds.), *Just Boys Doing Business: Men, Masculinities and Crime* (pp. 32–45). London: Routledge.

Stanley, L. and Wise, S. (1983) *Breaking Out: Feminist Consciousness and Feminist Research*. London: Routledge and Kegan Paul.

Stanley, L. and Wise, S. (1993). *Breaking Out Again: Feminist Ontology and Epistemology*. London: Routledge.

Star, B. (1978). Comparing battered and non-battered women. *Victimology*, 3 (1–2), 32–44.

Stark, E. and Flitcraft, A. (1988). Women and children at risk: a feminist perspective on child abuse. *International Journal of Health Services*, 18 (1), 97–118.

Steiner-Scott, E. (1997). 'To bounce a boot off her now and then . . .': domestic violence in post-famine Ireland. In M.G. Valiulis and M. O'Dowd (Eds.), *Women & Irish History* (pp. 125–143). Dublin: Wolfhound.

Stoltenberg, J. (1990). *Refusing to be a Man*. New York: Meridian.

Strand, F. (1983). *Physiology: A Regulatory Systems Approach* (2nd edn). New York: Macmillan.

Straus, M.A. (1977). Wife beating: how common and why? *Victimology*, 2 (3–4), 443–458.

Straus, M.A. (1979). Measuring intrafamily conflicts and violence: The Conflict Tactics (CTS) Scale. *Journal of Marriage and the Family*, 41, 75–88.

Straus, M.A. and Gelles, R.J. (1990). *Physical Violence in American Families: Risk Factors and Adaptations to Violence in 8,145 Families*. New Brunswick, NJ: Transaction.

Straus, M.A., Gelles, R.J. and Steinmetz, S. (1980). *Behind Closed Doors: Violence in the American Family*. New York Anchor Press.

Strauss, S. (1983). *'Traitors to the Masculine Cause': The Men's Campaigns for Women's Rights*. Westport, CT: Greenwood.

Suttie, I.D. (1935). *The Origins of Love and Hate*. Harmondsworth: Penguin; 1988 London: Free Association Books.

Sydie, R.A. (1987). *Natural Woman, Cultured Man*. Milton Keynes: Open University Press.

Taylor, L. (1972). The significance and interpretation of replies to motivational questionnaires: the case of sex offenders. *Sociology*, 6 (1), 23–39.

Thompson, S. (1990). Putting a big thing into a little hole: teenage girls' accounts of sexual initiation. *Journal of Sex Research*, 27 (3), 341–361.

Tifft, L. (1993). *Battering of Women: The Failure of Intervention and the Case for Prevention*. Boulder, CO: Westview.

Titterton, M. (1989). *The Management of Personal Welfare*. Report to the ESRC. Glasgow: Department of Social Administration and Social Work, University of Glasgow.

Titterton, M. (1992). Managing threats to welfare: the search for a new paradigm of welfare. *Journal of Social Policy*, 21 (1), 1–23.

Trew, T. (1979). What the papers say: linguistic variation and ideological difference. In R. Fowler, R. Hodge, G. Kress and T. Trew (Eds.), *Language and Control*. London: Routledge and Kegan Paul.

Van Hasselt, V., Morrison, R. and Bellack, A. (1985). Alcohol abuse in wife abusers and their spouses. *Addictive Behaviors*, 34 (3), 127–135.

Vessey, S.H. and Jackson, W.B. (1976). Animal behaviour and violence. In A.G. Neal (Ed.), *Violence in Animal and Human Societies* (pp. 35–47). Chicago: Nelson Hall.

Walby, S. (1986). *Patriarchy at Work*. Cambridge: Polity.

Walby, S. (1990). *Theorizing Patriarchy*. Oxford: Blackwell.

Walker, L. (1979). *The Battered Woman*. New York: Harper.

Waring, T. and Wilson, J. (1990). *Be Safe!* Rochdale: MOVE.

Warren, C. (1988). *Gender Issues in Field Research*. London and Beverly Hills, CA: Sage.

Weeks, J. (1977). *Coming Out: A History of Homosexual Politics from the Nineteenth Century*. London: Quartet.

Wetherell, M. and Potter, J. (1989). Narrative characters and accounting for violence. In J. Shotter and K.J. Gergen (Eds.), *Texts of Identity* (pp. 206–219). London: Sage.

Williams, J.F. (1992). *Structural Inequalities and the Management of Personal Welfare: A Selective Literature Review and Assessment*. Report for ESRC Management of Personal Welfare Initiative. Mimeo. Milton Keynes: Open University Press.

Williams, J.F. (1998). Social difference or social divisions? In F. Williams, J. Popay and A. Oakley (Eds.), *Welfare Research*. London: UCL Press.

Wise, S. and Stanley, L. (Eds.) (1984). *Women's Studies International Quarterly*, special issue 'sexual sexual politics', 7.

Wolf, D. (Ed.) (1996). *Feminist Dilemmas in Fieldwork*. Boulder, CO: Westview.

Wooden, W.S. and Parker, J. (1982). *Men Behind Bars: Sexual Exploitation in Prison*. New York: Plenum.

Yllö, K. and Bograd, M. (Eds.) (1988). *Feminist Perspectives on Wife Abuse*. Newbury Park, CA: Sage.

Zita, J.N. (1982). Historical amnesia and the lesbian continuum. In N.O. Keohane, M.Z. Roasalso and B.C. Gelpi (Eds.), *Feminist Theory* (pp. 161–176). Chicago: University of Chicago Press.

Index